KB100552

적중"100

영어 기출 문제집

중2

능률 | 김성곤

Best Collection

구성과 특징

교과서의 주요 학습 내용을 중심으로 학습 영역별 특성에 맞춰 단계별로 다양한 학습 기회를 제공하여 단원별 학습능력 평가는 물론 중간 및 기말고사 시험 등에 완벽하게 대비할 수 있도록 내용을 구성

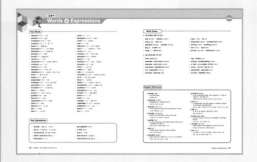

Words & Expressions

Step1 Key Words 단원별 핵심 단어 설명 및 풀이
Key Expression 단원별 핵심 숙어 및 관용어 설명
Word Power 반대 또는 비슷한 뜻 단어 배우기
English Dictionary 영어로 배우는 영어 단어

Step2 실력평가 단원별 수시평가 대비 주관식, 객관식 문제풀이

Step3 서술형 대비 학업성취도 및 수행능력평가 대비 서술형 문제풀이

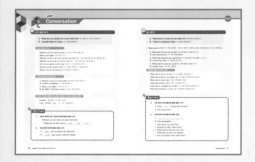

Conversation

Step1 핵심 의사소통 의사소통에 필요한 주요 표현 방법 요약
핵심 Check 기본적인 표현 방법 및 활용능력 확인

Step2 대화문 익히기 상황에 따른 대화문 활용 및 연습

Step3 기본평가 시험대비 기초 학습 능력 평가

Step4 실력평가 단원별 수시평가 대비 주관식, 객관식 문제풀이

Step5 서술형 대비 학업성취도 및 수행능력평가 대비 서술형 문제풀이

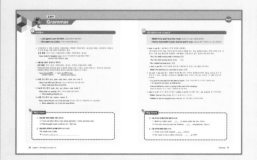

Grammar

Step1 주요 문법 단원별 주요 문법 사항과 예문을 알기 쉽게 설명
핵심 Check 기본 문법사항에 대한 이해 여부 확인

Step2 기본평가 시험대비 기초 학습 능력 평가

Step3 실력평가 단원별 수시평가 대비 주관식, 객관식 문제풀이

Step4 서술형 대비 학업성취도 및 수행능력평가 대비 서술형 문제풀이

Reading

Step1 구문 분석 단원별로 제시된 문장에 대한 구문별 분석과 내용 설명
확인문제 문장에 대한 기본적인 이해와 인지능력 확인

Step2 확인학습A 빈칸 채우기를 통한 문장 완성 능력 확인

Step3 확인학습B 제시된 우리말을 영어로 완성하여 작문 능력 키우기

Step4 실력평가 단원별 수시평가 대비 주관식, 객관식 문제풀이

Step5 서술형 대비 학업성취도 및 수행능력평가 대비 서술형 문제풀이
교과서 구석구석 교과서에 나오는 기타 문장까지 완벽 학습

Composition

|영역별 핵심문제|
단어 및 어휘, 대화문, 문법, 독해 등 각 영역별 기출문제의 출제 유형을 분석하여 실전에 대비하고 연습할 수 있도록 문제를 배열

|서술형 실전 및 창의사고력 문제|
학교 시험에서 점차 늘어나는 서술형 시험에 집중 대비하고 고득점을 취득하는데 만전을 기하기 위한 학습 코너

|단원별 예상문제|
기출문제를 분석한 후 새로운 시험 출제 경향을 더하여 새롭게 출제될 수 있는 문제를 포함하여 시험에 완벽하게 대비할 수 있도록 준비

|단원별 모의고사|
영역별, 단계별 학습을 모두 마친 후 실전 연습을 위한 모의고사

on the textbook
교과서 파헤치기

- **단어Test1~2** 영어 단어 우리말 쓰기와 우리말을 영어 단어로 쓰기
- **대화문Test1~2** 대화문 빈칸 완성 및 전체 대화문 쓰기
- **본문Test1~5** 빈칸 완성, 우리말 쓰기, 문장 배열연습, 영어 작문하기 복습 등 단계별 반복 학습을 통해 교과서 지문에 대한 완벽한 습득
- **구석구석지문Test1~2** 지문 빈칸 완성 및 전문 영어로 쓰기

이책의 차례 Contents

Lesson 3

Understand the World

🎙 의사소통 기능

- 경험 묻고 답하기

  A: Have you ever been to Brazil?

  B: Yes, I have. / No, I haven't.

- 의미 묻고 답하기

  A: What does that mean in Korea?

  B: It means good luck.

🎙 언어 형식

- 현재완료

  For a long time, Koreans **have thought** that fish are good guards.

- so ... that 구문

  It's **so** old **that** I can't really tell, but is it a fish?

  I'm enjoying this trip **so** much **that** I want to stay longer.

Words & Expressions

교과서

Key Words

- □ **arrive** [əráiv] 동 도착하다
- □ **bat** [bæt] 명 박쥐
- □ **beach** [biːtʃ] 명 해변, 바닷가
- □ **bow** [bau] 동 (인사를 위해) 머리를 숙이다, 절하다
- □ **calendar** [kǽləndər] 명 달력
- □ **Chinese** [tʃainíːz] 형 중국의 명 중국어
- □ **clothes** [klouz] 명 옷, 의복
- □ **colored** [kʌlərd] 형 채색된, 색깔이 있는
- □ **crow** [krou] 동 (닭이) 울다 명 까마귀
- □ **darkness** [dáːrknis] 명 어둠, 암흑
- □ **evil** [íːvəl] 형 사악한, 악마의
- □ **experience** [ikspíəriəns] 명 경험 동 경험하다
- □ **face** [feis] 동 ~을 향하다
- □ **festival** [féstəvəl] 명 축제
- □ **full moon** 보름달
- □ **gift shop** 선물 가게
- □ **good luck** 행운
- □ **greet** [griːt] 동 맞이하다, 환영하다
- □ **guard** [gaːrd] 명 보초, 경비병
- □ **guest** [gest] 명 손님
- □ **half moon** 반달
- □ **Indian** [índiən] 형 인도의, 인도 사람의
- □ **international** [ìntərnǽʃənəl] 형 국제적인, 세계적인
- □ **last** [læst] 동 계속되다, 지속되다
- □ **last year** 작년에
- □ **lock** [lak] 명 자물쇠 동 잠그다
- □ **luck** [lʌk] 명 운

- □ **musical** [mjúːzikəl] 명 뮤지컬
- □ **mean** [miːn] 동 의미하다
- □ **palm** [paːm] 명 손바닥, 야자나무
- □ **pay** [pei] 동 지불하다
- □ **peace** [piːs] 명 평화, 화해
- □ **pillow** [pílou] 명 베개
- □ **powder** [páudər] 명 가루, 분말
- □ **protect** [prətékt] 동 보호하다
- □ **remind** [rimáind] 동 생각나게 하다, 상기시키다
- □ **represent** [rèprizént] 동 나타내다, 상징하다
- □ **rooster** [rúːstər] 명 수탉
- □ **rude** [ruːd] 형 무례한
- □ **scary** [skέəri] 형 무서운, 두려운, 겁나는
- □ **separation** [sèpəréiʃən] 명 분리, 이별
- □ **shake** [artwərk] 동 흔들다, 흔들리다
- □ **sister school** 자매 학교
- □ **spirit** [spírit] 명 영혼, 정신
- □ **symbol** [símbəl] 명 상징(물), 기호
- □ **tell** [tel] 동 말하다, (정확히) 알다
- □ **toward** [tɔːrd] 전 ~쪽으로
- □ **traditional** [trədíʃənl] 형 전통의, 전통적인
- □ **try** [trai] 동 한번 해 보다
- □ **umbrella** [ʌmbrélə] 명 우산
- □ **valuable** [vǽljuəbl] 형 값비싼, 귀중한, 가치 있는
- □ **victory** [víktəri] 명 승리, 성공
- □ **Vietnamese** [viètnəːmíːz] 형 베트남의 명 베트남어

Key Expressions

- □ **be afraid of** ~을 두려워하다
- □ **be full of** ~으로 가득 차다
- □ **blow one's nose** 코를 풀다
- □ **go away** 사라지다, 떠나가다
- □ **have been to** 장소 ~에 가 본 적이 있다
- □ **listen to** ~을 듣다

- □ **point at** ~을 가리키다
- □ **remind A of B** A에게 B를 생각나게 하다
- □ **so** 형용사/부사 **that** 주어 동사 너무 ~해서 …하다
- □ **take off** (옷 등을) 벗다
- □ **talk about** ~에 대해 이야기하다
- □ **watch over** ~을 주시하다, 지키다

Word Power

※ 서로 비슷한 뜻을 가진 단어

□ **evil**(사악한, 악마의) – **wicked**(못된, 사악한)

□ **greet**(맞이하다, 환영하다) – **welcome**(환영하다)

□ **international**(국제적인, 세계적인) – **global**(세계적인)

□ **last**(계속되다, 지속되다) – **continue**(계속하다, 지속하다)

□ **remind**(생각나게 하다, 상기시키다) – **recall**(기억해 내다, 상기하다)

□ **represent**(나타내다, 상징하다) – **symbolize**(상징하다)

□ **go away** – **disappear**: 사라지다, 떠나가다

□ **rude**(무례한) – **impolite** (버릇없는, 무례한)

□ **separation**(분리, 이별) – **division** (분할)

□ **spirit**(영혼, 정신) – **soul**(정신, 마음)

□ **symbol**(상징(물), 기호) – **sign**(기호, 부호)

□ **traditional**(전통의, 전통적인) – **conventional**(전통적인)

□ **try**(한번 해 보다) – **attempt**(시도하다)

□ **victory**(승리, 성공) – **success**(성공, 성과)

□ **afraid**(두려워하는) – **frightened**(두려워하는)

□ **watch over** – **guard**: ~을 주시하다, 지키다

English Dictionary

□ **bow** (인사를 위해) 머리를 숙이다, 절하다
→ to lower your head or bend your body
머리를 낮추거나 몸을 구부리다

□ **crow** (닭이) 울다
→ to make the loud sound that a rooster makes 수탉이 내는 큰 소리를 만들다

□ **darkness** 어둠, 암흑
→ no light 빛이 없음

□ **evil** 사악한, 악마의
→ morally bad or wicked
도덕적으로 나쁘거나 사악한

□ **face** ~을 향하다
→ to have the front part toward something 앞 부분을 어떤 것 쪽으로 향하게 하다

□ **greet** 맞이하다, 환영하다
→ to say hello or welcome
안녕이라고 말하거나 환영하다

□ **last** 계속되다, 지속되다
→ to keep happening for a certain amount of time 일정의 시간 동안 계속 발생하다

□ **palm** 손바닥
→ the inside part of the hand between the wrist and the fingers 손목과 손가락 사이의 손 안쪽 부분

□ **pillow** 베개
→ a soft thing to put your head on while you sleep
자는 동안에 머리를 놓는 부드러운 것

□ **protect** 보호하다
→ to keep something or someone safe from danger
위험으로부터 사람이나 사물을 안전하게 지키다

□ **remind** 생각나게 하다, 상기시키다
→ to make someone remember something 누군가에게 무엇인가를 기억나게 만들다

□ **represent** 나타내다, 상징하다
→ to stand for something else 다른 무엇인가를 상징하다

□ **rooster** 수탉
→ a male chicken 수컷 닭

□ **scary** 무서운, 두려운, 겁나는
→ making people feel afraid, frightening 사람들을 두려워하고 겁나게 만드는

□ **separation** 분리, 이별
→ the act of moving two things or people apart
두 개의 사물이나 사람을 떨어지도록 움직이는 행위

□ **symbol** 상징(물), 기호
→ an object that represents something
무엇인가를 나타내는 물체

□ **traditional** 전통의, 전통적인
→ being part of something that people have done for a long time 오랜 시간 동안 사람들이 해 왔던 어떤 것의 일부인

□ **valuable** 값비싼, 귀중한, 가치 있는
→ very important or expensive 매우 중요하거나 비싼

□ **victory** 승리, 성공
→ success in defeating an opponent
상대방을 물리치는 데 있어서의 성공

01 다음 빈칸에 들어갈 말로 적절한 것은?

> In some cases, hiccups can _____ for days or even weeks!

① cause　　　② bring

③ invite　　　④ produce

⑤ last

[02~03] 다음 밑줄 친 부분과 의미가 가장 가까운 것은?

02

> All of us need to go out to meet and greet them.

① welcome　　② face

③ mean　　　④ try

⑤ say

03 중요

> The olive wreath stands for peace and it is still sometimes used today!

① shows　　　② represents

③ suggests　　④ stays

⑤ makes use of

04 다음 중 밑줄 친 부분의 뜻풀이가 바르지 <u>않은</u> 것은?

① I don't understand what you mean. (의미하다)

② A full moon is 9 times brighter than a half moon. (반달)

③ He tried praying, but that didn't ease his mind. (노력하다)

④ Meditation is helpful in training your body and spirit. (영혼, 정신)

⑤ I have to apologize to you for being rude. (무례한)

05 중요 다음 빈칸에 공통으로 들어갈 말로 알맞은 것은?

> • Be sure to _____ the door before you leave.
> • He observed the thief open the _____ of the door.

① lock　　　② turn

③ fix　　　　④ pull

⑤ rock

06 서답형 다음 빈칸에 들어갈 알맞은 단어를 〈보기〉에서 찾아 쓰시오. (형태 변화 가능)

> ┤ 보기 ├
> traditional　scary　international

(1) She told me some _____ stories.

(2) Export law became a key factor in _____ trade.

(3) She is wearing _____ Korean clothes.

07 서답형 다음 우리말과 일치하도록 괄호 안의 어구를 바르게 배열하시오.

(1) 토니는 어둠 속으로 사라졌다. (the darkness, in, got, Tony, lost)

➡ _____

(2) 그 소녀들은 베개 싸움을 하고 있다. (having, fight, the girls, a pillow, are)

➡ _____

08 다음 영영풀이에 해당하는 것은?

> in the direction of something

① against　② directly　③ far

④ toward　⑤ within

01 다음 〈보기〉와 같은 관계가 주어진 빈칸에 알맞은 말을 쓰시오. (주어진 철자로 시작할 것)

> ┤ 보기 ├
> good – nice

(1) impolite ➡ r_____
(2) attempt ➡ t_____
(3) wicked ➡ e_____
(4) success ➡ v_____

02 다음 빈칸에 알맞은 단어를 〈보기〉에서 골라 쓰시오.

> ┤ 보기 ├
> arrive   celebrate   experience   mean

(1) Staying curious allows me to continuously _____ the excitement of learning something new.
(2) That doesn't _____ that I'm lazy.
(3) What time does the next train _____?
(4) They _____ Christmas and New Year's Day together.

03 다음 주어진 우리말에 맞게 빈칸을 채우시오.

(1) 그 방은 해변을 향해 있나요?
   ➡ Does the room _____ the beach?
(2) 2년간의 이별 후에 그 부부는 다시 만날 수 있었다.
   ➡ After two years of _____, the couple was _____ to meet again.

04 다음 우리말에 맞게 주어진 단어를 이용해 빈칸을 완성하시오.

> 그는 항아리를 색깔이 있는 물로 채웠습니다.

➡ He filled a jar with _____ water. (color)

05 다음 〈보기〉에서 빈칸에 공통으로 들어갈 단어를 골라 쓰시오.

> ┤ 보기 ├
> in   about   at   from   of

(1) • I usually stay _____ home on Sundays.
   • It is rude to point _____ a person.
(2) • I am afraid _____ dogs when they bark.
   • Lemons remind people _____ things that are fresh and clean.

06 다음 우리말에 맞게 주어진 단어를 바르게 배열하시오.

(1) 그녀는 다정한 미소로 우리를 맞았다.
   (with, a, greeted, smile, kind, she, us)
   ➡ _____
(2) 그 회의는 세 시간 동안 계속되었다.
   (three, the, meeting, hours, lasted)
   ➡ _____
(3) 나는 그 동전을 그녀의 손바닥에 놓았다. (the, coin, I, her, put, palm, in)
   ➡ _____
(4) 붉은 깃발은 위험을 나타낸다.
   (a, danger, flag, represents, red)
   ➡ _____

Conversation

① 의미 묻고 답하기

    A What does that mean in Korea? 한국에서는 그게 어떤 의미니?
    B It means good luck. 행운을 뜻해.

■ 'What does that mean?'은 상대방의 말의 의도나 의미를 잘 이해하지 못할 때, 그 의도나 의미를 물어보는 표현이다. 대답할 때는 'It means ~.'로 의미를 설명해 준다.

의미를 묻는 표현

- What does that mean (in Korea)? (한국에서는) 그게 어떤 의미니?
- What is that exactly? 그것이 정확히 뭐니?
- I'd like to know what that means. 그것이 무슨 의미인지 알고 싶어.
- Could[Would/Will] you explain what that means? 그것이 무슨 의미인지 설명해 줄 수 있어?

■ Could[Can/Would/Will] you ~?'로 시작하는 의문문은 질문을 할 때도 쓰지만, 요청이나 부탁을 하는 경우에도 사용한다. 요청이나 부탁을 받았을 경우 꼭 Yes나 No로 대답할 필요는 없다.

    ex) A: Would you tell me what this sign means? (이 표지판이 무슨 의미인지 말해 줄래?)
        B: It means "no smoking." ('금연'이라는 뜻이야.)

핵심 Check

1. 주어진 문장에 이어질 대화의 순서를 바르게 배열하시오.

    I don't understand what this means.

    (A) Yes. What does that mean?

    (B) It means "very important person."

    (C) Are you talking about VIP?

    ➡ _____

2. 다음 우리말과 일치하도록 빈칸에 알맞은 말을 쓰시오.

    A: Could you _____ _____ the sign _____? (그 표지판이 무슨 의미인지 설명해 줄 수 있니?)

    B: It means "no parking." ('주차 금지'라는 의미야.)

3. 주어진 단어를 배열하여 대화를 완성하시오.

    A: It's about English sayings. Do you know the saying, "Look before you leap."?

    B: No. _____ (that, what, to, I'd, means, like, know)

    A: Sure. _____ before you do something. (you, it, think, carefully, means, should)

2 경험 묻고 답하기

> **A** Have you ever been to Brazil? 너는 브라질 가 봤니?
>
> **B** Yes, I have. / No, I haven't. 응. 가 봤어. / 아니, 못 가 봤어.

- 상대방의 경험에 대해 물어볼 때는, 현재완료 시제를 사용하여 'Have you 과거분사 ~?'라고 묻는다. 경험을 묻는 말에 긍정으로 대답할 경우에는 'Yes, I have.'로, 부정으로 대답할 때는 'No, I haven't.'로 대답한다.
- 완료 시제를 사용할 때는 ago, yesterday, when 등과 같이 명백한 과거를 나타내는 말과 같이 사용되지 않는다. ex) When have you met him? (×)   When did you meet him? (○)
- 경험을 나타내는 현재완료와 잘 사용하는 표현은 never(결코 ~ 않는), ever(어느 때고, 한 번이라도), once(한 번), twice(두 번), three times(세 번), before(전에) 등이 있다.
  ex) I have met him three times. (나는 그를 세 번 만난 적이 있다.)
- 'have been to 장소'는 '~에 가 본 경험이 있다'의 의미이고, 'have gone to 장소'는 '~에 갔다(그래서 지금 없다)'는 의미이다. ex) Have you gone to New York? (×)

경험을 묻는 표현

- Have you ever 과거분사 ~? (~해 본 적 있니?)
- Is this your first time -ing ~? (~해 보는 것이 처음이니?)
- Do you have any experience of -ing ~? (~해 본 경험이 있니?)

경험을 묻는 질문에 대답하는 표현

- I have never 과거분사. (한 번도 ~해 본 적이 없어.)
- I have a lot of experience. (나는 경험이 풍부해.)

핵심 Check

4. 다음 우리말과 일치하도록 빈칸에 알맞은 말을 쓰시오.

   A: _____ the movie *Aquaman*? (너는 영화 아쿠아맨을 본 적 있니?)

   B: Yes, I _____. _____ you? (응, 봤어. 너는 봤니?)

5. 대화의 순서를 바르게 배열하시오.

   (A) That sounds like fun.

   (B) No, I haven't.

   (C) I'm going to Japan with my friends this winter.

   (D) Have you been there before?

   ➡ _____

6. 주어진 단어를 배열하여 대화를 완성하시오.

   A: _____ (before, had, have, *gimchi*, you)

   B: Yes, I have.

A. Listen and Talk 1 A

G: ❶Have you ever been to Brazil?

B: No, I haven't. ❷Have you?

G: Yes, I have. I went there ❸last year. ❹There was a big samba festival.

B: That sounds interesting. I ❺hope to go there someday.

G: 너는 브라질 가 봤니?
B: 아니, 못 가 봤어. 너는 가 봤니?
G: 응. 가 봤어. 작년에 거기 갔었어. 큰 삼바 축제가 있었어.
B: 재미있게 들린다. 나도 언젠가 거기 가고 싶어.

❶ 'Have you ever p.p ~?'는 경험을 묻는 표현이다. 특히 'Have you ever been to 장소?'는 '~에 가 본 적 있니?'라는 뜻으로 어떤 곳에 가 본 경험에 대해 말할 때 사용하는 표현이다. 응답은 'Yes, I have.'또는 'No, I haven't.'로 하면 된다.

❷ Have you 뒤에 'ever been to Brazil'이 생략되어 있다.

❸ last year(작년)는 과거의 특정 시점이므로 과거형 동사를 사용해야 한다.

❹ There+be동사의 과거형(was, were): ~가 있었다 festival: 축제

❺ hope는 to부정사를 목적어로 받는다.

Check(√) True or False

(1) The boy has never been to Brazil.　　　　　T ☐　F ☐

(2) There was a samba festival in Brazil last year.　　　T ☐　F ☐

 B. Listen and Talk 1 B

W: ❶Welcome to the International Games Festival. ❷You can play many different traditional games here.

B: Wow! ❸It looks exciting! Which game should I play first?

W: Let's see. ❹Have you ever played *gorodki*?

B: No, I haven't. What is it?

W: It's a traditional game ❺from Russia.

B: How do I play it?

W: Put five sticks on the ground. Then ❻throw a bat at them.

B: That ❼sounds fun. I'll try that first.

W: 국제 게임 축제에 오신 걸 환영합니다. 당신은 여기서 많은 종류의 전통 게임을 할 수 있습니다.
B: 와! 재미있을 것 같아요! 어떤 게임 먼저 해야 하나요?
W: 한번 봅시다. 고로드키 게임 해 본 적 있나요?
B: 아니요. 그게 무엇인가요?
W: 러시아의 전통 게임이에요.
B: 어떻게 하나요?
W: 바닥에 다섯 개의 막대기를 놓으세요. 그리고 그것들을 향해 배트를 던지세요.
B: 재미있겠네요. 그거 먼저 할게요.

❶ welcome to ~: ~에 오신 걸 환영합니다

❷ can+동사원형: ~할 수 있다 traditional: 전통적인

❸ look + 형용사: ~하게 보이다 exciting: 흥미로운

❹ Have you ever p.p ~?: ~한 적 있니?

❺ from: (출처·기원) ~출신의[에서 온]

❻ throw: ~을 던지다 at: (방향) ~으로

❼ sound+형용사: ~하게 들리다

Check(√) True or False

(3) *Gorodki* is from France.　　　　　　T ☐　F ☐

(4) The boy is in the International Games Festival.　　　T ☐　F ☐

Listen and Talk 1 C

B: There is a Holi festival in Busan ❶this year.

G: A Holi festival? What is ❷that?

B: It's a traditional Indian festival. ❸People throw colored powder and water at each other.

G: That sounds exciting. ❹Have you ever been to a Holi festival?

B: No, I haven't. But my Indian friend told me a lot about it.

G: When is the festival?

B: ❺It's on the last full moon of the Hindu calendar. This year, it's ❻on March 21.

G: I'd like to go. ❼Should I bring anything?

B: No, but you should wear white clothes. Then the colored powder on your clothes will look more beautiful.

G: Okay. Thank you for the information.

❶ this year: 올해
❷ that은 'a Holi festival'을 의미한다.
❸ colored: 채색된, 색깔이 있는 at each other: 서로에게
❹ Have you ever been to 장소?: ~에 가 본 적 있니? festival: 축제
❺ Holi 축제가 언제인지에 대한 설명을 하고 있다 the last full moon: 마지막 보름달(이 뜨는 날)
❻ 날짜 앞에는 전치사 on을 사용한다.
❼ should+동사원형: ~해야 한다 Should I bring ~?: ~을 가져가야 하니?

Listen and Talk 2 A

G: Jinwoo, my Korean friend, ❶gave me *Yeot* as a gift. ❷What does that mean in Korea?

B: ❸It means good luck on a test.

❶ give는 4형식 동사로 간접목적어(~에게)와 직접목적어(~을[를]) 두 개를 받을 수 있다. as: ~으로
❷ What does that mean?: 그게 어떤 의미니? in Korea: 한국에서
❸ It은 Yeot을 의미한다. 주어 mean ~: 주어는 ~을 의미한다 good luck: 행운

Listen and Talk 2 B

B: Ling's birthday is ❶this Wednesday, ❷isn't it?

G: Yes. ❸I'm going to buy a book for her. What about you?

B: Well, ❹I'm thinking about buying her an

umbrella. I found a cute ❺one in a gift shop.

G: Oh, that's not a good gift for Chinese people. It means ❻something bad.

B: Really? What does an umbrella mean in China?

G: It means ❼separation. The words for *separation* and *umbrella* sound the same in Chinese.

B: I see. Then how about chocolate?

G: That's a good idea.

❶ this 요일: 이번 주 ~요일
❷ 부가의문문으로 말하는 이가 듣는 이에게 말한 내용을 확인하거나 동의를 구할 때 쓰며 '동사+주어(인칭대명사)'의 형태로 쓰인다. 앞 문장에 쓰인 동사가 be동사나 조동사이면 그대로, 일반동사이면 do동사로 쓰며, 앞 문장이 긍정이면 부정, 앞 문장이 부정이면 긍정으로 쓴다.
❸ be going to 동사원형: ~할 것이다, ~할 예정이다
❹ think about: ~에 대해 생각하다 about은 전치사이므로 뒤에 명사나 동명사가 올 수 있다. buy는 4형식 동사로 '~에게 …를 사 주다'의 의미로 사용되었다.
❺ one = umbrella
❻ -thing으로 끝나는 부정대명사(something, anything, nothing 등)는 보통 다른 명사들과 달리 형용사가 뒤에서 수식한다.
❼ separation: 분리, 이별

Listen and Talk 2 C

G: ❶What a nice picture! Are these your friends?

B: Yes. We ❷took this picture at the beach. ❸ We had a lot of fun.

G: Oh, ❹look at that boy. That's really ❺rude.

B: Which boy?

G: The boy ❻who is making the V sign. ❼His palm is facing toward himself.

B: What's wrong with that?

G: It has a bad meaning in England. But showing your palm and making a V sign is okay.

B: What does that mean?

G: It means victory or peace.

❶ 'What+a+형용사+명사!'(감탄문) What a nice picture!: 이 사진 정말 멋지다!
❷ take a picture: 사진을 찍다
❸ have fun: 재미있다, 즐거운 시간을 보내다
❹ look at: ~을 보다
❺ rude: 무례한
❻ who는 주격 관계대명사로 who is making the V sign은 앞의 the boy를 수식하고 있다.
❼ palm: 손바닥 face: ~을 향하다 toward: ~쪽으로

● 다음 우리말과 일치하도록 빈칸에 알맞은 말을 쓰시오.

Listen & Talk 1 A

G: _____ _____ ever _____ to Brazil?

B: No, I _____. _____ you?

G: Yes, I _____. I went there _____ _____. There _____ a big samba festival.

B: That _____ interesting. I hope _____ _____ there _____.

Listen & Talk 1 B

W: Welcome _____ the International Games _____. You can play _____ _____ _____ _____ here.

B: Wow! It _____ exciting! _____ game _____ I play first?

W: Let's see. _____ _____ _____ played *gorodki*?

B: _____, _____ _____. What is it?

W: It's a traditional game _____ Russia.

B: _____ do I play it?

W: Put five sticks _____ the ground. Then _____ a bat _____ them.

B: That _____ _____. I'll try that first.

Listen & Talk 1 C

B: _____ _____ a Holi festival _____ Busan _____ year.

G: A Holi festival? What is that?

B: It's _____ _____ _____ _____ _____. People throw _____ _____ and water at _____ other.

G: That _____ _____. _____ _____ _____ _____ to a Holi festival?

B: No, I haven't. But my Indian friend _____ _____ a lot about it.

G: _____ is the festival?

B: It's _____ the last full moon of the Hindu calendar. This year, it's _____ March 21.

G: I'd _____ to go. _____ I bring anything?

B: No, but you should wear white _____. Then _____ _____ _____ on your _____ will look more beautiful.

G: Okay. Thank you _____ the information.

해석

G: 너는 브라질 가 봤니?
B: 아니, 못 가 봤어. 너는 가 봤니?
G: 응. 가 봤어. 작년에 거기 갔었어. 큰 삼바 축제가 있었어.
B: 재미있게 들린다. 나도 언젠가 거기 가고 싶어.

W: 국제 게임 축제에 오신 걸 환영합니다. 당신은 여기서 많은 종류의 전통게임을 할 수 있습니다.
B: 와! 재미있을 것 같아요! 어떤 게임 먼저 해야 하나요?
W: 어디 봅시다. 고로드키 게임 해 본 적 있나요?
B: 아니요. 그게 무엇인가요?
W: 러시아의 전통 게임이에요.
B: 어떻게 하나요?
W: 바닥에 다섯 개의 막대기를 놓으세요. 그리고 그것들을 향해 배트를 던지세요.
B: 재미있겠네요. 그거 먼저 할게요.

B: 올해에는 부산에서 Holi Festival이 있어.
G: Holi Festival? 그게 뭐야?
B: 인도의 전통 축제야. 사람들은 서로에게 색 파우더와 물을 던지지.
G: 재미있겠다. Holi festival에 가 본 적 있니?
B: 아니, 없어. 근데 인도 친구가 그것에 대해 많이 이야기해 줬어.
G: 축제가 언제야?
B: 힌두교 달력으로 마지막 보름달이 뜨는 날이야. 올해는 3월 21일이네.
G: 가고 싶다. 나 뭐 가져가야 하니?
B: 아니, 하지만 하얀 옷을 입어야 돼. 그러면 네 옷에 묻은 색 파우더가 더 예쁘게 보일 거야.
G: 알겠어. 정보 알려줘서 고마워.

Listen and Talk 2 A

G: Jinwoo, my Korean friend, _____ _____ *Yeot* as a gift.
_____ _____ _____ _____ _____ _____ _____?

B: It _____ good luck on a test.

Listen and Talk 2 B

B: Ling's birthday is _____ Wednesday, _____ _____?
G: Yes. I'm going to buy a book for her. What about you?
B: Well, I'm thinking _____ _____ her an umbrella. I found a cute _____ in a gift shop.
G: Oh, that's not a good gift for Chinese people. It means _____ _____.
B: Really? _____ _____ an umbrella _____ _____ _____ _____?
G: It _____ _____. The words for _____ and *umbrella* sound the same in Chinese.
B: I see. Then how _____ chocolate?
G: That's a good idea.

Listen and Talk 2 C

G: _____ _____ nice picture! _____ these your friends?
B: Yes. We _____ this picture at the beach. We had a lot of fun.
G: Oh, _____ _____ that boy. That's really _____.
B: Which boy?
G: The boy _____ _____ the V sign. His _____ _____ _____ _____ himself.
B: What's wrong with that?
G: It has a bad _____ _____ England. But showing your palm and making a V sign is okay.
B: _____ _____ _____ _____ _____?
G: It means _____ _____ _____.

Do It Yourself

G: Hello, Santiago! What _____ you here today?
B: *Bienvenido*, Cathy. I came _____ see the Spanish festival.
G: Me, too. But what did you just say?
B: *Bienvenido*! It _____ "welcome" in Spanish. Look at those dancers. Their dance moves are so great.
G: Yes, they are.
B: _____ _____ _____ _____ _____ _____ a Spanish festival before?
G: No, _____ _____. Santiago, can you see the big letters on the stage? _____ _____ that mean?
B: Oh, gracias. That _____ "thank you."

해석

G: 내 한국인 친구인 진우가 선물로 엿을 줬어. 한국에서는 이게 어떤 의미니?
B: 시험 잘 보라는 뜻이야.

B: Ling의 생일이 이번 수요일이야, 그렇지 않니?
G: 응. 나는 그녀에게 책을 사 줄 거야. 너는?
B: 음, 나는 우산을 사려고 생각하고 있어. 선물 가게에서 귀여운 걸 찾았거든.
G: 어, 그건 중국 사람들에게 좋은 선물이 아니야. 뭔가 나쁜 걸 뜻하거든.
B: 진짜? 중국에서 우산이 뭘 의미하는데?
G: 이별을 뜻해. 중국에서는 이별을 뜻하는 단어와 우산을 뜻하는 단어의 발음이 같거든.
B: 알겠어. 그러면 초콜릿 어때?
G: 좋은 생각이야.

G: 이 사진 정말 멋지다! 네 친구들이니?
B: 응. 우리는 해변에서 이 사진을 찍었어. 정말 재미있었어.
G: 어, 저 남자애 봐. 정말 무례하다.
B: 누구?
G: V사인을 하고 있는 애. 손바닥이 자기 쪽을 향하고 있어.
B: 그게 뭐 잘못됐어?
G: 영국에서는 나쁜 뜻을 갖고 있어. 하지만 손바닥을 보여 주면서 V사인을 만드는 건 괜찮아.
B: 그건 무슨 뜻인데?
G: 승리나 평화를 뜻해.

G: 안녕, Santiago! 오늘 여기 어쩐 일이야?
B: Bienvenido, Cathy. 나는 스페인 축제를 보러 왔어.
G: 나도. 그런데 방금 뭐라고 말했니?
B: Bienvenido! 스페인어로 "환영합니다."라는 뜻이야. 저 무용수들을 봐. 그들의 춤 움직임은 정말 멋지다.
G: 응, 그렇네.
B: 전에 스페인 축제에 가 본 적 있니?
G: 아니, 가 본 적 없어. Santiago, 무대에 있는 큰 글씨들을 볼 수 있니? 무슨 뜻이야?
B: 아, gracias. 저건 "감사합니다."라는 뜻이야.

[01~02] 다음 대화의 빈칸에 알맞은 것으로 짝지어진 것은?

01

G: _____ you ever been to Brazil?

B: Yes, I _____ .

① Have/have ② Can/can ③ Did /did ④ Are/am ⑤ Do/do

02

A: What does that _____ in Korea?

B: It _____s good luck.

① make ② mean ③ stay ④ find ⑤ keep

03 다음 대화의 밑줄 친 부분의 의도로 알맞은 것은?

A: Have you ever listened to Spanish music?

B: Yes, I have.

① Asking about memories ② Giving advice

③ Asking about experiences ④ Requesting

⑤ Asking about the meanings

04 다음 대화의 순서를 바르게 배열한 것은?

(A) No, I haven't. What is it?

(B) It's a traditional game from Russia.

(C) Have you ever played *gorodki*?

① (A) - (C) - (B) ② (B) - (A) - (C)

③ (B) - (C) - (A) ④ (C) - (A) - (B)

⑤ (C) - (B) - (A)

05 다음 대화에서 어법상 어색한 것을 고르시오.

G: ①Have you ever gone to a Holi festival?

B: ②No, I haven't. ③But my Indian friend told me a lot about it.

G: ④When is the festival?

B: ⑤It's on the last full moon of the Hindu calendar. This year, it's on March 21.

①　　　　②　　　　③　　　　④　　　　⑤

01 빈칸 (A)와 (B)에 알맞은 말을 고르시오.

> **G:** Jinwoo, my Korean friend, (A) _____ *Yeot* as a gift. (B)_____ does that mean in Korea?
> **B:** It means good luck on a test.

	(A)	(B)
①	gave	How
②	gave me	How
③	gave me	What
④	gave to me	How
⑤	gave to me	What

 02 주어진 문장에 이어질 대화의 순서로 가장 적절한 것은?

> Have you ever been to Brazil?

> (A) Yes, I have. I went there last year. There was a big samba festival.
> (B) No, I haven't. Have you?
> (C) That sounds interesting. I hope to go there someday.

① (A) - (C) - (B)　　② (B) - (A) - (C)
③ (B) - (C) - (A)　　④ (C) - (A) - (B)
⑤ (C) - (B) - (A)

[03~06] 다음 대화를 읽고, 물음에 답하시오.

> **B:** ⓐLing's birthday is this Wednesday, isn't it? (①)
> **G:** Yes. ⓑI'm going to buy a book for her. (②)
> **B:** Well, ⓒI'm thinking about buying her an umbrella. I found a cute one in a gift shop. (③)

> **G:** Oh, that's not a good gift for Chinese people. ⓓIt means bad something. (④)
> **B:** Really? (an, mean, in, what, umbrella, China, does, ?)
> **G:** It means separation. ⓔThe words for *separation* and *umbrella* sounds the same in Chinese. (⑤)
> **B:** I see. Then how about chocolate?
> **G:** That's a good idea.

03 위 대화의 ①~⑤ 중 주어진 문장이 들어갈 알맞은 곳은?

> What about you?

①　　②　　③　　④　　⑤

서답형

04 위 대화의 괄호 안에 주어진 단어들을 바르게 배열하여 문장을 완성하시오.

➡ _____

중요

05 위 대화의 밑줄 친 ⓐ~ⓔ 중 어법상 틀린 개수를 고르시오.

① 1개　② 2개　③ 3개　④ 4개　⑤ 5개

06 위 대화를 읽고 답할 수 없는 질문을 모두 고르시오.

① What is the girl going to buy for Ling?
② What does a book mean in China?
③ When is Ling's birthday?
④ Where is the boy going to go to buy chocolate?
⑤ Is an umbrella a good present for Chinese people?

[07~08] 다음 대화를 읽고, 물음에 답하시오.

B: There is a Holi festival in Busan this year.
G: A Holi festival? (A)_____
B: It's a traditional Indian festival. People throw colored powder and water at each other.
G: That sounds exciting. (B)_____
B: No, I haven't. But my Indian friend told me a lot about it.
G: (C)_____
B: It's on the last full moon of the Hindu calendar. This year, it's on March 21.
G: I'd like to go. (D)_____
B: No, but you should wear white clothes. Then the colored powder on your clothes will look more beautiful.
G: Okay. Thank you for the information.

서답형
07 위 대화의 빈칸 (A)~(D)에 들어갈 말을 〈보기〉에서 골라 쓰시오.

┌─── 보기 ───┐
• Have you ever been to a Holi festival?
• What is Holi?
• What is that?
• When is the festival?
• Should I bring anything?
• Should I bring white clothes?
• What should I bring?
└──────────┘

➡ (A) _____
  (B) _____
  (C) _____
  (D) _____

08 위 대화의 내용과 일치하지 <u>않는</u> 것을 고르시오.

① A Holi festival will be held on March 21.
② At a Holi festival, people throw colored powder and water at each other.
③ The boy has an Indian friend.
④ At a Holi festival, people should wear colored clothes.
⑤ The boy has not been to a Holi festival.

[09~12] 다음 대화를 읽고, 물음에 답하시오.

W: Welcome to the International Games Festival. (①) You can play many different traditional games here.
B: Wow! ⓐIt looks (A)_____ (excite)! Which game should I play first? (②)
W: Let's see. (③)
B: No, I haven't. What is ⓑit? (④)
W: ⓒIt's a traditional game from Russia. (⑤)
B: How do I play ⓓit?
W: Put five sticks on the ground. Then throw a bat at them.
B: That sounds fun. I'll try ⓔthat first.

09 위 대화의 ①~⑤ 중 주어진 문장이 들어갈 알맞은 곳은?

┌────────────────────────┐
│ Have you ever played *gorodki*? │
└────────────────────────┘

①   ②   ③   ④   ⑤

서답형
10 위 대화의 빈칸 (A)에 주어진 단어를 이용하여 빈칸을 완성하시오.

➡ _____

중요
11 위 대화의 밑줄 친 ⓐ~ⓔ 중에서 가리키는 대상이 <u>다른</u> 하나는?

① ⓐ   ② ⓑ   ③ ⓒ   ④ ⓓ   ⑤ ⓔ

서답형
12 위 대화의 내용에 맞게 빈칸을 완성하시오.

┌────────────────────────┐
│ *G o r o d k i* is _____ _____ │
│ _____ _____ Russia. The way │
│ to _____ *gorodki* is _____ │
│ _____ _____ on the ground │
│ and _____ _____ _____ at │
│ them. │
└────────────────────────┘

[01~04] 다음 대화를 읽고, 물음에 답하시오.

G: ①What a nice picture! Are these your friends?

B: Yes. ②We took this picture at the beach. We had a lot of fun.

G: Oh, look at that boy. That's really rude.

B: Which boy?

G: ③The boy which is making the V sign. (A)_____

B: ④What's wrong with that?

G: It has a bad (B)_____(mean) in England. But showing your palm and making a V sign is okay.

B: ⑤What does that mean?

G: (C)It means victory or peace.

01 그림을 참고하고, 주어진 단어를 이용하여 빈칸 (A)에 알맞은 말을 쓰시오.

➡ _____

(toward, himself, palm, face)

02 주어진 단어를 이용하여 빈칸 (B)를 채우시오.

➡ _____

03  ①~⑤ 중 어법상 어색한 부분을 찾아 고치시오.

_____ ➡ _____

04 밑줄 친 (C)가 가리키는 것을 본문에서 찾아 쓰시오.

➡ _____

[05~07] 다음 대화를 읽고, 물음에 답하시오.

A: (A)_____ do you see in this picture?

B: The girl is ⓐ_____.

A: (B)_____ does ⓑ_____ mean in India?

B: 불운을 뜻해.

05 빈칸 (A)와 (B)에 공통으로 들어갈 단어를 쓰시오.

➡ _____

06 그림을 참고하고, 주어진 단어를 이용해 빈칸 ⓐ와 ⓑ에 공통으로 들어갈 말을 쓰시오. (7단어) (cut, on, hair, get)

➡ _____

07 밑줄 친 우리말을 영작하시오.

➡ _____

08 다음 대화의 밑줄 친 우리말을 영작하시오.

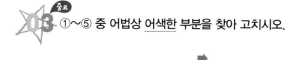

G: 너는 브라질에 가 봤니?

B: No, I haven't.

➡ _____

교과서
Grammar

① 현재완료

- For a long time, Koreans **have thought** that fish are good guards.
  오랜 세월 동안, 한국인들은 물고기가 훌륭한 파수꾼이라고 생각해 왔다.

- **Have** you ever **visited** Paris before? 너는 전에 파리에 가 본 적이 있니?

■ 현재완료는 'have[has] + 과거분사'의 형태로 과거의 일이 현재까지 영향을 주는 동작 · 상태의 의미를 나타낸다.

■ 부정형은 'have[has] not + 과거분사'이며, 의문형은 'Have[Has] + 주어 + 과거분사 ~?'로 나타낸다.
  - I **haven't completed** the work yet. 나는 일이 아직 안 끝났다.
  - How long **have** you **lived** together? 당신들은 얼마 동안 함께 살았습니까?

■ 현재완료는 '완료(지금[막] …했다), 경험(…해 본 적이 있다), 계속((지금까지) …해 왔다), 결과(…해서 (그 결과) 지금 ~하다)'의 네 가지 용법으로 쓰인다.
  완료 용법은 보통 'just, already, yet'과 같은 부사와 함께 쓰이며, 경험 용법은 'ever, never, once, before' 등과 같은 부사와 함께 쓰인다.
  계속 용법은 보통 'for+기간 명사'나 'since+시간 명사'와 함께 쓰이며 결과 용법은 과거에 발생한 사건이 현재 미치고 있는 결과를 포함한다.
  - They **have** already **finished** their lunch. 〈완료〉 그들은 이미 점심식사를 끝마쳤다.
  - I **have** never **been** here before. 〈경험〉 저는 이곳이 처음입니다.
  - He **has been** missing since last month. 〈계속〉 그는 지난달부터 실종되었다.
  - She **has lost** her purse. 〈결과〉 그녀는 지갑을 잃어버렸다. (그 결과 (지갑이) 지금 없다.)

  *have[has] been to vs. have[has] gone to
  have[has] been to는 '~에 가 본적이 있다'는 경험을 나타내고, have[has] gone to는 '~에 가고 없다' 는 결과를 나타낸다. 그러므로 have[has] gone to는 3인칭만 주어로 쓸 수 있다.

■ 현재완료는 과거의 일이 현재까지 영향을 주는 동작 · 상태를 나타내므로 과거를 나타내는 어구와 함께 쓸 수 없다.
  - We **ate** lunch an hour ago.　　　(○)
  - We have eaten lunch an hour ago. (×)

핵심 Check

1. 주어진 동사를 어법에 맞게 쓰시오.
   (1) They _____ _____ to Seoul. So you cannot meet them now. (go)
   (2) I _____ never _____ Seoul. (visit)
   (3) _____ you ever _____ *The Little Prince*? (read)

2 결과를 나타내는 so ... that 구문

- It's **so** old **that** I can't really tell, but is it a fish?
  그것은 매우 오래되어서 정말 알 수가 없는데, 그건 물고기인가요?

- This book was **so** sad **that** I cried. 이 책이 매우 슬퍼서 나는 울었어.

■ 'so+형용사[부사]+that+주어+동사'의 형태로 '매우 …해서 ~하다'라는 의미이며 원인과 그에 따른 결과를 서술할 때 쓰인다.

■ so 뒤의 형용사나 부사는 원인을 나타내며, 접속사 that 뒤에 나오는 내용은 그에 따른 결과를 나타낸다.
  - I was **so** tired **that** I couldn't exercise. 나는 너무 피곤해서 운동할 수 없었다.
  - He was **so** happy **that** he danced. 그는 너무 기뻐 춤을 추었다.

■ 'so ... that' 구문에서 that 앞에 형용사나 부사 대신 명사가 오면 so 대신 such를 쓴다.
  - He was **such** a good runner **that** I couldn't catch him. 그가 너무 빨리 달려 나는 그를 따라잡을 수가 없었다.

■ 'so+형용사[부사]+that+주어+can ~'는 '형용사[부사]+enough+to 동사원형'으로 바꿔 쓸 수 있으며, 'so+형용사[부사]+that+주어+can't ~'는 'too+형용사[부사]+to 동사원형'으로 바꿔 쓸 수 있다.

  - She is **so** kind **that** she can help her friends.
    = She is kind **enough to** help her friends.

  - He was **so** sick **that** he couldn't go out.
    = He was **too** sick **to** go out.

핵심 Check

2. 다음 우리말에 맞게 빈칸에 알맞은 말을 쓰시오.

(1) 나는 오늘 너무 바빠서 갈 수가 없어.

I'm _____ _____ _____ I can't go today.

(2) 그의 모자는 너무 커서 그것은 그의 눈을 가렸다.

His hat was _____ _____ _____ it covered his eyes.

01 다음 문장에서 어법상 어색한 부분을 바르게 고쳐 쓰시오.

(1) I have visit there many times.

_____ ➡ _____

(2) She has finished the work yesterday.

_____ ➡ _____

(3) Do you have cleaned your room?

_____ ➡ _____

(4) I'm so busy what I can't go out today.

_____ ➡ _____

(5) The room was very dirty that it smelled bad.

_____ ➡ _____

(6) Sam has lived with his pet dog for 2015.

_____ ➡ _____

(7) The man have lived with them for a long time.

_____ ➡ _____

02 다음 중 어법상 어색한 것은?

① I've never heard that before.
② Have you finished your homework?
③ Joel has work for 6 hours straight.
④ The bus has just arrived.
⑤ Linda has lost her smartphone.

03 다음 대화의 빈칸에 들어갈 말로 알맞은 것은?

M: How was your trip to Vietnam?
W: It was great!
M: Did you visit Danang?
W: Yes, of course. The place was _____ beautiful that I stayed a few more days.

① so   ② such   ③ very
④ too   ⑤ enough

01 다음 빈칸에 알맞은 말이 순서대로 바르게 짝지어진 것은?

> • _____ you ever visited Tibet?
> • I have never _____ to Rome.

① Were – gone
② Were – been
③ Have – gone
④ Have – been
⑤ Did – being

02 다음 문장의 밑줄 친 부분 중에서 어법상 잘못된 곳을 고르시오.

> Amy was ①too ②sick yesterday ③that she ④couldn't take part ⑤in the meeting.

03 다음 질문에 대한 응답으로 알맞은 것은?

> Has Chris ever visited Seoul?

① Yes, he is.
② Yes, he does.
③ No, he isn't.
④ No, he doesn't.
⑤ No, he hasn't.

04 다음 빈칸에 알맞은 말이 바르게 짝지어진 것은?

> Steve was _____ hungry _____ he ate all the food on the table.

① as – as   ② such – as
③ so – that   ④ too – to
⑤ enough – to

서답형

05 다음 괄호 안에서 알맞은 말을 고르시오.

(1) I have (visited / visit) Phuket, Thailand.
(2) She (have / has) gone to Jeju.
(3) You can't meet her now. She has (been / gone) to China.
(4) Ann has been to Paris (before / ago).
(5) He (doesn't have / hasn't) read *The Little Prince*.

06 다음 중 어법상 바르지 <u>않은</u> 것은?

① Dad's explanation was too clear that we could understand it easily.
② They have lived there since 2010.
③ The math problems were so easy that we could solve them.
④ Evan has just finished his homework.
⑤ Emma felt so sick that she couldn't even breathe.

07 다음 우리말을 영어로 바르게 옮긴 것은?

> 나는 전에 스페인 음식을 먹어본 적이 없다.

① I didn't eat Spanish food ago.
② I don't eat Spanish food before.
③ I have never eat Spanish food before.
④ I don't have eaten Spanish food before.
⑤ I have never eaten Spanish food before.

08 다음 괄호 안에서 알맞은 말을 고르시오.

(1) Jack was (so / such) witty that he became popular among us.

(2) *Mona Lisa* is so wonderful (that / what) people love it.

(3) It gave him (so / such) a shock that his face turned white.

(4) The boxes were so heavy that I (wouldn't / couldn't) carry them.

09 다음 빈칸에 알맞은 말이 순서대로 짝지어진 것은?

• Ben has lived in Jeonju _____ 5 years.
• Ben has lived in Jeonju _____ 2005.

① after – for   ② for – after
③ since – for   ④ for – since
⑤ as – for

10 다음 두 문장을 한 문장으로 바르게 연결한 것은?

• Amanda studied very hard.
• So she got an A⁺.

① Amanda studied very hard that she got an A⁺.

② Amanda studied so hard that she got an A⁺.

③ Amanda studied hard so that she got an A⁺.

④ Amanda studied hard enough that she got an A⁺.

⑤ Amanda studied too hard that she could get an A⁺.

11 다음 중 밑줄 친 부분의 용법이 <u>다른</u> 하나는?

① I have already eaten dinner.
② Have you ever played golf before?
③ Harry has not written his report yet.
④ The train has just left the platform.
⑤ Emily has just finished her homework.

12 다음 문장을 주어진 어휘를 이용하여 같은 의미가 되도록 바꿔 쓰시오.

(1) Julia got so angry that she couldn't speak. (too)
➡ _____

(2) Sean is so rich that he can buy the expensive car. (enough)
➡ _____

(3) The panda is so cute that I can't take my eyes off him. (to)
➡ _____

(4) The house was so nice that Melanie wanted to live there. (to)
➡ _____

13 다음 두 문장을 한 문장으로 바르게 바꾼 것은?

• Paulinya went to Russia.
• And she still stays there.

① Paulinya went to Russia.
② Paulinya has been to Russia.
③ Paulinya hasn't gone to Russia.
④ Paulinya has gone to Russia.
⑤ Paulinya hasn't come back yet.

They go outside and walk around the garden.

Peter: What is on that piece of paper? It looks scary.
= sheet   감각동사 look 뒤에는 형용사가 온다.

Grandfather: Do you mean this painting of a rooster?
목적격 관계를 나타내는 전치사. …을, …의

Peter: Oh, is it a rooster?

Grandfather: Yes, it is. Roosters crow every morning.

Their crowing means that a new day is beginning. For many years,
= Roosters'   접속사

Koreans have believed evil spirits go away when a rooster crows.
have believed는 현재완료 시제로, 여기서는 과거의 일이 현재까지 계속됨을 나타낸다.
evil spirits go away는 목적어로 쓰인 명사절이고, evil 앞에 접속사 that이 생략되어 있다.

Mina: Really? I've never heard that before.

Peter: Actually, I'm afraid of darkness and evil spirits. Could you
= In fact   be afraid of: ~을 무서워하다

draw a rooster for me, Mina?

Mina: Sure. I'll draw a big rooster for you!

Grandfather: Put the drawing above your door. Then it will protect

you.

Peter: Yes, I will.

Peter's Diary   May 28

I'm enjoying this trip so much that I want to stay longer. I love
원인과 결과를 나타내는 so … that 구문으로, so 다음에 부사 much가 쓰였다. '너무 …해서 ~하다'라는 의미이다.

all the traditional Korean symbols in this house. Now I understand

a lot of them. I want to visit Korea again with my family.

rooster 수탉
crow (닭이) 울다
evil 사악한, 악마의
spirit 정신, 영혼
go away 사라지다, 떠나가다
protect 보호하다

확인문제

● 다음 문장이 본문의 내용과 일치하면 T, 일치하지 않으면 F를 쓰시오.

1   Peter asks what is on that piece of paper. ☐

2   Roosters' crowing means that a new day is ending. ☐

3   Koreans have believed evil spirits appear when a rooster crows. ☐

4   Peter is afraid of darkness and evil spirits. ☐

5   Mina will draw a big rooster for Peter. ☐

6   Peter wants to visit Korea again with his friends. ☐

● 우리말을 참고하여 빈칸에 알맞은 말을 쓰시오.

1 _____ Korean Symbols

2 Peter is visiting Korea to meet a friend, Mina, _____ _____ _____ _____.

3 Peter is going to _____ _____ her grandfather's house _____ _____ _____ _____.

4 When he arrives, Mina shows _____ _____ _____.

5 Peter, you will _____ _____.

6 This guest room _____ _____ _____ traditional Korean things.

7 _____ _____ this pillow.

8 What are _____ _____?

9 _____ bats.

10 Bats _____ _____ _____? That's _____!

11 _____ _____. In Korea, bats are _____ _____ luck and a long life.

12 That's _____. In many Western countries, bats _____ people _____ darkness and scary things.

13 Mina _____ Peter her grandfather's room.

14 Peter and Mina's grandfather _____ and _____ _____ _____.

15 Hi, Peter! _____ _____ _____ _____ this kind of lock before?

16 No, I _____. It's _____ old _____ I can't really tell, but is it a fish?

17 Yes. _____ _____ _____ _____, Koreans have thought that fish are _____ _____.

1	전통적인 한국의 상징물
2	피터는 자매 학교 친구인 미나를 만나기 위해 한국을 방문 중이다.
3	피터는 일주일간 미나네 할아버지 댁에 머무를 것이다.
4	그가 도착하자, 미나가 그에게 손님방을 보여준다.
5	피터, 넌 여기에 머무르게 될 거야.
6	이 손님방은 한국의 전통 물건들로 가득 차 있어.
7	이 베개를 봐.
8	이것들은 뭐야?
9	그건 박쥐들이야.
10	내 베개 위에 박쥐가? 그거 겁나는데!
11	그렇지 않아. 한국에서는 박쥐가 행운과 장수의 상징이거든.
12	그거 놀라운 일인데. 서구의 많은 나라들에서 박쥐는 사람들에게 어둠과 무서운 것들을 상기시키거든.
13	미나는 피터에게 할아버지의 방을 보여준다.
14	피터와 미나의 할아버지가 만나서 서로 인사한다.
15	안녕, 피터! 너는 이런 종류의 자물쇠를 전에 본 적 있니?
16	아니요, 본 적 없어요. 그 자물쇠는 너무 오래되어서 사실 알아볼 수가 없는데, 그건 물고기인가요?
17	맞아. 오랜 세월 동안, 한국인들은 물고기가 훌륭한 파수꾼이라고 생각해 왔단다.

18 Fish don't _____ _____ _____, even when they sleep.

19 That's _____.

20 We think fish can _____ _____ valuable things. _____ _____ this lock looks _____ a fish.

21 Now I _____.

22 They go outside and _____ _____ the garden.

23 What is on _____ _____ _____ _____? It looks scary.

24 _____ _____ _____ this painting of a rooster?

25 Oh, is it _____ _____?

26 Yes, it is. Roosters _____ every morning.

27 Their crowing means that _____ _____ _____ is beginning.

28 For many years, Koreans have believed evil spirits _____ _____ when a rooster _____.

29 Really? _____ _____ _____ that before.

30 _____, I'm _____ of darkness and evil spirits.

31 Could you draw a rooster _____ _____, Mina?

32 Sure. I'll _____ _____ _____ _____ for you!

33 _____ the drawing _____ your door. Then it will _____ you.

34 Yes, I _____.

35 I'm enjoying this trip _____ _____ _____ I want to stay longer.

36 I love all the _____ _____ _____ in this house.

37 Now I understand _____ _____ _____ _____.

38 I want to visit Korea again _____ _____ _____.

18 물고기는 잘 때도 눈을 감지 않거든.

19 그거 재미있군요.

20 우리는 물고기가 귀중품을 지킬 수 있다고 생각해. 그것이 이 자물쇠가 물고기 모양으로 생긴 이유란다.

21 이제 이해가 되는군요.

22 그들은 밖에 나가서 정원을 걷는다.

23 저 종이에는 무엇이 그려져 있는 거죠? 무서워 보여요.

24 이 수탉 그림을 말하는 거니?

25 오, 그게 수탉이에요?

26 응, 그렇단다. 수탉은 매일 아침 울지.

27 수탉의 울음은 새로운 날이 시작하는 것을 의미해.

28 오랫동안 한국인들은 수탉이 울 때 악령이 물러간다고 믿어 왔단다.

29 정말요? 전 그런 말을 들어본 적이 없어요.

30 사실 전 어둠과 악령을 무서워해요.

31 미나야, 날 위해 수탉을 그려 줄 수 있니?

32 물론이지. 내가 널 위해 커다란 수탉을 그려줄게!

33 그 그림을 네 문 위에 걸어 놓으렴. 그러면 그게 널 지켜 줄 거야.

34 네, 그럴게요.

35 난 이번 여행이 매우 즐거워서 더 오래 머무르고 싶다.

36 난 이 집의 모든 전통적인 한국의 상징물들이 아주 마음에 든다.

37 나는 이제 그것들을 많이 알게 되었다.

38 난 우리 가족과 함께 한국을 다시 방문하고 싶다.

● 우리말을 참고하여 본문을 영작하시오.

1 ▷ 전통적인 한국의 상징물

➡ _____

2 ▷ 피터는 자매 학교 친구인 미나를 만나기 위해 한국을 방문 중이다.

➡ _____

3 ▷ 피터는 일주일간 미나네 할아버지 댁에 머무를 것이다.

➡ _____

4 ▷ 그가 도착하자, 미나가 그에게 손님방을 보여준다.

➡ _____

5 ▷ 피터, 넌 여기에 머무르게 될 거야.

➡ _____

6 ▷ 이 손님방은 한국의 전통 물건들로 가득 차 있어.

➡ _____

7 ▷ 이 베개를 봐.

➡ _____

8 ▷ 이것들은 뭐야?

➡ _____

9 ▷ 그건 박쥐들이야.

➡ _____

10 ▷ 내 베개 위에 박쥐가? 그거 겁나는데!

➡ _____

11 ▷ 그렇지 않아. 한국에서는 박쥐가 행운과 장수의 상징이거든.

➡ _____

12 ▷ 그거 놀라운 일인데. 서구의 많은 나라들에서 박쥐는 사람들에게 어둠과 무서운 것들을 상기시키거든.

➡ _____

13 ▷ 미나는 피터에게 할아버지의 방을 보여준다.

➡ _____

14 ▷ 피터와 미나의 할아버지가 만나서 서로 인사한다.

➡ _____

15 ▷ 안녕, 피터! 너는 이런 종류의 자물쇠를 전에 본 적 있니?

➡ _____

16 ▷ 아니요, 본 적 없어요. 그 자물쇠는 너무 오래되어서 사실 알아볼 수가 없는데, 그건 물고기인가요?

➡ _____

17 ▷ 맞아. 오랜 세월 동안, 한국인들은 물고기가 훌륭한 파수꾼이라고 생각해 왔단다.

➡ _____

dance. One of the most famous dances is the lion dance. In this dance, two dancers dress and act like lions. They usually dance on special days, such as New Year's Day. I think their dance moves are great. I hope to practice this dance someday.

18 위 글의 빈칸 ⓐ에 들어갈 알맞은 말을 고르시오.

① However　　② In other words
③ Therefore　　④ In addition
⑤ For example

서답형

19 다음 문장에서 위 글의 내용과 <u>다른</u> 부분을 찾아서 고치시오. (두 군데)

A lion dance is a traditional Chinese dance and people usually perform it at any time. In this dance, three dancers dress and act like lions.

➡ (1) _____
　(2) _____

[20~21] 다음 글을 읽고, 물음에 답하시오.

My trip to Korea was great. My friend Mina and her grandfather were very kind to me. (A)[During / For] my trip, I learned (B)[a lot / a lot of] about traditional Korean symbols. That was so (C)[interesting / interested] that I want to visit Korea again with my family.
　　　　　　　　　　　　　　I: Peter

서답형

20 위 글의 괄호 (A)~(C)에서 어법상 알맞은 낱말을 골라 쓰시오.

➡ (A)_____ (B)_____ (C)_____

중요

21 위 글을 읽고 피터의 여행에 대해 알 수 없는 것을 고르시오.

① 여행 장소　　② 여행 기간
③ 같이 지낸 사람들　　④ 여행에서 배운 것
⑤ 여행에 대한 느낌

[22~24] 다음 글을 읽고, 물음에 답하시오.

Peter: What is on that piece of paper? It looks scary.
Grandfather: Do you mean this painting of a rooster?
Peter: Oh, is it a rooster?
Grandfather: Yes, it is. Roosters crow every morning. Their crowing means that a new day is (A)[beginning / ending]. For many years, Koreans have believed evil spirits go away when a rooster crows.
Mina: Really? I've never heard that before.
Peter: ⓐActually, I'm afraid of darkness and evil spirits. ⓑCould you draw a rooster for me, Mina?
Mina: Sure. I'll draw a big rooster for you!
Grandfather: Put the drawing above your door. Then it will (B)[prevent / protect] you.
Peter: Yes, I (C)[do / will].

서답형

22 위 글의 괄호 (A)~(C)에서 문맥이나 어법상 알맞은 낱말을 골라 쓰시오.

➡ (A)_____ (B)_____ (C)_____

23 위 글의 밑줄 친 ⓐActually와 바꿔 쓸 수 있는 말을 <u>모두</u> 고르시오.

① As a result　　② In fact
③ Above all　　④ In other words
⑤ As a matter of fact

서답형

24 다음 빈칸 (A)와 (B)에 들어갈 알맞은 단어를 본문에서 찾아, Peter가 밑줄 친 ⓑ처럼 말한 이유를 완성하시오.

Because Peter is (A)_____ of darkness and evil spirits and he wants them to (B)_____ _____ thanks to the painting of a rooster.

[01~03] 다음 글을 읽고, 물음에 답하시오.

Peter is visiting Korea to meet a friend, Mina, from a sister school. Peter is going to stay at her grandfather's house for a week. When he arrives, ⓐMina shows him the guest room.

Mina: Peter, you will stay here. This guest room is full of traditional Korean things. Look at this pillow.
Peter: What are these things?
Mina: They're bats.
Peter: Bats on my pillow? That's scary!
Mina: Not really. In Korea, bats are symbols of luck and a long life.
Peter: That's surprising. In many Western countries, bats remind people of darkness and scary things.

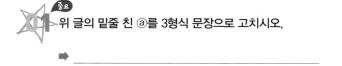

01 위 글의 밑줄 친 ⓐ를 3형식 문장으로 고치시오.

➡ _____

02 다음 질문에 대한 알맞은 대답을 주어진 단어로 시작하여 쓰시오. (5 단어)

Q: What do bats symbolize in Korea?
A: They symbolize _____.

03 다음 문장에서 위 글의 내용과 다른 부분을 찾아서 고치시오.

Bats remind people of happiness and pleasant things in many Western countries.

_____ ➡ _____

[04~07] 다음 글을 읽고, 물음에 답하시오.

Mina shows Peter her grandfather's room. ⓐPeter and Mina's grandfather meet and greet to each other.
Grandfather: Hi, Peter! ⓑ너는 이런 종류의 자물쇠를 전에 본 적 있니?
Peter: No, I haven't. It's so old that I can't really tell, but is it a fish?
Grandfather: Yes. For a long time, Koreans have thought that fish are good guards. Fish don't close their eyes, even when they sleep.
Peter: That's interesting.
Grandfather: We think fish can watch over valuable things. That's why this lock looks like a fish.
Peter: Now I understand.

04 위 글의 밑줄 친 ⓐ에서 어법상 틀린 부분을 찾아 고치시오.

_____ ➡ _____

05 위 글의 밑줄 친 ⓑ의 우리말에 맞게 한 단어를 보충하여, 주어진 어휘를 알맞게 배열하시오.

seen / lock / this / you / kind / ever / of / have

➡ _____

06 다음 질문에 대한 알맞은 대답을 주어진 단어로 시작하여 쓰시오. (9 단어)

Q: Why have Koreans thought that fish are good guards?
A: Because _____
_____.

15 다음 우리말을 영어로 바르게 옮긴 것은?

> 그는 너무 천천히 걸어서 회의에 늦었다.

① He walked too slowly as he was late for the meeting.
② He walked slowly so that he was late for the meeting.
③ He walked so slowly that he was late for the meeting.
④ He walked slowly enough that he was late for the meeting.
⑤ He walked too slowly to be late for the meeting.

16 다음 중 어법상 어색한 것은?

① When have you visited London?
② Have you watched *The Wizard of Oz*?
③ Lindsay has visited Korea twice.
④ We have known her since she was a little girl.
⑤ Jake has been sick for two weeks.

17 다음 두 문장을 한 문장으로 바르게 연결한 것은?

> • Mom became very angry.
> • Mom yelled at me.

① Mom became very angry that she yelled at me.
② Mom became enough angry to yell at me.
③ Mom became too angry to yell at me.
④ Mom became angry as that she yelled at me.
⑤ Mom became so angry that she yelled at me.

18 다음 우리말에 맞게 빈칸에 알맞은 말을 쓰시오.

> Sonya는 너무 피곤해서 곧 잠이 들었다.

➡ Sonya was _____ tired _____ she fell asleep in a moment.

19 다음 우리말과 의미가 같도록 빈칸에 알맞은 말을 쓰시오.

(1) 그는 인도를 방문해 본 적이 없다.
　➡ He _____ never _____ to India.
(2) Shirley는 영국에 가서 여기 없다.
　➡ Shirley _____ _____ to England.

20 다음 중 어법상 어색한 것은?

① He is so smart that he can solve all these math problems without a calculator.
② Nicole was very tired that she couldn't go shopping.
③ Ms. Winslet is such a nice teacher that she gives all her students gifts.
④ The little boy was too short to reach the shelf.
⑤ Edan studied hard enough to pass the math test.

21 괄호 안에 주어진 어휘를 이용하여 다음을 영작하시오.

(1) 그 차는 너무 빨라서 경찰은 그것을 잡을 수 없었다. (the car, fast, that, the police, catch)
　➡ _____
(2) 그 콘서트는 너무 좋아서 많은 사람들이 그것을 다시 보러 갔다. (the concert, good, that, see, again)
　➡ _____

22 주어진 두 문장을 현재완료를 이용해 한 문장으로 만드시오.

(1) Lin spent all the money for shopping. So she doesn't have any money now.

➡ _____

(2) Jeremy started to play the piano six years ago. And he still plays the piano.

➡ _____

Reading

[23~24] 다음 글을 읽고, 물음에 답하시오.

Peter is visiting Korea ⓐto meet a friend, Mina, from a sister school. Peter is going to stay at her grandfather's house for a week. When he arrives, Mina shows him the guest room.

Mina: Peter, you will stay here. This guest room is full of (A)[modern / traditional] Korean things. Look at this pillow.

Peter What are these things?

Mina: They're bats.

Peter: Bats on my pillow? That's (B)[scary / terrific]!

Mina: Not really. In Korea, bats are symbols of luck and a long life.

Peter: That's surprising. In many Western countries, bats (C)[remind / remain] people of darkness and scary things.

23 위 글의 밑줄 친 ⓐto meet과 to부정사의 용법이 같은 것을 모두 고르시오.

① I went to the store to buy some eggs.
② It wasn't easy to solve the problem.
③ He wanted to get a good grade.
④ I have some questions to ask her.
⑤ He studied hard to be a scientist.

24 위 글의 괄호 (A)~(C)에서 문맥상 알맞은 낱말을 골라 쓰시오.

➡ (A)_____ (B)_____ (C)_____

[25~27] 다음 글을 읽고, 물음에 답하시오.

Mina shows Peter her grandfather's room. Peter and Mina's grandfather meet and greet each other.

Grandfather: Hi, Peter! Have you ever seen this kind of lock before?

Peter: No, I haven't. It's ⓐ old ⓑ I can't really tell, but is it a fish?

Grandfather: Yes. For a long time, Koreans have thought that fish are good guards. Fish don't close their eyes, even when they sleep.

Peter: ⓒThat's interesting.

Grandfather: We think fish can watch over valuable things. That's why this lock looks like a fish.

Peter: Now I understand.

25 위 글의 빈칸 ⓐ와 ⓑ에 들어갈 알맞은 말을 고르시오.

① such – that   ② too – as
③ enough – that   ④ so – that
⑤ so – as

26 위 글의 밑줄 친 ⓒThat이 가리키는 것을 본문에서 찾아 쓰시오.

➡ _____

27 위 글의 주제로 알맞은 것을 고르시오.

① the reason Mina shows Peter her grandfather's room
② the most popular kind of lock in Korea
③ the reason fish don't close their eyes
④ various kinds of locks in traditional Korean houses
⑤ the reason the lock looks like a fish

[28~30] 다음 글을 읽고, 물음에 답하시오.

Peter: What is on that piece of paper? It looks scary.
Grandfather: Do you mean this painting of a rooster?
Peter: Oh, is it a rooster?
Grandfather: Yes, it is. Roosters crow every morning. Their crowing means that a new day is beginning. For many years, Koreans have believed ⓐ_____ when a rooster crows.
Mina: Really? I've never heard that before.
Peter: Actually, I'm afraid _____ⓑ darkness and evil spirits. Could you draw a rooster _____ⓒ me, Mina?
Mina: Sure. I'll draw a big rooster _____ⓒ you!
Grandfather: Put the drawing above your door. Then it will protect you.
Peter: Yes, I will.

28 위 글의 빈칸 ⓐ에 들어갈 알맞은 말을 고르시오.

① evil spirits go away
② darkness follows
③ people go to sleep
④ evil spirits arrive
⑤ it gets dark

29 위 글의 빈칸 ⓑ와 ⓒ에 들어갈 전치사가 바르게 짝지어진 것은?

① in – to   ② of – at
③ of – for   ④ for – to
⑤ in – for

30 위 글의 내용과 일치하지 않는 것은?

① 피터는 종이 위에 있는 그림을 무서워한다.
② 피터는 종이 위에 수탉 그림이 있는 것을 알고 있었다.
③ 수탉의 울음은 새로운 날이 시작하는 것을 의미한다.
④ 피터는 어둠과 악령을 무서워한다.
⑤ 미나는 피터를 위해 커다란 수탉을 그려줄 것이다.

[31~32] 다음 일기를 읽고, 물음에 답하시오.

Peter's Diary

May 28

I'm enjoying this trip so much that I want ⓐto stay longer. I love all the traditional Korean symbols in this house. ⓑNow I understand a lot of it. I want to visit Korea again with my family.

31 아래 〈보기〉에서 위 일기의 밑줄 친 ⓐto stay와 문법적 쓰임이 같은 것의 개수를 고르시오.

┌─ 보기 ─┐
① It is time to go to bed.
② She decided to meet him again.
③ I worked hard to pass the test.
④ He is the last man to tell a lie.
⑤ It is good to help the old.
└─────┘

① 1개   ② 2개   ③ 3개   ④ 4개   ⑤ 5개

32 위 일기의 밑줄 친 ⓑ에서 어법상 틀린 부분을 찾아 고치시오.

_____ ➡ _____

[01~02] 주어진 문장의 뒤에 나올 대화의 순서를 알맞게 쓰시오.

출제율 90%

01

There is a Holi festival in Busan this year.

(A) That sounds exciting. Have you ever been to a Holi festival?

(B) It's a traditional Indian festival. People throw colored powder and water at each other.

(C) A Holi festival? What is that?

(D) No, I haven't. But my Indian friend told me a lot about it.

➡ _____

출제율 85%

02

Oh, look at that boy. That's really rude.

(A) What's wrong with that?

(B) It has a bad meaning in England. But showing your palm and making a V sign is okay.

(C) It means victory or peace.

(D) Which boy?

(E) What does that mean?

(F) The boy who is making the V sign. His palm is facing toward himself.

➡ _____

[03~04] 다음 대화를 읽고, 물음에 답하시오.

G: Have you ever been to Brazil?

B: No, I (A)_____. (B)_____ you?

G: Yes, I (C)_____. I went there last year. There (D)_____ a big samba festival.

B: That (E)_____ interesting. I hope (F)_____ there someday.

출제율 100%

03 빈칸 (A)~(C)에 들어갈 단어를 쓰시오. (각 1 단어)

➡ (A)_____ (B)_____ (C)_____

출제율 90%

04 빈칸 (D)~(F)에 들어갈 말이 바르게 짝지어진 것은?

	(D)	(E)	(F)
①	is	sounds	go
②	is	sounds like	to go
③	was	sounds like	going
④	was	sounds	to go
⑤	were	sounds like	going

[05~07] 다음 대화를 읽고, 물음에 답하시오.

B: Ling's birthday is this Wednesday, isn't it?

G: Yes. I'm going to buy a book for her. (①) What about you?

B: Well, I'm thinking about buying her an umbrella. I found a cute one in a gift shop. (②)

G: Oh, that's not a good gift for (A)_____ people. (③) It means something bad.

B: Really? What does an umbrella mean in China?

G: (④) The words for *separation* and *umbrella* sound the same in (B)_____.

B: I see. (⑤) Then how about chocolate?

G: That's a good idea.

Peter is visiting Korea to meet a friend, Mina, from a sister school. Peter is going to stay at her grandfather's house (A)[during / for] a week. When he arrives, Mina shows (B)[him / to him] the guest room.

Mina: Peter, you will stay here. This guest room is full of traditional Korean things. Look at this pillow.
Peter: What are these things?
Mina: They're bats.
Peter: Bats on my pillow? That's scary!
Mina: Not really. In Korea, bats are symbols of luck and a long life.
Peter: ⓐThat's (C)[surprising / surprised]. In many Western countries, bats remind people of darkness and scary things.

07 위 글의 괄호 (A)~(C)에서 어법상 알맞은 낱말을 골라 쓰시오.

➡ (A)_____ (B)_____ (C)_____

08 위 글의 밑줄 친 ⓐThat이 가리키는 것을 본문에서 찾아 쓰시오.

➡ _____

09 위 글을 읽고, 한국과 서구의 많은 나라들에서 박쥐가 상징하는 것이 어떻게 다른지 우리말로 쓰시오.

➡ 한국: _____

서구의 많은 나라들: _____

_____

Peter: What is on that piece of paper? It looks scary.
Grandfather: ⓐ이 수탉 그림을 말하는 거니?
Peter: Oh, is it a rooster?
Grandfather: Yes, it is. Roosters crow every morning. Their crowing means that a new day is beginning. For many years, Koreans have believed evil spirits go away when a rooster crows.
Mina: Really? I've never heard ⓑthat before.
Peter: Actually, I'm afraid of darkness and evil spirits. Could you draw a rooster for me, Mina?
Mina: Sure. I'll draw a big rooster for you!
Grandfather: Put the drawing above your door. Then it will protect you.
Peter: Yes, I will.

10 위 글의 밑줄 친 ⓐ의 우리말에 맞게 한 단어를 보충하여, 주어진 어휘를 알맞게 배열하시오.

| mean / painting / you / rooster / this / do / a |

➡ _____

11 다음 문장에서 위 글의 내용과 다른 부분을 찾아서 고치시오. (본문의 단어를 사용하시오.)

The meaning of roosters' crowing is that the sun is setting. For many years, Koreans have believed evil spirits disappear with the crowing of roosters.

_____ ➡ _____

12 위 글의 밑줄 친 ⓑthat이 가리키는 것을 본문에서 찾아 쓰시오.

➡ _____

01 다음 주어진 단어와 그림을 참고하여 대화를 완성하시오.

visit a Spanish festival

A: Have you ever _____?

B: No, _____. Have you?

A: Yes, I have. I _____ last year. (visit) There was a La Tomatina festival.

B: What is La Tomatina festival?

A: It's _____ festival. People _____.

B: _____?

A: It's the last Tuesday in August.

B: I'd like to go. It sounds interesting.

---

02 다음 내용을 바탕으로 학급 신문에 다른 나라의 전통 문화를 소개하는 글을 쓰시오.

1. Q: What do you want to talk about?

   A: I want to talk about traditional Chinese dances.

2. Q: What are some examples?

   A: There are a lion dance, a fan dance, and an umbrella dance.

3. Q: Choose one and search for more information about it.

   A: In the lion dance, two dancers dress and act like lions. They do the dance on special days.

4. Q: What do you think of it?

   A: I think their dance moves are great.

An Amazing Traditional Chinese Dance

Do you know about (A)_____ Chinese dances? There are many kinds. For example, there are a lion dance, a fan dance, and an umbrella dance. One of the most famous dances (B)_____ the lion dance. In this dance, two dancers dress and act (C)_____ lions. They usually dance on (D)_____ days, such as New Year's Day. I think their dance moves are great. I hope (E)_____ this dance someday.

Lesson 4

Go Green Together

 의사소통 기능

- 걱정 표현하기
  I'm worried about the Earth.

- 방법 묻기
  Can you tell me how to make the bag?

언어 형식

- 수동태
  The waste **is turned** into food for the plants by bacteria.

- 비교급 강조
  The plants grow **much** faster than plants in soil.

Words & Expressions

교과서

Key Words

- **air conditioner** 에어컨
- **amazing** [əméiziŋ] 형 놀라운
- **any** [əni] 형 어떤, 무슨
- **anywhere** [énihwɛər] 부 어디든
- **article** [ɑ́ːrtikl] 명 (신문) 기사
- **bottom** [bɑ́təm] 명 바닥, 맨 아래
- **chemical** [kémikəl] 명 화학 물질
- **clay** [klei] 명 점토
- **connect** [kənékt] 동 연결하다
- **consume** [kənsúːm] 동 섭취하다, 먹다, 소모하다
- **difficult** [dífkʌlt] 형 어려운
- **disappear** [dìsəpíər] 동 사라지다
- **documentary** [dkjuméntəri] 명 다큐멘터리, 기록물
- **enough** [inʌf] 형 충분한 부 충분히
- **environment** [inváiərənmənt] 명 환경
- **experiment** [ikspérəmənt] 명 실험
- **fan** [fæn] 명 선풍기, 부채
- **feed(-fed-fed)** [fiːd] 동 먹이를 주다, 먹이다
- **fix** [fiks] 동 고정하다
- **gardening** [ɡɑ́ːrdniŋ] 명 정원 가꾸기, 원예
- **global** [ɡlóubəl] 형 지구의
- **grow** [ɡrou] 동 재배하다
- **hang** [hæŋ] 동 매달려 있다
- **healthy** [hélθi] 형 건강한, 건강에 좋은
- **helpful** [hélpfəl] 형 도움이 되는, 유용한
- **hole** [houl] 명 구멍
- **information** [infərméiʃən] 명 정보
- **instead** [instéd] 부 대신에
- **interesting** [íntərəstiŋ] 형 흥미로운
- **island** [áilənd] 명 섬
- **leave** [liːv] 동 남기다, ~을 떠나다
- **lid** [lid] 명 뚜껑
- **nervous** [nə́ːrvəs] 형 초조한, 긴장된
- **plate** [pleit] 명 접시
- **pot** [pɑt] 명 화분, 그릇
- **pollution** [pəlúːʃən] 명 오염
- **problem** [prɑ́bləm] 명 문제
- **process** [prɑ́ses] 명 과정
- **produce** [prədjúːs] 동 생산하다, 만들다
- **productive** [prədʌ́ktiv] 형 생산적인
- **put** [put] 동 두다, 놓다
- **raise** [reiz] 동 기르다, 키우다
- **repeat** [ripíːt] 동 반복하다
- **say** [sei] 동 ~라고 쓰여 있다
- **sea level** 해수면
- **sew** [sou] 동 바느질하다
- **should** [səd] 조 ~해야 한다
- **speech contest** 말하기 대회
- **solution** [səlúːʃən] 명 해결책
- **soil** [sɔil] 명 토양, 흙
- **solve** [sɑlv] 동 해결하다
- **space** [speis] 명 공간
- **terrible** [térəbl] 형 끔찍한
- **too** [tuː] 부 너무, 지나치게
- **traditional** [trədíʃnl] 형 전통적인
- **warming** [wɔ́ːrmiŋ] 명 온난화
- **waste** [weist] 동 낭비하다 명 쓰레기, 폐기물
- **water** [wɔ́ːtər] 동 물을 주다

Key Expressions

- **be about ~** ~에 관한 것이다
- **be worried about** ~에 관해 걱정하다
- **cut A into B** A를 B로 자르다
- **fill A with B** A를 B로 채우다
- **get+비교급** 점점 ~해지다
- **go up** 올라가다, 상승하다
- **how to+동사원형** ~하는 방법
- **in danger** 위험에 처한
- **in place** 제자리에
- **look+형용사** ~처럼 보이다

- **right away** 즉시, 당장(=at once)
- **remind A of B** A에게 B를 상기시키다
- **run out** (시간이) 다 되다
- **throw away** 버리다
- **try to+동사원형** ~하려고 노력하다[애쓰다]
- **turn A into B** A를 B로 바꾸다
- **turn off** (전기, 가스, 수도 등을) 끄다
- **turn on** (전기, 가스, 수도 등을) 켜다
- **What[How] about ~?** ~은 어때?
- **Why don't you+동사원형 ~?** ~하는 게 어때?

Word Power

※ 서로 반대되는 뜻을 가진 단어

- □ **waste** (낭비하다) ↔ **save** (절약하다)
- □ **disappear** (사라지다) ↔ **appear** (나타나다)
- □ **turn off** (끄다) ↔ **turn on** (켜다)
- □ **near** (가까운) ↔ **far** (먼)
- □ **fill** (채우다) ↔ **empty** (비우다)
- □ **bottom** (바닥) ↔ **top** (꼭대기)

- □ **much** (양이 많은) ↔ **little** (양이 적은)
- □ **lose** (잃다) ↔ **gain** (얻다)
- □ **enough** (충분한) ↔ **short; lacking** (부족한)
- □ **difficult** (어려운) ↔ **easy** (쉬운)
- □ **without** (~ 없이) ↔ **with** (~이 있는, ~을 가지고)
- □ **productive** (생산적인) ↔ **unproductive** (비생산적인)

※ 서로 비슷한 뜻을 가진 단어

- □ **nervous : anxious** (초조한, 걱정하는)
- □ **danger : jeopardy** (위험)
- □ **connect : link** (연결하다)
- □ **produce : create** (만들어 내다)
- □ **solution : answer** (해결책, 해답)

- □ **raise : rear** (키우다, 기르다)
- □ **consume : eat** (섭취하다, 먹다)
- □ **choose : select** (고르다, 선택하다)
- □ **disappear : vanish** (사라지다)
- □ **amazing : astonishing** (놀라운)

English Dictionary

- □ **chemical** 화학 물질
  - → a substance used in chemistry or produced by a chemical process
    화학에서 사용되거나 화학 과정에서 만들어지는 물질
- □ **connect** 연결하다
  - → to join or be joined with something else 다른 무언가와 연결하거나 연결되다
- □ **consume** 먹다
  - → to eat or drink, especially a lot of something 어떤 것을 많이 먹거나 마시다
- □ **documentary** 다큐멘터리
  - → a film or a television or radio programme that gives detailed information about a particular subject 특별한 주제에 관해 상세한 정보를 제공하는 영화나 TV 또는 라디오 프로그램
- □ **feed** 먹이를 주다
  - → to give food to a person or animal 사람이나 동물에게 먹이를 주다
- □ **fix** 고정시키다
  - → to fasten something in position so that it cannot move
    움직이지 못하도록 무언가를 자리에 고정시키다

- □ **hole** 구멍
  - → an empty space in an object, usually with an opening to the object's surface 물체의 빈 공간, 대개 물체의 표면에 있는 틈
- □ **raise** 기르다, 키우다
  - → to take care of a person, or an animal or plant, until they are completely grown 완전히 자랄 때까지 사람이나 동물, 또는 식물을 돌보다
- □ **produce** 생산하다
  - → to make something or bring something into existence
    어떤 것을 만들거나 존재하게 하다
- □ **productive** 생산적인
  - → producing or achieving a lot
    많은 것을 생산하거나 성취[달성]하는
- □ **repeat** 반복하다
  - → to happen, or to do something, more than once
    한 번 이상 어떤 일이 일어나거나 어떤 것을 하다
- □ **water** 물을 주다
  - → to pour water onto plants or the soil that they are growing in 식물이 자라고 있는 토양이나 식물에 물을 붓다

서답형

01 다음 짝지어진 두 단어의 관계가 같도록 빈칸에 알맞은 단어를 주어진 글자로 시작하여 쓰시오.

> nervous : anxious – eat : c_____

02 다음 빈칸에 공통으로 들어갈 말은?

> • They turn off their lights for an hour to _____ people of our environmental problems.
> • This song _____s me of my first date.

① hang   ② remind   ③ make
④ fill   ⑤ leave

03 다음 중 밑줄 친 단어의 우리말 뜻이 **잘못된** 것은?

① Why don't you make a bag?
   왜 하지 않았니
② In some countries, people are in danger.
   위험에 처한
③ I am worried about my homework.
   ~에 관해 걱정하다
④ I want to talk about soil pollution.
   토양 오염
⑤ We should also use fans instead of air conditioners.   ~ 대신에

[04~05] 다음 영영풀이에 해당하는 단어를 고르시오.

04

> to happen, or to do something, more than once

① fix   ② produce
③ repeat   ④ connect
⑤ waste

05

> to fasten something in position so that it cannot move

① water   ② produce
③ sew   ④ fix
⑤ feed

서답형

06 다음 우리말에 맞게 빈칸에 알맞은 단어를 쓰시오.

> 그것을 사용하는 법을 말해 줄 수 있니?

➡ Can you tell me _____ _____ _____ it?

07 다음 빈칸에 들어갈 말이 알맞게 짝지어진 것은?

> • Cut them _____ small pieces.
> • We should not put too much food _____ our plates.

① with – for   ② into – in
③ from – at   ④ to – on
⑤ into – on

08 다음 우리말에 맞게 빈칸에 들어갈 말이 알맞게 짝지어진 것은?

> 한 가지 장치만으로도 식물과 물고기를 동시에 키울 수 있어.
> We can _____ plants and _____ fish in just one system.

① rise – raise   ② produce – fix
③ grow – raise   ④ consume – raise
⑤ grow – try

01 다음 빈칸에 들어갈 말을 〈보기〉에서 찾아 쓰시오. (필요하면 변형하여 쓰시오.)

┤ 보기 ├
article   turn   consume   water
appear   produce

(1) The plants clean the water by _____ the food.
(2) I'm reading an _____ about aquaponics.
(3) Aquaponics is a much more _____ way of growing food.
(4) The waste is _____ into food for the plants by bacteria.

02 다음 문장에 어울리는 단어를 〈보기〉에서 찾아 쓰시오. (필요하면 변형하여 쓰시오.)

┤ 보기 ├
connect   feed   bottom   solution

(1) After you _____ the fish, they produce waste.
(2) The speeches are about environmental problems and their _____.
(3) I used the tube to _____ the pump to the pot.
(4) I made holes in the _____ of a pot.

03 다음 우리말과 같은 표현이 되도록 문장의 빈칸을 채우시오.

(1) 나 다음 주에 있을 웅변대회 때문에 걱정이야.
➡ I'm _____ _____ the speech contest next week.
(2) 사람들은 한 시간 동안 불을 끈다.
➡ People _____ _____ their lights for an hour.
(3) 지구가 점점 더워지고 있어.
➡ The Earth is _____ _____.

04 다음 그림에 해당하는 단어를 주어진 철자로 시작하여 쓰시오.

(1)
➡ g_____

(2)
➡ t_____

(3)
➡ _____ d_____

(4)
➡ h_____

05 다음 영영풀이에 알맞은 단어를 〈보기〉에서 찾아 쓰시오.

┤ 보기 ├
chemical   disappear   raise

(1) _____ : to take care of a person, or an animal or plant, until they are completely grown
(2) _____ : to become impossible to see any longer

Conversation

1 걱정 표현하기

> **I'm worried about the Earth.** 나는 지구가 걱정돼.

- 'I'm worried about ~'은 걱정을 나타내는 표현으로 'I'm worried about' 뒤에 명사나 대명사, 동명사를 써서 '나는 ~에 대해 걱정한다.'라는 의미를 나타낸다.

■ 걱정이나 두려움을 표현할 때는 I'm worried about ~., I worry about ~., I'm concerned about[for] ~., I'm nervous about[of] ~., I'm anxious about[for] ~. 등으로 말할 수 있다

- I'm nervous about the exam. (나는 시험이 걱정돼.)
- I'm concerned about my health. (나는 내 건강이 걱정돼.)
- I feel uneasy about this matter. (나는 이 문제가 염려돼.)

■ 걱정을 표현한 상대에게 해 줄 수 있는 대답

- Don't worry. (걱정하지 마.)
- Try not to get worried. You'll do fine. (걱정하지 마. 넌 잘할 거야.)
- Take it easy. (마음 편히 가져.)
- Everything will be all right. (모든 게 괜찮아질 거야.)

핵심 Check

1. 다음 대화의 빈칸에 알맞은 말은?

   A: What's wrong?

   B: My math exam was very difficult. _____

   ① Don't worry.

   ② I'm worried about the result.

   ③ Mathematics is one of my favorites.

   ④ How about studying together?

   ⑤ I'm concerned about you.

2. 다음 우리말과 같은 의미가 되도록 주어진 단어를 이용하여 빈칸을 채우시오.

   음식 낭비가 걱정이야. (worry, waste)

   ➡ I'm _____ _____ _____ food.

② 방법 묻기

Can you tell me how to make the bag? 가방을 어떻게 만드는지 알려 줄 수 있니?

- 상대방에게 무엇인가를 하는 방법을 물을 때는 '~하는 방법'이라는 의미의 'how to+동사원형' 구문을 사용하여, 'Do you know how to+동사원형 ~?', 'Can you tell me how to+동사원형 ~?' 또는 'Can you explain (to me) how to+동사원형~?' 등과 같이 말할 수 있다.

- Do you know how to make a cake? (너는 케이크 만드는 방법을 아니?)
- Can you explain how to fix this radio? (이 라디오를 고치는 방법을 설명해 주겠니?)
- Can you tell me how to use a microwave? (전자레인지 사용하는 법을 나한테 말해 주겠니?)
- Do you know how to play the violin? (너는 바이올린을 연주하는 법을 아니?)

- 'how+to부정사'는 'how+주어+should+동사원형'으로 바꿔 쓸 수 있다.

- Do you know how to swim? (너는 수영하는 방법을 아니?)
  = Do you know how you should swim?
- Can you tell me how to make the bag? 가방을 어떻게 만드는지 알려 줄 수 있니?
  = Can you tell me how I should make the bag?

핵심 Check

3. 다음 대화의 밑줄 친 부분과 바꾸어 쓸 수 있는 것은?

    A: Are you good at cooking?

    B: Yes, I know <u>how I should make</u> cookies and sandwiches.

    ① how to should make   ② how to making

    ③ what to make   ④ how to make

    ⑤ how I to make

4. 다음 빈칸에 들어갈 알맞은 것은?

    Do you know _____ to make cheese?

    ① what   ② why   ③ when

    ④ where   ⑤ how

5. 다음 우리말에 맞게 주어진 단어를 이용하여 빈칸을 채우시오.

    눈사람 그리는 방법을 말해 주겠니? (how, draw)

    Can you tell me _____ _____ _____ a snowman?

🎤 **Listen and Talk 1 Get Ready**

> **B:** In my school, ❶students leave so much food on their plates. ❷I'm worried about wasting food.
> **G:** Right, that's a big problem. ❸We should not put too much food on our plates.
> **B:** You're right. ❹We shouldn't.

B: 우리 학교에서, 학생들이 그릇에 너무 많은 음식을 남겨. 나는 음식 낭비가 걱정이야.
G: 맞아. 큰 문제야. 우리가 접시에 너무 많은 음식을 담으면 안 돼.
B: 맞아. 우리는 그러면 안 돼.

❶ leave는 '~을 남기다'는 뜻이고, so는 부사로 much를 수식한다.
❷ be worried about은 '~에 대해 걱정하다'는 뜻이고, 전치사 about 뒤에는 명사나 동명사를 사용한다.
❸ should not은 '~해서는 안 된다'는 의미고, put A on B는 'A를 B에 놓다[두다]'는 뜻이다.
❹ We shouldn't.는 We shouldn't put too much food on our plates.를 줄인 말이다.

Check(√) True or False

(1) The boy is worried about wasting food.　　　　T ☐ F ☐

(2) The girl doesn't agree with the boy's opinion.　　T ☐ F ☐

🎤 **Listen and Talk 1 Listen and Check**

> **G:** Did you watch the documentary last night?
> **B:** No, I didn't. What was it about?
> **G:** ❶It was about global warming. ❷The Earth is getting hotter, and sea levels are going up. I'm worried about the Earth.
> **B:** Oh, I've heard about that problem before. ❸Some islands are disappearing, so people are losing their homes.
> **G:** Yes. It is terrible.
> **B:** ❹Is there any way to stop it?
> **G:** We can save energy. We should turn off the lights when we don't need them. ❺We should also use fans instead of air conditioners.
> **B:** Those are great ideas. I'll try to do those things right away.

G: 어젯밤에 다큐멘터리 봤어?
B: 아니, 못봤어. 무슨 내용이었어?
G: 지구 온난화에 대한 내용이었어. 지구가 점점 더워지면서, 해수면이 올라가고 있대. 나는 지구가 걱정돼.
B: 어, 나도 그 문제에 대해 들어본 적 있어. 몇몇 섬들이 사라져서, 사람들이 자기 집을 잃고 있대.
G: 맞아. 끔찍해.
B: 그걸 막을 방법이 있을까?
G: 에너지를 아끼는 방법이 있지. 우리는 전등을 필요하지 않을 때 꼭 꺼야 해. 그리고 우리는 또한 에어컨보다는 선풍기를 써야 해.
B: 좋은 생각이다. 그것들을 바로 시도해 봐야겠다.

❶ be about은 '~에 관한 것이다'라는 뜻이다.
❷ 'get+비교급' 형태로 '점점 ~해지다'는 뜻이다.
❸ so는 결과를 나타내는 접속사로 '그래서'의 의미이다. 앞 문장에는 원인이 나온다.
❹ to stop은 명사 way를 수식하는 형용사적 용법이다.
❺ instead of는 '~ 대신에'라는 뜻이다.

Check(√) True or False

(3) The boy watched the documentary about global warming.　　T ☐ F ☐

(4) Because of global warming, people are losing their homes.　　T ☐ F ☐

[01~02] 다음 대화를 읽고 물음에 답하시오.

G: You look upset. What's going on?

B: (A)_____ I need to make a short video about saving the environment. But making a video is difficult.

G: Well, how about using this application? It's easy.

B: (B)Can you tell me how to use it?

G: Sure! Open the application. Add your photos and choose some music. Then it will make a video with your photos.

B: Wow, that sounds easy. I'll try it now. Thanks.

01 위 대화의 빈칸 (A)에 들어갈 말로 알맞은 것은?

① I'm worried about using an application.

② Do you know how to write it?

③ I am worried about my science homework.

④ Why don't you go see a doctor?

⑤ I am worried about the environment.

02 위 대화의 밑줄 친 (B)와 같은 의미가 되도록 문장의 빈칸을 채우시오.

➡ Can you tell me _____?

[03~05] 다음 대화를 읽고 물음에 답하시오.

B: I like your bag, Jenny. Where did you get it?

G: (A)내가 직접 만들었어.

B: You made it yourself? That's amazing.

G: Why don't you make ⓐone? It's not difficult.

B: Really? Can you tell me (B)_____?

G: Sure. Find some old jeans. Cut them into small pieces. Then sew the pieces together.

B: That sounds easy. I'll make ⓐone as a birthday present for my sister.

위 대화의 밑줄 친 (A)를 영어로 바르게 나타낸 것을 모두 고르시오.

① I myself made it.

② I was making it to me.

③ I made me it.

④ I made it myself.

⑤ I made myself to it.

04 위 대화의 빈칸 (B)에 들어갈 말로 알맞은 것은?

① how easy it is   ② what to make

③ where to get it   ④ how to use it

⑤ how to make it

05 위 대화의 밑줄 친 ⓐ가 공통으로 가리키는 것을 찾아 두 단어로 쓰시오.

➡ _____

다음 대화의 빈칸에 공통으로 들어갈 말은?

G: Did you watch the documentary last night?

B: No, I didn't. What was it _____?

G: It was _____ global warming.

① about   ② for   ③ at   ④ in   ⑤ on

[07~08] 다음 대화를 읽고 물음에 답하시오.

B: In my school, students leave so much food on their plates. I'm worried about (A)_____.

G: Right, that's a big problem. We should not put too much food on our plates.

B: You're right. (B)We shouldn't.

07 위 대화의 빈칸 (A)에 들어갈 말로 알맞은 것은?

① saving energy ② wasting food
③ eating too much ④ plastic waste
⑤ the trash in cafeteria

08 위 대화의 밑줄 친 (B)의 의도로 알맞은 것은?

① 음식물 쓰레기를 버리지 말자.
② 음식물 잔반 처리를 잘하자.
③ 먹을 수 있는 만큼만 음식을 담자.
④ 식판 대신에 다른 식기를 사용하자.
⑤ 음식을 많이 담는 것은 큰 문제가 아니다.

09 중요 다음 중 짝지어진 대화가 어색한 것을 고르시오.

① A: I'm worried about soil pollution.
  B: Me, too.
② A: I made a bag with some old jeans.
  B: Can you tell me how to make it?
③ A: What does it mean?
  B: It means we are wasting paper.
④ A: Can you tell me how to use it?
  B: Sure.
⑤ A: How much chocolate is produced in a day?
  B: Our chocolate is made by robots.

[10~12] 다음 대화를 읽고 물음에 답하시오.

G: Have you heard of Earth Hour before?

B: No, I haven't. What is it?

G: It's a global environmental event. People (a)_____ their lights for an hour.

B: Why do they do that?

G: (A)사람들에게 환경문제에 대해서 상기시키기 위해서지. They believe such a small action can change the world.

B: Oh, I see. Can you tell me how to join it?

G: Sure. Just turn off your lights from 8:30 p.m. to 9:30 p.m. on the last Saturday in March.

B: That's easy. I will join the next Earth Hour.

서답형

10 위 대화의 빈칸 (a)에 들어갈 단어에 대한 영어 설명을 읽고 알맞은 단어를 쓰시오.

to make a machine, a television, an engine, or a light etc. stop operating by pushing a button

➡ _____

서답형

11 위 대화의 우리말 (A)에 맞게 주어진 문장의 빈칸을 채우시오.

➡ They do it _____ _____ people _____ our environmental problems.

12 위 대화의 Earth Hour에 관한 내용으로 어색한 것은?

① Earth Hour는 세계 환경 행사다.
② 참가자들은 1시간 동안 불을 끈다.
③ 참가자들은 그들의 행동이 세상을 바꿀 수 있다고 믿는다.
④ 매달 8시 30분부터 9시 30분까지 참가 가능하다.
⑤ Earth Hour는 1년에 한 번 열린다.

[01~02] 다음 대화를 읽고 물음에 답하시오.

B: I like your bag, Jenny. Where did you get it?

G: I made it myself.

B: You made it yourself? That's amazing.

G: Why don't you make one? It's not difficult.

B: Really? (A)어떻게 만드는지 알려줄 수 있니?(can, tell, me, how, to)

G: Sure. Find some old jeans. Cut them into small pieces. Then sew the pieces together.

B: That sounds easy.

중요
01 위 대화의 밑줄 친 (A)의 우리말에 맞게 주어진 단어를 이용하여 영어로 쓰시오.

➡ _____

02 위 대화를 읽고 아래 그림의 빈칸을 채우시오.

(1) ___ ___ ___ a bag

Find some (2)___ jeans.   (3) ___ the jeans ___ small pieces.   (4) ___ the pieces together.

➡ (1) _____
➡ (2) _____ (3) _____ , _____
   (4) _____

[03~04] 다음 대화를 읽고 물음에 답하시오.

G: Did you watch the documentary last night?

B: No, I didn't. What was it about?

G: It was about global warming. The Earth is getting hotter, and sea levels are going up. (A)나는 지구가 걱정이 돼. (am, worry, the Earth)

B: Oh, I've heard about that problem before. Some islands are disappearing, so people are losing their homes.

G: Yes. It is terrible.

B: Is there any way to stop it?

G: We can save energy. We should turn off the lights when we don't need them. We should also use fans instead of air conditioners.

B: Those are great ideas. I'll try to do those things.

03 위 대화의 밑줄 친 (A)의 우리말에 맞게 주어진 단어를 이용하여 영작하시오.

➡ _____

중요
04 위 대화에서 두 사람이 나누는 문제점과 그것의 해결책을 찾아 아래 문장을 완성하시오.

• Problem
Because the Earth is _____ _____ and sea levels are _____ _____ , some islands are _____ .
• Solutions
_____ _____ the lights when you _____ _____ them. And _____ fans _____ _____ air conditioners.

05 다음 대화의 밑줄 친 (A)를 완전한 문장으로 다시 쓰시오.

B: In my school, students leave so much food on their plates. I'm worried about wasting food.

G: Right, that's a big problem. We should not put too much food on our plates.

B: You're right. (A)We shouldn't.

➡ _____

Grammar

① 수동태

> • He found the treasure.   <능동태> 그가 그 보물을 발견했다.
> • The treasure **was found** by him. <수동태> 그 보물은 그에 의해 발견되었다.

■ 수동태는 '주어+be동사+동사의 과거분사+by+행위자'의 형식을 가지며 '…에 의해 ~되다[당하다]'라는 의미로 주어가 동사가 나타내는 행위를 당하거나 행동의 영향을 받는 것을 나타낸다. 수동태 문장의 주어 자리에는 능동태 문장의 목적어가 오고, by 다음에는 능동태 문장의 주어를 쓴다. 누가 그 동작을 했는지 중요하지 않거나 잘 모를 때, 수동태 문장으로 표현한다. 수동태는 현재, 과거, 미래 시제로 쓸 수 있고, 'be동사+동사의 과거분사'에서 be동사로 시제를 표현한다.

> • This process **is repeated** again and again! 이러한 과정이 계속해서 반복된다!

■ 4형식 문장의 수동태는 간접목적어와 직접목적어 각각을 주어로 하는 수동태가 가능하다. 직접목적어를 주어로 한 수동태에서는 간접목적어 앞에 특정한 전치사를 써야 한다.

전치사 to를 쓰는 동사는 'give, send, tell, teach, show, bring' 등이고, 전치사 for를 쓰는 동사는 'buy, make, choose, cook, get' 등이며, 전치사 of를 쓰는 동사는 'ask' 등이 있다. 또한 make, buy, read, write 등은 직접목적어를 주어로 하는 수동태만 가능하다.

> • A computer **was bought** for me by Mom. 컴퓨터가 엄마에 의해 나에게 사주어졌다.

■ 조동사가 있는 문장의 수동태는 '조동사+be+p.p.' 형식을 갖는다.

> • A book **will be read** to us by Mom. 책이 엄마에 의해 우리에게 읽힐 것이다.

■ 목적격보어가 원형부정사인 경우, 수동태 문장에서는 to부정사로 바뀐다.

> • Ted **was made** to clean the car by his dad. Ted는 그의 아빠에 의해 세차하도록 시켜졌다.

■ by 이외의 전치사를 사용하는 수동태에 유의한다.

> • be interested in: ~에 흥미가 있다   • be filled with: ~로 가득 차다
>
> • be covered with: ~로 덮여 있다   • be surprised at: ~에 놀라다
>
> • be made of: ~로 만들어지다(물리적 변화)   • be made from: ~로 만들어지다(화학적 변화)
>
> • be satisfied with: ~에 만족하다   • be pleased with: ~에 기뻐하다

핵심 Check

1. 다음 괄호 안에서 알맞은 말을 고르시오.

(1) The ring (found / was found) by them.

(2) A letter was written (for / to) her by Jim.

(3) The room was filled (by / with) many books.

❷ 비교급 강조

> • The plants grow **much** faster than plants in soil.
> 그 식물들은 흙에서 자라는 식물들보다 훨씬 빨리 자란다.
>
> • It will get **even** bigger. 그것은 한층 더 커질 것이다.

■ 비교급을 강조할 때는 비교급 앞에 much, still, even, far, a lot 등의 부사를 쓰며 '(…보다) 훨씬 더 ~한'이라는 의미를 갖는다.
  • A tiger is stronger than a cat. 호랑이는 고양이보다 더 강하다.
  • A tiger is **much** stronger than a cat. 호랑이는 고양이보다 훨씬 더 강하다.
  • Mary is prettier than Kim. Mary가 Kim보다 더 예쁘다.
  • Mary is **a lot** prettier than Kim. Mary가 Kim보다 훨씬 더 예쁘다.

■ very는 원급의 형용사[부사]를 수식하며, 비교급은 수식하지 않는다.
  • She is **very** beautiful. 〈원급 강조〉 그녀는 매우 예쁘다
  • She is **much** more beautiful than her sister. 〈비교급 강조〉 그녀는 자기 여동생보다 훨씬 더 예쁘다.

cf. She is very more beautiful than her sister. (×)

핵심 Check

2. 다음 괄호 안에서 알맞은 말을 고르시오.

(1) Dan is (very / far) wiser than Josh.

(2) This computer is (lot / even) newer than that one.

(3) My smartphone is (much / many) nicer than yours.

01 다음 빈칸에 알맞은 것은?

> He built the house.
> → The house _____ by him.

① builds ② built ③ has built
④ is built ⑤ was built

02 다음 빈칸에 들어갈 말로 적절하지 <u>않은</u> 것은?

> They choose aquaponics because it is _____ easier than traditional gardening.

① even ② very ③ a lot
④ still ⑤ far

03 다음 우리말에 맞게 빈칸에 알맞은 말을 쓰시오.

productive: 생산적인
source: 공급원

(1) 그 창문은 Mike에 의해 깨졌다.
➡ The window _____ _____ by Mike.
(2) 노인과 바다는 Hemingway에 의해 쓰여졌다.
➡ *The Old Man and the Sea* _____ _____ by Hemingway.
(3) 그것은 식량을 재배하는 훨씬 더 생산적인 방법이다.
➡ It is a _____ more productive way of growing food.
(4) 인터넷은 훨씬 더 좋은 뉴스 공급원이다.
➡ The Internet is a _____ better source for news.

04 다음 문장에서 어법상 어색한 부분을 바르게 고쳐 쓰시오.

(1) Laura is very kinder than Bill.
_____ ➡ _____
(2) Her room cleans every day by her.
_____ ➡ _____

05 다음 우리말을 괄호 안에 주어진 어구를 이용하여 영작하시오.

(1) 이 드레스는 내 친구에 의해 디자인되었다. (this dress)

➡ _____

(2) *Charlie and the Chocolate Factory*는 William Shakespeare에 의해 쓰여지지 않았다. (write)

➡ _____

_____

(3) 인터뷰는 한국어와 영어로 진행됐다. (the interview, carry, both, in, out)

➡ _____

_____

(4) 이러한 항목들이 각 응답자에게 물어졌다. (items, ask, each respondent)

➡ _____

(5) 그는 그녀에게 긴 편지를 썼다. (write) (수동태로 쓸 것.)

➡ _____

(6) Annabel은 그녀의 서울에서의 생활에 만족했다. (satisfy, her life in Seoul)

➡ _____

06 다음 문장에서 어법상 어색한 부분을 찾아 바르게 고치시오.

(1) The problem of control is many more important.

(2) You look too smarter than your picture.

(3) It seemed ever more difficult than I had expected.

(4) Was it very bigger than your dog?

(5) This hat is lots cheaper than that.

➡ _____

_____

07 다음 우리말을 괄호 안에 주어진 어구를 이용하여 영작하시오.

(1) 이 탑은 저 탑보다 훨씬 더 높다. (this tower, high, lot)

➡ _____

(2) 내 남동생은 나보다 훨씬 더 높게 뛴다. (jump, even, I)

➡ _____

(3) 그녀는 그녀의 오빠보다 훨씬 더 활동적이다. (much, active, her brother)

➡ _____

(4) Brenda는 전보다 훨씬 더 친절하다. (kinder, far, before)

➡ _____

(5) 민주주의는 공산주의보다 훨씬 더 낫다. (democracy, communism, good, still)

➡ _____

08 다음 문장을 수동태로 바꿔 쓰시오.

(1) Amanda taught me math last year. (두 가지로 쓸 것.)

➡ _____

_____

(2) Teresa chose us a chocolate cake.

➡ _____

(3) Ann asked me a question.

➡ _____

09 다음 그림을 보고 주어진 단어를 이용하여 비교하는 문장을 쓰시오. (fast, much)

Yuri
Sumi

➡ _____

My Science Project: Home Aquaponics

Jennifer: What are you reading?

Eric: I'm reading an article about aquaponics. It's a way of growing
plants without soil. We can also grow plants and raise fish in just one
system.
= aquaponics   _동격의 전치사_
_흙 없이_

Jennifer: Is that possible?
We can also grow plants and raise fish in just one system.

Eric: We'll see. I'm going to try it at home for my science project.
_곧 알게 될 거야._

Fish, bacteria, and plants are the main parts of aquaponics.
bacterium의 복수

After you feed the fish, they produce waste. The waste is turned
수동태 문장으로 '…으로 바뀌다'라는 의미이다.
into food for the plants by bacteria. The plants clean the water by
by를 사용하여 행위의 주체가 bacteria임을 나타내고 있다.
consuming the food. This process is repeated again and again!
동명사(전치사의 목적어)   _= over and over (again) = repeatedly_

raise 기르다
bacteria 박테리아, 세균
produce 생산하다
turn into ~이 되다, ~로 변하다
consume 먹다, 소비하다, 소모하다

확인문제

● 다음 문장이 본문의 내용과 일치하면 T, 일치하지 않으면 F를 쓰시오.

1 Aquaponics is a way of growing plants without soil. ☐

2 We can grow plants and raise fish in two systems. ☐

3 Fish, bacteria, and plants are the main parts of aquaponics. ☐

4 The waste is turned into food for the plants by fish. ☐

Home Aquaponics   by Eric Jackson

Questions: How can I make an aquaponics system at home?
집에서

Why is aquaponics good?

Period: From May 15 to August 15
_└ ,~부터 ~까지 ,┘_

Materials: a pot & small stones, a fish tank, a plastic tube, a water
pump, plants, some fish, a box cutter, clay

Steps:

1. I made holes in the bottom of a pot. Then I put small stones and
   ~의 바닥에
   plants in it.
   = the pot

2. I made a big hole in the lid of the fish tank and put the pot in the
   made와 병렬구문을 이루도록 과거시제로 쓴 것임.
   hole.

hole 구멍
lid 뚜껑
fix 고정하다, 수리하다
connect 연결하다

3. I fixed the pot <u>in place</u> with clay.
제자리에

4. I made <u>another hole</u> in the lid and put a tube through <u>it</u>.
another+단수명사 =the hole

5. I put a water pump in the fish tank. I used the tube <u>to connect</u> the
부사적 용법(목적)

pump to the pot.

6. I <u>filled</u> the fish tank <u>with</u> water and put some fish in it. Then I
fill A with B: A를 B로 채우다

<u>turned on</u> the pump.
turn on: 켜다. 작동하다

확인문제

● 다음 문장이 본문의 내용과 일치하면 T, 일치하지 <u>않으면</u> F를 쓰시오.

1 Eric made holes in the bottom of a pot. ☐
2 Eric put a water pump in the pot. ☐
3 Eric used a tube to connect the pump to the pot. ☐

Results: From this experiment, I grew my plants and raised fish with
aquaponics. I <u>just</u> fed the fish, but the plants <u>have grown</u> 17 centimeters
단지. 그저   have grown은 현재완료로 '…해서 그 결과 ~하다'라는 의미이다.
in three months. The fish <u>stay healthy</u> and the water is clean <u>all the time</u>.
stay+형용사 보어   항상

Conclusion: Some important things about aquaponics <u>were learned</u>
수동태 문장으로 주어가 복수이고 시제는 과거이므로 be동사는 were를 쓴다.
from this experiment. First, water is saved because the plants don't

<u>need watering</u>. Second, <u>it is good for</u> the environment because no
need watering=need to be watered ~에 좋다
chemicals <u>are used</u>. Finally, you can do aquaponics anywhere because
수동태
it doesn't need much space.

I found out...

Some farmers use aquaponics <u>to produce</u> vegetables and raise
부사적 용법(목적)
fish. They choose aquaponics because it is <u>far</u> easier than traditional
far가 비교급 easier의 의미를 강조하여 '훨씬 더 …한'이라는 뜻이다.
gardening. Also, it is a <u>much</u> more productive way of growing food.
much가 비교급 more productive의 의미를 강조하여 '훨씬 더 …한'이라는 뜻이다.
The plants grow much faster than plants in soil, and it <u>saves</u> space.
절약한다
I hope more food <u>is produced</u> in this way in the future because it is
수동태
healthy for us and the environment.

result 결과
water (식물 등에) 물을 주다
chemical 화학 물질, 화학 제품
productive 생산적인, 생산력 있는
future 미래

확인문제

● 다음 문장이 본문의 내용과 일치하면 T, 일치하지 <u>않으면</u> F를 쓰시오.

1 The fish stay healthy and the water is clean all the time. ☐
2 Water is wasted because the plants need watering. ☐
3 The plants in soil grow faster than the plants in aquaponics. ☐

● 우리말을 참고하여 빈칸에 알맞은 말을 쓰시오.

1   My _____ _____ : Home Aquaponics

2   _____ are you reading?

3   I'm reading _____ _____ about aquaponics.

4   It's a way of growing plants _____ _____ .

5   We can also grow plants and raise fish _____ _____ _____ _____ .

6   Is that _____?

7   We'll see. I'm _____ _____ _____ it at home for my science project.

8   Fish, bacteria, and plants are _____ _____ _____ of aquaponics.

9   After you _____ the fish, they produce _____ .

10 The waste _____ _____ _____ food for the plants by bacteria.

11 The plants clean the water _____ _____ the food.

12 This process _____ _____ again and again!

13 _____ _____ by Eric Jackson

14 Questions: _____ can I make an aquaponics system at home?

15 _____ is aquaponics good?

16 Period: _____ May 15 _____ August 15

17 _____ : a pot & small stones, a fish tank, a plastic tube, a water pump, plants, some fish, _____ _____ _____ , clay

1	나의 과학 프로젝트: 가정용 아쿠아포닉스
2	무엇을 읽고 있니?
3	아쿠아포닉스에 관한 기사를 읽고 있어.
4	흙 없이 식물을 재배할 수 있는 방법이야.
5	또 한 가지 장치만으로도 식물과 물고기를 동시에 키울 수 있어.
6	그게 가능하니?
7	곧 알게 될 거야. 내가 과학 프로젝트로 집에서 해 볼 예정이거든.
8	물고기, 박테리아, 식물이 아쿠아포닉스의 주요 부분이다.
9	물고기에게 먹이를 주면, 그것들은 배설물을 만들어 낸다.
10	이 배설물은 박테리아에 의해 식물의 먹이로 바뀐다.
11	식물은 그 먹이를 먹음으로써 물을 정화한다.
12	이러한 과정이 계속해서 반복된다!
13	가정용 아쿠아포닉스 에릭 잭슨
14	질문: 집에서 아쿠아포닉스 장치를 어떻게 만들 수 있을까?
15	아쿠아포닉스가 왜 좋은가?
16	기간: 5월 15일부터 8월 15일까지
17	재료: 화분과 작은 돌들, 어항, 플라스틱 관, 수중 펌프, 식물, 물고기, 커터칼, 찰흙

18 _____ : I made holes in the _____ of a pot.

19 _____ I _____ small stones and plants _____ it.

20 I made a big hole in _____ _____ of the fish tank and _____ the pot _____ the hole.

21 I _____ the pot in place _____ clay.

22 I made _____ _____ in the lid and put a tube _____ it.

23 I _____ a water pump _____ the fish tank.

24 I used the tube _____ _____ the pump _____ the pot.

25 I _____ the fish tank _____ water and put some fish in it.

26 Then I _____ _____ the pump.

27 Results: From this experiment, I grew my plants and raised fish _____ _____ .

28 I just _____ the fish, but the plants _____ _____ 17 centimeters _____ three months.

29 The fish stay _____ and the water is clean _____ _____ _____ .

30 Conclusion: Some important things about aquaponics _____ _____ from this experiment.

31 First, water _____ _____ because the plants don't need watering.

32 Second, it is good for the environment because no chemicals _____ _____ .

33 _____ , you can do aquaponics _____ because it doesn't need much space.

34 *I found out...* Some farmers use aquaponics _____ _____ vegetables and raise fish.

35 They choose aquaponics because it is _____ _____ _____ traditional gardening.

36 Also, it is a _____ _____ _____ way of growing food.

37 The plants grow _____ _____ _____ plants in soil, and it saves space.

38 I hope more food _____ _____ in this way in the future because it is _____ _____ us and the environment.

18 절차: 화분 바닥에 구멍들을 뚫었다.

19 그런 후에 화분에 작은 돌들을 넣고 식물을 심었다.

20 어항 덮개에 큰 구멍을 내고 구멍에 그 화분을 넣었다.

21 찰흙으로 화분을 제자리에 고정하였다.

22 덮개에 또 다른 구멍을 하나 만들고 그 안에 관을 넣었다.

23 어항에 수중 펌프를 넣었다.

24 관을 이용하여 펌프를 화분에 연결하였다.

25 어항에 물을 채우고 물고기 몇 마리를 거기에 넣었다.

26 그리고 나서 펌프를 작동하였다.

27 결과: 이 실험으로 나는 아쿠아포닉스로 식물과 물고기를 키웠다.

28 나는 그저 물고기에 먹이만 주었는데도 식물은 석 달 동안 17cm나 자랐다.

29 물고기는 건강을 유지하며 물은 항상 깨끗하다.

30 결론: 아쿠아포닉스에 관한 몇 가지 중요한 사항이 이 실험에서 발견되었다.

31 첫째, 식물에 물을 줄 필요가 없으므로 물이 절약된다.

32 둘째, 화학 물질이 사용되지 않으므로 아쿠아포닉스는 환경에 이롭다.

33 끝으로, 넓은 공간이 필요하지 않으므로 당신은 어디에서나 아쿠아포닉스를 쉽게 할 수 있다.

34 나는 알게 되었다... 몇몇 농부들은 채소를 생산하고 물고기를 키우는 데 아쿠아포닉스를 이용한다.

35 그들은 아쿠아포닉스가 전통 재배 방식보다 훨씬 더 쉽기 때문에 그것을 선택한다.

36 또한, 아쿠아포닉스는 식량을 재배하는 훨씬 더 생산적인 방법이다.

37 식물들이 흙에서 자라는 식물보다 훨씬 빠르게 자라고 공간도 절약한다.

38 그것은 우리와 환경에 훨씬 건강하기 때문에 나는 미래에 더 많은 식량이 이런 방식으로 생산되기를 희망한다.

• 우리말을 참고하여 본문을 영작하시오.

1 나의 과학 프로젝트: 가정용 아쿠아포닉스

➡ _____

2 무엇을 읽고 있니?

➡ _____

3 아쿠아포닉스에 관한 기사를 읽고 있어.

➡ _____

4 흙 없이 식물을 재배할 수 있는 방법이야.

➡ _____

5 또 한 가지 장치만으로도 식물과 물고기를 동시에 키울 수 있어.

➡ _____

6 그게 가능하니?

➡ _____

7 곧 알게 될 거야. 내가 과학 프로젝트로 집에서 해 볼 예정이거든.

➡ _____

8 물고기, 박테리아, 식물이 아쿠아포닉스의 주요 부분이다.

➡ _____

9 물고기에게 먹이를 주면, 그것들은 배설물을 만들어 낸다.

➡ _____

10 이 배설물은 박테리아에 의해 식물의 먹이로 바뀐다.

➡ _____

11 식물은 그 먹이를 먹음으로써 물을 정화한다.

➡ _____

12 이러한 과정이 계속해서 반복된다!

➡ _____

13 가정용 아쿠아포닉스   에릭 잭슨

➡ _____

14 질문: 집에서 아쿠아포닉스 장치를 어떻게 만들 수 있을까?

➡ _____

15 아쿠아포닉스가 왜 좋은가?

➡ _____

16 기간: 5월 15일부터 8월 15일까지

➡ _____

17 재료: 화분과 작은 돌들, 어항, 플라스틱 관, 수중 펌프, 식물, 물고기, 커터칼, 찰흙

➡ _____

18 절차: 화분 바닥에 구멍들을 뚫었다.

➡ _____

19 그런 후에 화분에 작은 돌들을 넣고 식물을 심었다.

➡ _____

20 어항 덮개에 큰 구멍을 내고 구멍에 그 화분을 넣었다.

➡ _____

21 찰흙으로 화분을 제자리에 고정하였다.

➡ _____

22 덮개에 또 다른 구멍을 하나 만들고 그 안에 관을 넣었다.

➡ _____

23 어항에 수중 펌프를 넣었다.

➡ _____

24 관을 이용하여 펌프를 화분에 연결하였다.

➡ _____

25 어항에 물을 채우고 물고기 몇 마리를 거기에 넣었다.

➡ _____

26 그러고 나서 펌프를 작동하였다.

➡ _____

27 결과: 이 실험으로 나는 아쿠아포닉스로 식물과 물고기를 키웠다.

➡ _____

28 나는 그저 물고기에 먹이만 주었는데도 식물은 석 달 동안 17cm나 자랐다.

➡ _____

29 물고기는 건강을 유지하며 물은 항상 깨끗하다.

➡ _____

30 결론: 아쿠아포닉스에 관한 몇 가지 중요한 사항이 이 실험에서 발견되었다.

➡ _____

31 첫째, 식물에 물을 줄 필요가 없으므로 물이 절약된다.

➡ _____

32 둘째, 화학 물질이 사용되지 않으므로 아쿠아포닉스는 환경에 이롭다.

➡ _____

33 끝으로, 넓은 공간이 필요하지 않으므로 당신은 어디에서나 아쿠아포닉스를 쉽게 할 수 있다.

➡ _____

34 나는 알게 되었다... 몇몇 농부들은 채소를 생산하고 물고기를 키우는 데 아쿠아포닉스를 이용한다.

➡ _____

35 그들은 아쿠아포닉스가 전통 재배 방식보다 훨씬 더 쉽기 때문에 그것을 선택한다.

➡ _____

36 또한, 아쿠아포닉스는 식량을 재배하는 훨씬 더 생산적인 방법이다.

➡ _____

37 식물들이 흙에서 자라는 식물보다 훨씬 빠르게 자라고 공간도 절약한다.

➡ _____

38 그것은 우리와 환경에 훨씬 건강하기 때문에 나는 미래에 더 많은 식량이 이런 방식으로 생산되기를 희망한다.

➡ _____

[01~03] 다음 글을 읽고 물음에 답하시오.

Jennifer: What are you reading?
Eric: I'm ⓐreading an article about aquaponics. ⓑIt's a way of ⓒgrowing plants without soil. We can also grow plants and raise fish in just one system.
Jennifer: Is that possible?
Eric: We'll see. I'm going to try it at home for my science project.

서답형
01 위 글의 밑줄 친 ⓐ, ⓒ와 문법적 쓰임이 같은 것을 각각 아래 〈보기〉에서 모두 골라 쓰시오.

┌─── 보기 ───
① Studying English is interesting.
② I heard him crying in the room.
③ The girl standing at the door is my sister.
④ Have you finished cleaning the room?
⑤ His hobby is collecting stamps.
└──────────

➡ ⓐ와 쓰임이 같은 것: _____
ⓒ와 쓰임이 같은 것: _____

서답형
02 위 글의 밑줄 친 ⓑIt이 가리키는 것을 본문에서 찾아 쓰시오.

➡ _____

03 위 글의 내용과 일치하지 않는 것은?

① 에릭은 아쿠아포닉스에 관한 기사를 읽고 있다.
② 아쿠아포닉스는 흙 없이 식물을 재배할 수 있는 방법이다.
③ 아쿠아포닉스는 두 가지 장치로 식물과 물고기를 동시에 키울 수 있다.
④ 제니퍼는 아쿠아포닉스가 가능한지를 묻고 있다.
⑤ 에릭은 과학 프로젝트로 아쿠아포닉스를 집에서 해 볼 예정이다.

[04~06] 다음 글을 읽고 물음에 답하시오.

Fish, (A)[bacteria / bacterias], and plants are the main parts of aquaponics. After you feed the fish, they produce waste. The waste is turned (B)[by / into] food for the plants by bacteria. The plants clean the water by (C)[consuming / saving] the food. This process is repeated ⓐagain and again!

서답형
04 위 글의 괄호 (A)~(C)에서 문맥이나 어법상 알맞은 낱말을 골라 쓰시오.

➡ (A)_____ (B)_____ (C) _____

서답형
05 본문의 내용과 일치하도록 다음 빈칸 (A)와 (B)에 알맞은 단어를 쓰시오.

┌────────────────────────┐
│ The main parts of aquaponics are │
│ (A)_____, (B)_____ and (C)_____. │
└────────────────────────┘

중요
06 위 글의 밑줄 친 ⓐagain and again과 바꿔 쓸 수 없는 말을 고르시오.

① repeatedly   ② time after time
③ relatively   ④ over and over
⑤ time and time again

[07~09] 다음 글을 읽고 물음에 답하시오.

Home Aquaponics   by Eric Jackson
Questions: How can I make an aquaponics system at home?
          Why is aquaponics good?
Period: From May 15 to August 15
Materials: a pot & small stones, a fish tank, a plastic tube, a water pump, plants, some fish, a box cutter, clay

07 위 글의 밑줄 친 ⓐ~ⓒ의 it이 가리키는 것을 본문에서 찾아 각각 쓰시오.

➡ ⓐ _____ ⓑ _____

ⓒ _____

08 다음 문장에서 위 글의 내용과 다른 부분 두 군데를 찾아서 고치시오.

> • Eric put a water pump in the pot and connected it to the fish tank by using the tube.

➡ _____

[09~10] 다음 글을 읽고 물음에 답하시오.

Results:

From this experiment, I grew my plants and raised fish with aquaponics. ⓐ나는 그저 물고기에 밥만 주었는데도 식물은 석 달 동안 17cm나 자랐다. The fish stay healthy and the water is clean all the time.

Conclusion:

Some important things about aquaponics were learned from this experiment. First, water is saved because the plants don't need watering. Second, it is good for the environment because no chemicals are used. Finally, you can do aquaponics anywhere because it doesn't need much space.

I = Eric

09 위 글의 밑줄 친 ⓐ의 우리말에 맞게 한 단어를 보충하여, 주어진 어구를 알맞게 배열하시오.

> have grown / fed / the fish / just / 17 centimeters / three months / the plants / but / I

➡ _____

_____

10 위 글을 읽고 아쿠아포닉스의 장점 세 가지를 우리말로 쓰시오.

➡ (1) _____

(2) _____

(3) _____

[11~13] 다음 글을 읽고, 물음에 답하시오.

Home Aquaponics   by Eric Jackson
Questions: How can I make an aquaponics system at home?
     Why is aquaponics good?
Period: From May 15 to August 15
Materials: a pot & small stones, a fish tank, a plastic tube, a water pump, plants, some fish, a box cutter, clay

Steps:

1. I made holes in the ⓐ(top, bottom) of a pot. Then I put small stones and plants in it.
2. I made a big hole in the lid of the fish tank and put the pot in the hole.
3. I fixed the pot in place with clay.
4. I made another hole in the lid and put a tube through it.
5. I put a water pump in the fish tank. ⓑ관을 이용하여 펌프를 화분에 연결하였다.
6. I filled the fish tank with water and put some fish in it. Then I turned on the pump.

11 다음 질문에 대한 알맞은 대답을 빈칸에 쓰시오.

> **Q:** How long did Eric do the experiment?
> **A:** About _____ months.

12 위 글의 괄호 ⓐ에서 알맞은 것을 고르시오.

➡ _____

13 위 글의 밑줄 친 ⓑ의 우리말에 맞게 주어진 어휘를 이용하여 11 단어로 영작하시오.

> connect, to

➡ _____

After You Read

Window Farming

Do you want to grow plants in your house? Then try window farming! You
want는 부정사(to+동사원형)를 목적어로 취하는 동사이다.　　　　　　시도하다
can do it anywhere near a window with plastic bottles. Each bottle hangs from
　　=window farming　(전) ~ 가까이　　　　　　each는 단수 명사를 취하며 단수 동사가 온다.
the one above, so you don't need much space.

구문해설　· farming 농업, 농사　· anywhere 어디에서나　· hang 매달리다　· above 위에　· space 공간

창문 농경
집에서 식물을 기르고 싶나
요? 그렇다면 창문 농경을 해
보세요! 플라스틱 병으로 창
문 근처 어디에서나 그것을
할 수 있습니다. 각각의 병은
위에 매달려 있어서 많은 공
간을 필요로 하지 않아요.

Think and Write

Let's Make Our School Green!

Lots of energy is wasted around us. To solve this problem, let's do these
= Much　　　　수동태　　　　　부사적 용법(목적)
things. First, we should turn off the lights when we leave our classrooms.
　　　　　　　　　　~을 끄다　　　　　　접속사
Next, we should turn off the classroom computers when we are not using
　　　　　　　~을 끄다
them.
= the classroom computers
Lastly, we should close the doors and windows when we use air conditioners.
= Finally　　　　　닫다(동사)
Doing these things will be helpful to our school and the environment.
동명사(주어)　　　　　　　~에 도움이 되다

구문해설　· waste: 낭비하다.　· leave: 떠나다.　· helpful: 도움이 되는.　· environment: 환경

우리 학교를 친환경적으로 만
듭시다!
우리 주변에서 많은 에너지가
낭비되고 있습니다. 이 문제
를 해결하기 위해, 다음과 같
은 일들을 해 봅시다. 먼저 우
리가 교실을 나갈 때 전깃불
을 꺼야 합니다. 다음 우리가
교실 컴퓨터를 사용하지 않을
때 그것들을 꺼야 합니다. 마
지막으로 에어컨을 사용할 때
교실 문과 창문을 닫아야 합
니다. 이런 일들을 하는 것은
우리 학교와 환경에 도움이
될 것입니다.

Culture Link

This refrigerator works without electricity. It is powered by dirty water. It is
　　　　　　　　작동하다　~이 없이　　　　　　수동태
useful for countries that have little electricity.
~에 유용하다　　　　　　　거의 없는(부정문)
When you need water, just have this water drop! It reduces the use of plastic
　　　　　　　　　　　명령문　　　　물방울
bottles.
This special tower is the Warka Water Tower. Thanks to this tower, people can
　　　　　　　　　　　　　　　　　　　　= because of
get water from the air. It saves water.
~부터 …를 얻다

구문해설　· power: ~에 동력을 공급하다　· thanks to: ~ 덕분에

이 냉장고는 전력 없이 작동된다.
그것은 더러운 물에 의해 동력을
공급받는다. 이것은 전력이 거의
없는 나라에 유용하다.
당신이 물이 필요할 때, 그냥 이
물방울을 마셔라! 이것은 플라스
틱 병의 사용을 줄인다.
이 특별한 탑은 와카 워터 타워이
다. 이 탑 덕분에 사람들은 공기
로부터 물을 얻을 수 있다. 이것
은 물을 절약한다.

Words & Expressions

01 다음 짝지어진 두 단어의 관계가 같도록 빈칸에 알맞은 단어를 쓰시오.

waste : save – far : _____

02 다음 대화의 빈칸 ⓐ와 ⓑ에 들어갈 말이 바르게 짝지어진 것은?

G: Look at this ball. Can you tell me how
ⓐ _____ it?
M: Just play soccer for thirty minutes, and
the light will ⓑ _____ . You can use
the light anywhere.
G: Wow, that's interesting.

① using – turn up
② to use – turn off
③ to make – go up
④ making – run out
⑤ to use – turn on

[03~04] 다음 영영풀이에 해당하는 것을 고르시오.

03

to make something or bring something
into existence

① fix
② sew
③ produce
④ connect
⑤ feed

04

to pour water onto plants or the soil that
they are growing in

① water
② waste
③ reuse
④ use
⑤ solve

05 다음 빈칸에 들어갈 말이 바르게 짝지어진 것은?

• _____ the cup with water.
• Time is running _____ for the Earth.

① Put – on
② Fill – out
③ Make – in
④ Put – to
⑤ Fill – of

06 다음 밑줄 친 부분의 뜻이 잘못된 것은?

① It's a way of growing plants without soil.
토양, 흙
② This process is repeated again and again.
반복되다
③ I feed the fish. ~을 먹다
④ I fixed the pot in place with clay.
고정시켰다
⑤ Each bottle hangs from the one above.
매달려 있다

Conversation

[07~08] 다음 대화를 읽고 물음에 답하시오.

Jenny: You look upset. What's going on?
Ben: (A)나는 과학 숙제가 걱정이 돼. I need to
make a short video about saving the
environment. But making a video is
difficult.
Jenny: Well, how about using this application?
It's easy.
Ben: Can you tell me how to use it?
Jenny: (1)_____
Ben: Wow, that sounds easy. I'll try it now.
Thanks.

07 위 대화의 (A)의 우리말에 맞게 영어로 쓰시오.

➡ _____

08 Ben의 질문에 대한 Jenny의 대답을 빈칸 (1)에 넣을 때 알맞은 순서는?

> (A) Then it will make a video with your photos.
> (B) Add your photos and choose some music.
> (C) Sure! Open the application.

① (A)-(B)-(C)
② (B)-(A)-(C)
③ (B)-(C)-(A)
④ (C)-(A)-(B)
⑤ (C)-(B)-(A)

[09~11] 다음 대화를 읽고 물음에 답하시오.

> G: Have you heard of Earth Hour before?
> B: No, I ⓐhaven't. What is it?
> G: It's a global environmental event. People ⓑturn off their lights for an hour.
> B: Why do they do that?
> G: They do it to ⓒremind people of our environmental problems. They believe (A)such a small action can ⓓexchange the world.
> B: Oh, I see. (B)_____
> G: Sure. Just turn off your lights from 8:30 p.m. to 9:30 p.m. on the last Saturday in March.
> B: ⓔThat's easy. I will join the next Earth Hour.

09 위 대화의 밑줄 친 (A)에 해당하는 행동을 우리말로 구체적으로 쓰시오.

➡ _____
_____

10 위 대화의 빈칸 (B)에 들어갈 알맞은 것은?

① Do you know how to use it?
② Can you explain how to make it?
③ Can you tell me how to join it?
④ Can you tell me where to join it?
⑤ Can you tell me when to begin?

11 위 대화의 흐름상 밑줄 친 ⓐ~ⓔ 중, 어휘의 쓰임이 어색한 것은?

① ⓐ
② ⓑ
③ ⓒ
④ ⓓ
⑤ ⓔ

[12~13] 다음 대화를 읽고 물음에 답하시오.

> G: Did you watch the documentary last night?
> B: No, I didn't. What was it about?
> G: It was about global warming. (A)지구가 점점 더워지면서, 해수면이 올라가고 있대. I'm worried about the Earth.
> B: Oh, I've heard about that problem before. Some islands are disappearing, so people are losing their homes.
> G: Yes. It is terrible.
> B: Is there any way to stop it?
> G: We can save energy. We should turn off the lights when we don't need them. We should also use fans (B)_____ air conditioners.
> B: Those are great ideas. I'll try to do those things.

12 위 대화의 밑줄 친 (A)의 우리말에 맞게 주어진 문장의 빈칸을 채우시오.

➡ The Earth is _____ _____, and sea levels are _____ _____.

13 위 대화의 빈칸 (B)에 들어갈 알맞은 것은?

① because of
② instead of
③ thanks to
④ during
⑤ despite

Grammar

14 다음 중 어법상 올바른 것은?

① The cat was more bigger than yours.

② Blue whales are considered to be the biggest animals.

③ The car in the show room was far expensive than I thought.

④ My brother wasn't made wash the car by my dad.

⑤ The waste turned into food for the plants by bacteria.

15 다음 밑줄 친 부분과 바꿔 쓸 수 있는 것은?

> The line on the blackboard is <u>much</u> longer than the line on the desk.

① very   ② so   ③ lot

④ even   ⑤ too

16 다음 빈칸에 들어갈 말을 순서대로 바르게 짝지은 것을 고르시오.

> • This scarf looks _____ on you than that one.
> • Many dolls _____ in the factory by them.

① too nice – made

② very nicer – were made

③ far nicer – were made

④ far nicer – made

⑤ very nicer – made

17 다음 문장에서 어법상 틀린 것을 고쳐 다시 쓰시오.

(1) I heard 17 trees use to make one ton of paper.

➡ _____

(2) A car accident was happened a few days ago in front of the school.

➡ _____
_____

(3) A beautiful dress is being made to her daughter by Angie.

➡ _____

(4) The tree is planted her grandfather right after he bought the house.

➡ _____
_____

(5) Yesterday Don was seen cross the road by Bella.

➡ _____
_____

(6) The expensive car will buy by someone for whom money grows on trees.

➡ _____
_____

18 다음 빈칸에 들어갈 전치사가 나머지와 다른 것은?

① Our chocolate is made _____ robots.

② The telephone was invented _____ Alexander Bell.

③ *Romeo and Juliet* was written _____ Shakespeare.

④ The pictures in this album were taken _____ Sam.

⑤ Are you satisfied _____ your job as a tour guide?

19 다음 우리말을 괄호 안에 주어진 어구를 이용하여 영작하시오.

(1) 낮은 여름보다 겨울에 훨씬 짧다. (days, much, in winter, 9 단어)

➡ _____

(2) Ann은 코미디언보다 훨씬 더 유머가 있다. (far, humorous, comedians, 7 단어)

➡ _____

(3) 한국에서 축구는 야구보다 훨씬 인기 있다. (soccer, even, popular, 9 단어)

➡ _____

Reading

[20~22] 다음 글을 읽고 물음에 답하시오.

Fish, bacteria, and plants are the main parts of aquaponics. After you feed the fish, they produce ⓐwaste. ⓑThe waste is turned into food for the plants by bacteria. The plants clean the water by consuming the food. This process ___ⓒ___ again and again!

20 위 글의 밑줄 친 ⓐwaste와 같은 의미로 쓰인 것을 고르시오.

① Don't waste your time trying it.
② It's a waste of time to do the thing.
③ I didn't waste a good opportunity.
④ We must use waste talents.
⑤ Let's recycle the industrial waste.

21 위 글의 밑줄 친 ⓑ를 능동태로 고치시오.

➡ _____

22 위 글의 빈칸 ⓒ에 repeat를 알맞은 형태로 쓰시오.

➡ _____

[23~24] 다음 글을 읽고 물음에 답하시오.

Home Aquaponics by Eric Jackson
Questions: How can I make an aquaponics system at home?
Why is aquaponics good?
Period: From May 15 to August 15
Materials: a pot & small stones, a fish tank, a plastic tube, a water pump, plants, some fish, a box cutter, clay
Steps:
1. I made holes in the bottom of a pot. Then I put small stones and plants in it.
2. I made a big hole in the lid of the fish tank and put the pot in the hole.
3. I fixed the pot in place with clay.
4. I made another hole in the lid and put a tube through it.
5. I put a water pump in the fish tank. I used the tube ⓐto connect the pump to the pot.
6. I filled the fish tank with water and put some fish in it. Then I turned on the pump.

23 위 글의 밑줄 친 ⓐto connect와 to부정사의 용법이 다른 것을 모두 고르시오.

① He smiled to see the puppy.
② It is necessary to use the dictionary.
③ She must be honest to say so.
④ I have some letters to write.
⑤ This water is not good to drink.

24 위 글의 내용과 일치하지 않는 것은?

① 에릭은 집에서 아쿠아포닉스 장치를 어떻게 만들 수 있을지와 아쿠아포닉스가 왜 좋은지를 알기 위해 실험을 했다.
② 에릭은 5월 15일부터 8월 15일까지 실험을 했다.
③ 어항 바닥에 큰 구멍을 내고 구멍에 화분을 넣었다.
④ 어항에 수중 펌프를 넣고 관을 이용하여 펌프를 화분에 연결하였다.
⑤ 어항에 물을 채우고 물고기 몇 마리를 거기에 넣었다.

[25~26] 다음 글을 읽고 물음에 답하시오.

Results:

From this experiment, I grew my plants and raised fish with aquaponics. I just fed the fish, but the plants have grown 17 centimeters ⓐ_____ three months. The fish stay healthy and the water is clean all the time.

Conclusion:

Some important things about aquaponics were learned from this experiment. First, water is saved because the plants don't need watering. Second, it is good ⓑ_____ the environment because no chemicals are used. Finally, you can do aquaponics anywhere because it doesn't need much space.

I = Eric

25 위 글의 빈칸 ⓐ와 ⓑ에 들어갈 전치사가 바르게 짝지어진 것은?

① in – for
② for – at
③ at – for
④ for – to
⑤ in – at

26 위 글을 읽고 대답할 수 <u>없는</u> 질문은?

① Did Eric grow his plants and raise fish at the same time?
② How is the water quality with aquaponics?
③ Why is water saved with aquaponics?
④ Why is aquaponics good for the environment?
⑤ What do you need to do aquaponics?

[27~29] 다음 글을 읽고 물음에 답하시오.

I found out...

Some farmers use aquaponics to produce vegetables and raise fish. They choose aquaponics because it is far ⓐ_____ than traditional gardening. Also, it is a much ⓑ_____ way of growing food. The plants grow much ⓒ_____ than plants in soil, and it saves space. I hope ⓓ_____ food is produced in ⓔ<u>this way</u> in the future because it is healthy for us and the environment.

27 위 글의 빈칸 ⓐ~ⓓ에 각각 easy, productive, fast, much의 비교급을 쓰시오.

➡ ⓐ _____ ⓑ _____
　 ⓒ _____ ⓓ _____

28 위 글의 밑줄 친 ⓔthis way가 가리키는 것을 본문에서 찾아 쓰시오.

➡ _____

29 위 글을 읽고 아쿠아포닉스의 장점이 <u>아닌</u> 것을 고르시오.

① 전통적인 재배 방식보다 훨씬 쉽다.
② 식량을 재배하는 훨씬 더 생산적인 방법이다.
③ 화학 물질의 사용을 줄여준다.
④ 식물들이 흙에서 자라는 식물보다 훨씬 빠르게 자라고 공간도 절약한다.
⑤ 우리와 환경에 훨씬 건강하다.

출제율 95%

01 다음 짝지어진 단어의 관계가 같도록 빈칸에 알맞은 말을 쓰시오.

> choose : select = link : _____

출제율 90%

02 다음 영영풀이에 해당하는 단어는?

> an empty space in an object, usually with an opening to the object's surface

① plant   ② system   ③ hole
④ space   ⑤ bottle

출제율 85%

03 다음 빈칸에 우리말에 맞게 알맞은 단어를 쓰시오.

> • 나는 찰흙으로 화분을 제자리에 고정하였다 .
> (A) I _____ the pot in _____ with clay.
> • 식물에 물을 줄 필요가 없으므로 물이 절약된다.
> (B) Water is saved because the plants don't need _____.

출제율 90%

04 다음은 Home Aquaponics에 관한 글이다. 알맞은 단어를 골라 쓰시오.

> Fish, bacteria, and plants are the main parts of aquaponics. After you (A)[feed / consume] the fish, they produce waste. The waste is turned into food for the (B) [fish / plants] by bacteria. The plants clean the water by consuming the food. This (C)[process / produce] is repeated again and again.

➡ (A)_____ (B)_____ (C)_____

[05~06] 다음 대화를 읽고 물음에 답하시오.

> G: Did you watch the documentary last night?
> B: No, I didn't. What was it about?
> G: It was about global warming. The Earth is getting hotter, and sea levels are going up. (A)_____
> B: Oh, I've heard about that problem before. Some islands are (B)_____, so people are losing their homes.
> G: Yes. It is terrible.

출제율 90%

05 위 대화의 빈칸 (A)에 들어갈 말로 가장 적절한 것은?

① I'm worried about the trash on the street.
② I'm worried about the Earth.
③ The documentary was very interesting.
④ How high are sea levels going up?
⑤ How is the weather?

출제율 100%

06 위 대화의 빈칸 (B)에 들어갈 말로 알맞은 것은?

① appearing   ② expanding
③ warming   ④ developing
⑤ disappearing

[07~09] 다음 대화를 읽고 물음에 답하시오.

> Boy: You look nervous. What's wrong?
> Girl: I'm worried about the speech contest next week. The speeches are about environmental problems and their solutions.
> Boy: What are you going to talk about?
> Girl: I want to talk about soil pollution, but I can't find enough information.

Boy: What about water problems (A)_____? I read an article, and it said we don't have enough water. I'm really worried about it. I think we have to do something about that problem.

Girl: But isn't there enough water for everyone?

Boy: No. In some countries, people are in danger (B)_____ they don't have enough water. Our country could have this problem in the near future.

Girl: Oh, I didn't know that. I will talk about that problem and its solutions. Thank you for your advice!

출제율90%

07 What topic did the girl want to talk about at first? (Write in a full sentence.)

➡ _____

출제율95%

08 위 대화의 빈칸 (A)와 (B)에 들어갈 말이 알맞게 짝지어진 것은?

① however – though ② instead – so
③ instead – because ④ however – so
⑤ therefore – because

출제율95%

09 위 대화의 내용과 일치하지 <u>않는</u> 것은?

① The girl looks nervous because she has the speech contest next week.
② The girl doesn't have enough information about soil pollution.
③ The boy is worried about not having enough water.
④ The girl knew that there isn't enough water for everyone.
⑤ The girl will talk about water shortage instead of soil pollution.

출제율90%

10 다음 대화의 빈칸 ⓐ와 ⓑ에 들어갈 단어가 알맞게 짝지어진 것은?

Boy: In my school, students ⓐ_____ so much food on their plates. I'm worried about wasting food.

Girl: Right, that's a big problem. We should not ⓑ_____ too much food on our plates.

Boy: You're right. We shouldn't.

① leave – put   ② put – put
③ take – turn   ④ make – leave
⑤ leave – fill

출제율95%

11 다음 중 밑줄 친 부분이 어법상 <u>잘못된</u> 것은?

① Jake <u>was chosen</u> as our class leader.
② The work <u>must be finished</u> before noon.
③ He <u>was given</u> a reward by the king.
④ The children <u>looked after</u> by their mother.
⑤ The kids <u>are surprised</u> at his grades.

출제율90%

12 다음 빈칸에 들어갈 수 <u>없는</u> 것을 고르시오.

Tigers are _____ faster than pigs.

① very   ② much   ③ far
④ still   ⑤ a lot

13 다음 중 수동태로 바꿔 쓴 것이 <u>잘못된</u> 것은?

① Joe ate a cake.

= A cake was eaten by Joe.

② A cat chases a mouse.

= A mouse is chased by a cat.

③ They take good care of old people at home.

= Old people are taken good care by them at home.

④ The police found the missing boy last Saturday.

= The missing boy was found by the police last Saturday.

⑤ Marc Chagall painted *I and the Village* in 1911.

= *I and the Village* was painted by Marc Chagall in 1911.

14 다음 주어진 단어들을 이용하여 빈칸을 알맞게 채우시오.

• (fast, cheap)

(1) Light travels _____ _____ than sound.

(2) Vegetables are _____ _____ than beef.

➡ (1) _____

(2) _____

15 다음 문장과 같은 뜻이 되도록 빈칸을 채우시오.

(1) Sandra will see the movie *Avatar* tonight.

➡ The movie *Avatar* _____

_____ .

(2) John Logie Baird invented the TV in 1925.

➡ The TV _____

_____ .

16 우리말 의미에 맞도록 괄호 안의 어구를 알맞게 배열하시오.

(1) laptop이 컴퓨터보다 훨씬 더 유용하다.

(the laptop, the computer, more, is, useful, much, than).

➡ _____

(2) 그녀는 여동생보다 훨씬 더 젊어 보인다. (she, even, sister, her, younger, little, looks, than)

➡ _____

[17~19] 다음 글을 읽고 물음에 답하시오.

Fish, bacteria, and plants are the main parts of aquaponics. After you feed the fish, ⓐthey produce waste. The waste is turned into food for the plants by bacteria. The plants clean the water by consuming ⓑthe food. This process is repeated again and again!

17 위 글의 밑줄 친 ⓐthey가 가리키는 것을 본문에서 찾아 쓰시오.

➡ _____

18 다음 빈칸에 알맞은 단어를 넣어 ⓑthe food에 대한 소개를 완성하시오.

After _____ is produced by the fish, bacteria turn it into food for the plants.

➡ _____

19 위 글의 내용과 일치하지 <u>않는</u> 것은?

① 물고기, 박테리아, 식물이 아쿠아포닉스의 주요 부분이다.

② 물고기에게 먹이를 주면, 그것들은 배설물을 만들어 낸다.

③ 이 배설물은 물고기에 의해 식물의 먹이로 바뀐다.

④ 식물은 그 먹이를 먹음으로써 물을 정화한다.

⑤ 이러한 과정이 계속해서 반복된다.

[20~22] 다음 글을 읽고 물음에 답하시오.

Steps:

1. I made holes in the bottom of a pot. ⓐThen I put small stones and plants in it.
2. I made a big hole in the lid of the fish tank and put the pot in the hole.
3. I (A)[fixed / repaired] the pot in place ⓑ_____ clay.
4. I made another hole in the lid and put a tube (B)[threw / through] it.
5. I put a water pump in the fish tank. I used the tube to connect the pump to the pot.
6. I filled the fish tank ⓒ_____ water and put some fish in it. Then I turned (C)[on / off] the pump.

20 위 글의 밑줄 친 ⓐThen을 다음과 같이 바꿔 쓸 때 빈칸에 들어갈 알맞은 말을 쓰시오.

➡ After _____

21 위 글의 괄호 (A)~(C)에서 문맥상 알맞은 낱말을 골라 쓰시오.

➡ (A)_____ (B)_____ (C)_____

22 위 글의 빈칸 ⓑ와 ⓒ에 공통으로 들어갈 알맞은 전치사를 고르시오.

① to　　② on　　③ at
④ by　　⑤ with

[23~25] 다음 글을 읽고 물음에 답하시오.

Results:

From this experiment, I grew my plants and raised fish with aquaponics. I just fed the fish, but the plants ①have grown 17 centimeters in three months. The fish stay ②healthily and the water is clean all the time.

Conclusion:

Some important things about aquaponics ③was learned from this experiment. First, water ⓐ_____ because the plants don't need ④being watered. Second, it is good for the environment because no chemicals are used. Finally, you can do aquaponics ⑤anywhere because it doesn't need much space.

I = Eric

23 위 글의 밑줄 친 ①~⑤ 중 어법상 <u>틀린</u> 것의 개수를 고르시오.

① 1개　　② 2개　　③ 3개　　④ 4개　　⑤ 5개

24 위 글의 빈칸 ⓐ에 save를 알맞은 형태로 쓰시오.

➡ _____

25 다음 문장에서 위 글의 내용과 <u>다른</u> 부분을 찾아서 고치시오.

• From this experiment, the plants have grown 17 centimeters in three months because Eric watered the plants.

➡ _____

_____

01 다음 그림을 보고 대화의 빈칸을 완성하시오.

flower pot

1. Make holes in the bottom.
2. Fill the cup with soil and plants.

A: I made _____ _____ _____ with a plastic cup.

B: Can you tell me _____ _____ _____ it?

A: Sure. Make holes in _____ _____. Then _____ the cup _____ soil and plants.

02 다음은 수질 오염에 관한 그림이다. 〈보기〉에서 알맞은 해결책을 골라 대화를 완성하시오.

water pollution

┌──── 보기 ────┐
recycle   plant many trees
use less water   use less soap
└──────────────┘

A: I am worried about (A)_____ these days.

B: Me, too. We should (B)_____ to solve this problem.

➡ (A) _____
  (B) _____

03 다음은 어떤 환경 문제에 관한 대화이다. 빈칸 (A)에는 언급하고 있는 문제를, (B)에는 해결책을 주어진 단어를 이용하여 쓰시오.

G: Did you watch the documentary last night?

B: No, I didn't. What was it about?

G: It was about (A)_____. The Earth is getting hotter, and sea levels are going up. I'm worried about the Earth.

B: Is there any way to stop it?

G: We can save energy. We should (B)_____ (the lights) when we don't need them. We should also use fans instead of air conditioners.

B: Those are great ideas. I'll try to do those things.

➡(A) _____ (B) _____

04 다음 주어진 문장을 능동태는 수동태로, 수동태는 능동태로 바꾸시오.

(1) What did he do last weekend?
  ➡ _____

(2) Van Gogh painted these paintings.
  ➡ _____

(3) My father gave me that watch years ago.
  ➡ _____
  _____

05 다음 문장에서 **틀린** 것을 고쳐 다시 쓰시오.

(1) He is very tall than his son.

➡ _____

(2) Sue uses too much water than Nick.

➡ _____

[06~08] 다음 글을 읽고 물음에 답하시오.

Home Aquaponics   by Eric Jackson

Questions: ⓐ   can I make an aquaponics
system at home?

Why is aquaponics good?

Steps:

1. I made holes in the bottom of a pot. Then I put small stones and plants in it.

2. I made a big hole in the lid of the fish tank and put the pot in the hole.

3. I fixed the pot in place with clay.

4. I made another hole in the lid and put a tube through it.

5. I put a water pump in the fish tank. I used the tube ⓑ_____.

6. I filled the fish tank with water and put some fish in it. ⓒThen I turned on the pump.

06 위 글의 빈칸 ⓐ에 들어갈 알맞은 말을 쓰시오.

➡ _____

07 그림을 참조하여 위 글의 빈칸 ⓑ에 들어갈 알맞은 말을 쓰시오. (7 단어)

➡ _____

08 위 글의 밑줄 친 ⓒThen을 다음과 같이 바꿔 쓸 때 빈칸에 들어갈 알맞은 말을 쓰시오.

➡ _____ I filled the fish tank with water and put some fish in it

[09~11] 다음 글을 읽고 물음에 답하시오.

Conclusion:

ⓐSome important things about aquaponics were learned from this experiment. First, water is saved because the plants don't need ⓑwatering. Second, it is good for the environment because no chemicals are used. Finally, you can do aquaponics anywhere because it doesn't need much space.

09 위 글의 밑줄 친 ⓐ를 I를 주어로 하여 능동태로 고치시오.

➡ _____

_____

10 위 글의 밑줄 친 ⓑ를 to부정사를 사용하여 고치시오.

➡ _____

11 본문의 내용과 일치하도록 다음 빈칸 (A)~(C)에 알맞은 단어를 넣어 아쿠아포닉스의 장점을 정리하시오.

(1) You need not water the plants in aquaponics.

➡ You can (A)_____.

(2) You need not (B)_____ in aquaponics.

➡ Aquaponics is good for the environment.

(3) You don't need (C)_____ in aquaponics.

➡ You can do aquaponics anywhere.

01 다음은 일상생활에서 발생할 수 있는 문제와 해결책에 관한 문장이다. 〈보기〉를 참고하여, 문제점과 그에 대한 해결책으로 알맞은 두 문장 이상의 대화를 완성하시오.

<문제점>

a park in my town – It is full of trash. / my brother – He always buys too many things. /

my cat – He is missing. / my friend – She uses her smartphone too often.

<해결책>

We should clean up the park together. / He should make a shopping list.

You should put up posters to find him. / She should find a new hobby.

<보기>

A: I'm worried about a park in my town. It is full of trash.

Can you tell me how to solve this problem?

B: I think we should clean up the park together.

---

02 다음 내용을 바탕으로 학교에서 환경을 보호하는 방법을 친구들에게 제안하는 글을 쓰시오.

Problem

Lots of energy is wasted.

Solutions

• Turn off the lights.

• Turn off the classroom computers.

• Close the doors and windows when we use air conditioners.

Let's Make Our School Green!

Lots of energy (A)_____ around us. To solve this problem, let's do these things. First, we should (B)_____ the lights when we leave our classrooms. Next, we should turn off the classroom computers when we are not (C)_____ them. Lastly, we should (D)_____ the doors and windows when we use air conditioners. Doing these things will be (E)_____ to our school and the environment.

단원별 모의고사

01 다음 단어에 대한 영어 설명이 어색한 것은?

① in place: in the correct position

② productive: producing or achieving a lot

③ consume: to eat or drink, especially a lot of something

④ reuse: to use something again

⑤ remind: to make someone forget something that they must do

02 다음 짝지어진 단어의 관계가 같도록 빈칸에 알맞은 말을 쓰시오.

> turn off : turn on = appear : _____

03 다음 영영풀이에 해당하는 단어를 고르시오.

> a cover for the open part of a pot, box, or container, etc.

① lid ② tank

③ article ④ cup

⑤ project

04 다음 글의 빈칸에 들어갈 말이 바르게 짝지어진 것은?

> Time is (A)_____ for the Earth. Remember the Earth is (B)_____. Keep the Earth green!

① getting – dangerous

② polluting – clean

③ making up – safe

④ turning on – going up

⑤ running out – in danger

[05~06] 다음 대화를 읽고 물음에 답하시오.

B: I like your bag, Jenny. Where did you get ⓐit?

G: I made ⓑit myself.

B: You made ⓒit yourself? That's amazing.

G: Why don't you make one? ⓓIt's not difficult.

B: Really? Can you tell me how to make ⓔit?

G: Sure. Find some old jeans. (A)그걸 작은 조각으로 잘라. Then sew the pieces together.

B: That sounds easy. I'll make one as a birthday present for my sister.

05 위 대화의 밑줄 친 ⓐ~ⓔ 중, 가리키는 대상이 다른 하나는?

① ⓐ ② ⓑ ③ ⓒ ④ ⓓ ⑤ ⓔ

06 위 대화의 밑줄 친 (A)의 우리말에 맞게 주어진 단어를 이용하여 영어로 쓰시오.

➡ _____

(cut, into, pieces)

07 다음 대화의 빈칸 (A)에 들어갈 말을 주어진 단어를 이용하여 영어로 쓰시오.

> G: Earth Hour is a global environmental event. People turn off their lights for an hour.
>
> B: Why do they do that?
>
> G: They do it to remind people of our environmental problems.
>
> B: Oh, I see. (A)_____
>
> (can, tell, how, join, it)
>
> G: Sure. Just turn off your lights from 8:30 p.m. to 9:30 p.m. on the last Saturday in March.
>
> B: That's easy.

➡ _____

[08~10] 다음 대화를 읽고 물음에 답하시오.

Ben: You look nervous. What's wrong?

Jenny: I'm worried about the speech contest next week. The speeches are about environmental problems and their solutions.

Ben: What are you going to talk about?

Jenny: I want to talk about soil pollution, but I can't find enough information.

Ben: What about water problems instead? I read an article, and ⓐit said we don't have enough water. I'm really worried about ⓑit. I think we have to do something about ⓒthat problem.

Jenny: But isn't there enough water for everyone?

Ben: No. In some countries, (A)물이 부족해서 사람들이 위험에 처하기도 해. Our country could have ⓓthis problem in the near future.

Jenny: Oh, I didn't know that. I will talk about ⓔthat problem and its solutions. Thank you for your advice!

08 위 대화를 읽고 답할 수 없는 질문은?

① What topic will Jenny talk about?

② Why is Jenny going to talk about soil pollution?

③ What is Ben worried about?

④ When is the speech contest?

⑤ Is there enough water for everyone?

09 위 대화의 밑줄 친 ⓐ~ⓔ 중, 가리키는 대상이 다른 하나는?

① ⓐ   ② ⓑ   ③ ⓒ   ④ ⓓ   ⑤ ⓔ

10 위 대화의 밑줄 친 (A)의 우리말에 맞게 주어진 어구를 이용하여 영어로 쓰시오.

(are, danger, because, they, enough water)

➡ _____

_____

11 다음 밑줄 친 부분 중 생략할 수 있는 것은?

① The airplane was invented by the Wright brothers in 1903.

② *Harry Potter* was written by J. K. Rowling.

③ The bike was fixed by my elder brother.

④ English is spoken in Australia by them.

⑤ The children weren't taught by him.

12 다음 〈보기〉의 표현이 빈칸에 들어갈 수 없는 문장은?

┌─ 보기 ─┐

much   far

① This dictionary is _____ heavier than that book.

② Taking a bus is _____ cheaper than taking a taxi.

③ She felt _____ great after taking a sound sleep.

④ My brother jumps _____ higher than I.

⑤ Lisa dances _____ harder than me.

13 다음 밑줄 친 부분의 쓰임이 나머지 넷과 다른 것은?

① The bike was repaired by my brother.
② This chocolate cake was cooked for me by my mother.
③ Water is saved because the plants don't need watering.
④ She often avoided replying to our comments.
⑤ The pictures were drawn by my daughter.

14 다음 그림을 보고 주어진 단어를 이용하여 비교하는 문장을 쓰시오.

➡ _____

(feather, stone, much)

15 다음 문장에서 틀린 것을 고쳐 다시 쓰시오.

(1) Paper is made of wood.
➡ _____

(2) Olivia was cooked the chicken soup by her mother.
➡ _____

(3) A man was appeared on the stage slowly.
➡ _____

(4) I didn't know you were interested by Latin dance.
➡ _____

(5) Some birds were heard sing on the tree.
➡ _____

[16~17] 다음 글을 읽고 물음에 답하시오.

> Jennifer: What are you reading?
> Eric: I'm reading an article about aquaponics. It's a way of growing plants (A)[with / without] soil. We can also grow plants and (B)[rise / raise] fish in just one system.
> Jennifer: Is ⓐthat possible?
> Eric: We'll (C)[see / show]. I'm going to try it at home for my science project.

16 위 글의 괄호 (A)~(C)에서 문맥이나 어법상 알맞은 낱말을 골라 쓰시오.

➡ (A)_____ (B)_____ (C)_____

17 위 글의 밑줄 친 ⓐthat이 가리키는 것을 본문에서 찾아 쓰시오.

➡ _____
_____

[18~19] 다음 글을 읽고 물음에 답하시오.

> Steps:
> 1. I made holes in the bottom of a pot. Then I put small stones and plants ①_____ it.
> 2. I made a big hole ②_____ the lid of the fish tank and put the pot in the hole.
> 3. ⓐ찰흙으로 화분을 제자리에 고정하였다.
> 4. I made another hole in the lid and put a tube through it.
> 5. I put a water pump ③_____ the fish tank. I used the tube to connect the pump ④_____ the pot.
> 6. I filled the fish tank with water and put some fish ⑤_____ it. Then I turned on the pump.

18 위 글의 빈칸 ①~⑤에 들어갈 전치사가 나머지 넷과 다른 것은?

①   ②   ③   ④   ⑤

19 위 글의 밑줄 친 ⓐ의 우리말에 맞게 한 단어를 보충하여, 주어진 어휘를 알맞게 배열하시오.

> with / the / fixed / I / clay / pot / in

➡ _____

[20~21] 다음 글을 읽고 물음에 답하시오.

> **Results:**
>
> From this experiment, I grew my ___ⓐ___ and raised ___ⓑ___ with aquaponics. I just fed the fish, but the plants have grown 17 centimeters in three months. The fish stay healthy and the water is clean all the time.
>
> **Conclusion:**
>
> Some important things about aquaponics were learned from this experiment. First, water is saved because the plants don't need watering. Second, it is good for the environment because no chemicals are used. Finally, you can do aquaponics anywhere because it doesn't need much space.
>
>   I = Eric

20 다음 그림을 참조하여 위 글의 빈칸 ⓐ와 ⓑ에 들어갈 알맞은 말을 쓰시오.

➡ ⓐ _____ ⓑ _____

21 위 글의 내용과 일치하지 않는 것은?

① 에릭은 그저 물고기에 밥만 주었는데도 식물은 석 달 동안 17cm나 자랐다.

② 아쿠아포닉스로 물고기는 건강을 유지하며 물은 항상 깨끗하다.

③ 아쿠아포닉스에서는 식물에 물을 자주 주어야 하므로 물이 많이 소비된다.

④ 화학 물질이 사용되지 않으므로 아쿠아포닉스는 환경에 이롭다.

⑤ 넓은 공간이 필요하지 않으므로 당신은 어디에서나 아쿠아포닉스를 쉽게 할 수 있다.

[22~23] 다음 글을 읽고 물음에 답하시오.

> *I found out...*
>
> Some farmers use aquaponics to produce vegetables and raise fish. They choose aquaponics because it is ⓐfar easier than traditional gardening. Also, it is a much more productive way of growing food. The plants grow much faster than plants in soil, and it saves space. I hope more food is produced in this way in the future because it is healthy for us and the environment.

22 위 글의 밑줄 친 ⓐ와 바꿔 쓸 수 있는 것은?

① so   ② very   ③ too

④ much   ⑤ lot

23 다음 문장에서 위 글의 내용과 다른 부분을 찾아서 고치시오.

> The plants in soil grow much faster than the plants in aquaponics system.

➡ _____

_____

Lesson 5

Give a Helping Hand

 의사소통 기능

- 도움 요청하고 답하기
  A: Can you help me move these books?
  B: Sure. / I'm sorry, but I can't.

- 제안하기
  Why don't we donate our clothes to the community center?

언어 형식

- 목적격 관계대명사
  The little black dress **which** she wore in a movie is famous even today.

- 감정을 나타내는 과거분사
  She was **shocked** because their lives were very difficult.

Words & Expressions

교과서

Key Words

- **accident** [ǽksidənt] 명 사고
- **alive** [əláiv] 형 살아 있는, 존속하는
- **beauty** [bjú:ti] 명 아름다움, 미(美)
- **blind** [blaind] 형 눈 먼, 장님의
- **carry** [kǽri] 동 나르다, 운반하다
- **collect** [kəlékt] 동 모으다, 수집하다
- **donate** [dóuneit] 동 기부하다
- **elderly** [éldərli] 형 나이가 지긋한
- **fame** [feim] 명 명성
- **favor** [féivər] 명 호의, 친절
- **feed** [fi:d] 동 먹이를 주다
- **fire** [faiər] 명 화재
- **following** [fálouiŋ] 형 (그) 다음의
- **goodwill ambassador** 친선 대사
- **grass** [græs] 명 풀, 잔디
- **hold** [hould] 동 열다, 개최하다
- **homeless** [hóumlis] 형 집 없는, 노숙자의
- **honor** [ánər] 동 예우하다, 존중하다
- **international** [intərnǽʃənəl] 형 국제적인
- **item** [áitəm] 명 항목, 물품
- **kind** [kaind] 명 종류, 유형

- **luckily** [lʌkili] 부 운이 좋게도, 다행스럽게도
- **medicine** [medisn] 명 약
- **mission** [míʃən] 명 임무, 사명
- **moment** [móumənt] 명 순간, 잠깐
- **nursing home** 양로원
- **plant** [plænt] 동 (식물을) 심다
- **praise** [preiz] 동 칭찬하다
- **raise** [reiz] 동 들어 올리다, (자금을) 모으다
- **realize** [rí:əlàiz] 동 깨닫다, 알아차리다
- **respect** [rispékt] 동 존경하다
- **return** [ritə́:rn] 동 돌아오다, 반납하다
- **saying** [séiiŋ] 명 속담, 격언
- **serve** [sə:rv] 동 (음식을) 제공하다
- **spirit** [spírit] 명 마음, 정신, 영혼
- **statue** [stǽtʃu:] 명 조각상
- **support** [səpɔ́:rt] 동 지지하다, 원조하다
- **survive** [sərváiv] 동 살아남다, 생존하다
- **turning point** 전환점
- **volunteer** [vàləntíər] 형 자원봉사의 명 자원 봉사자
- **walk** [wɔ:k] 동 산책시키다, (사람·동물을) 걷게 하다
- **worldwide** [wə́:rldwaid] 형 세계적인

Key Expressions

- **all the time**: 늘, 내내
- **be going to** 동사원형: ~할 것이다
- **be in a hurry**: 서두르다
- **break one's arm**: 팔이 부러지다
- **clean up**: ~을 치우다, 청소하다
- **fall down**: 넘어지다
- **give a hand**: ~을 돕다
- **hand out**: 나누어 주다
- **have to** 동사원형: ~해야 한다
- **help** 목적어 (**to**) 동사원형: …가 ~하는 것을 돕다

- **hold a party**: 파티를 열다
- **in need**: 어려움에 처한
- **pass away**: 죽다, 사망하다
- **raise money**: 돈을 모금하다
- **search for**: ~을 찾다
- **take care of**: ~을 돌보다
- **thanks to**: ~ 덕분에
- **What[How] about** 동명사 ~?: ~하는 게 어떨까?
- **what kinds of** ~: 어떤 종류의
- **Why don't we** ~?: ~하는 게 어떨까?

Word Power

※ 명사 – 형용사
- □ **beauty**(아름다움, 미(美)) – **beautiful**(아름다운)
- □ **favor**(호의, 친절) – **favorable**(호의적인)
- □ **respect**(존경) – **respectful**(존경심이 가득한, 존경하는), **respectable**(존경할 만한)

※ 서로 반대되는 뜻을 가진 단어
- □ **alive**(살아 있는, 존속하는) ↔ **dead**(죽은)
- □ **beauty**(아름다움) ↔ **ugliness**(추함)
- □ **luckily**(운이 좋게도) ↔ **unluckily**(불행히도)

※ 서로 비슷한 뜻을 가진 단어
- □ **following**((그) 다음의) : **next**(다음의)
- □ **collect**(모으다) : **gather**(모으다)
- □ **thanks to**(~ 덕분에) : **because of**, **due to**(~ 때문에)
- □ **pass away**(죽다) : **die**(죽다)

※ 사람의 성격을 묘사할 때 쓸 수 있는 형용사
- □ **nice[kind/friendly]**(상냥한, 다정한)
- □ **wise**(현명한)
- □ **curious**(호기심 많은)
- □ **funny**(재미있는)
- □ **polite**(공손한)
- □ **patient**(끈기 있는)
- □ **gentle**(온화한)
- □ **honest**(정직한)
- □ **creative**(창의적인)
- □ **generous**(관대한)
- □ **lively**(쾌활한)

English Dictionary

□ **accident** 사고
→ a sudden event that causes damage
손상[손해]을 유발하는 갑작스러운 일

□ **blind**: 눈 먼, 장님의
→ not able to see anything
어떤 것도 볼 수 없는

□ **collect**: 모으다, 수집하다
→ to put things together in one place
한 장소에 사물들을 함께 두다

□ **donate**: 기부하다
→ to give something to help people
사람들을 돕기 위해 무언가를 주다

□ **fame**: 명성
→ the state of being famous
유명한 상태

□ **honor**: 예우하다, 존중하다
→ to treat someone with respect
존경심을 가지고 누군가를 대하다

□ **international**: 국제적인
→ involving more than one country
하나 이상의 나라를 포함한

□ **mission**: 임무, 사명
→ a special task to be accomplished
달성되어야 할 특별한 일

□ **moment**: 순간, 잠깐
→ a particular point in time
시간 상의 특정한 시점

□ **nursing home**: 양로원
→ a place where people who are too old or sick to take care of themselves live
너무 나이 들거나 병이 들어서 스스로 돌볼 수 없는 사람들이 사는 장소

□ **praise**: 칭찬하다
→ to say nice things about someone
어떤 사람에 대해 좋은 점을 말하다

□ **realize**: 깨닫다, 알아차리다
→ to suddenly know something
갑자기 무언가를 알다

□ **respect**: 존경하다
→ to admire or look up to somebody
누군가를 존경하거나 우러러보다

□ **statue**: 조각상
→ a sculpture of a person made from stone or metal
돌이나 금속으로 만든 사람의 조각품

□ **support**: 지지하다, 원조하다
→ to provide with assistance
도움을 제공하다

□ **survive**: 살아남다, 생존하다
→ to continue to live after something bad happens
어떤 나쁜 일이 일어난 후에 계속 살다

□ **turning point**: 전환점
→ a time when a huge change takes place
큰 변화가 발생하는 때

□ **volunteer**: 자원 봉사자
→ someone who is willing to do a job without getting paid
돈을 받지 않고 기꺼이 어떤 일을 하는 사람

01 다음 중 성격이 <u>다른</u> 하나를 고르시오.

① creative ② generous ③ lively
④ lucky ⑤ passionate

[02~03] 다음 빈칸에 들어갈 말로 가장 적절한 것을 고르시오.

02
Please don't _____ the animals in the zoo.

① feed ② blow ③ cost
④ fall ⑤ find

This box is so heavy that I can't _____ it alone.

① carry ② wear ③ play
④ try ⑤ break

[04~06] 다음 밑줄 친 단어와 바꿔 쓸 수 있는 것을 고르시오.

04
I bought these <u>items</u> at a low price because they are used ones.

① sites ② stops
③ goods ④ markets
⑤ views

He <u>died</u> at the hospital last night.

① passed over ② passed away
③ got over ④ gave up
⑤ got back

06
I want to meet many people and travel <u>all over the world</u>.

① nationally ② internationally
③ worldwide ④ global
⑤ variously

07 다음 중 밑줄 친 부분의 뜻풀이가 바르지 <u>않은</u> 것은?

① I'd like to make an <u>international</u> call. (국제적인)
② Her <u>mission</u> was to establish schools for children. (임무)
③ The man keeps his family's tradition <u>alive</u>. (살아 있는)
④ She's gone but her <u>spirit</u> is right here with us. (정신)
⑤ They will <u>raise</u> money to help the poor. (들어 올리다)

[08~09] 다음 영영풀이에 해당하는 단어를 고르시오.

08
a time when a huge change takes place

① turning point ② schedule
③ timetable ④ moment
⑤ honor

09
a particular point in time

① second ② plan
③ moment ④ motive
⑤ respect

01 다음 짝지어진 두 단어의 관계가 같도록 빈칸에 알맞은 단어를 쓰시오. (주어진 철자로 시작할 것)

> luckily: unluckily - a_____ : dead

02 다음 밑줄 친 부분과 의미가 가장 가까운 것을 주어진 철자로 시작하여 쓰시오.

> We'll never forget his <u>soul</u>.

➡ s_____

[03~04] 다음 빈칸에 공통으로 들어갈 말을 쓰시오.

03
> • Can you drive faster? I'm _____ a hurry.
> • I helped the people _____ need.

04
> • The kind girl _____ some money to the poor old man.
> • He came to us and _____ a hand.

05 다음 빈칸에 알맞은 단어를 〈보기〉에서 골라 쓰시오. (형태 변화 가능)

> ┌─ 보기 ─┐
> break   hand   search   take

(1) Please _____ care of my son while I'm not here.

(2) He _____ his arm a week ago.

(3) Santa Claus _____ out gifts to the children last Christmas.

(4) Would you help me _____ for more information about these?

06 우리말에 맞게 주어진 단어를 바르게 배열하시오.

(1) 네 충고 덕택에 기분이 나아졌다.
(thanks, advice, I, to, your, feel, better)
➡ _____

(2) 그녀는 지난달에 세상을 떠났다.
(month, passed, last, away, she)
➡ _____

(3) 정부는 노인들을 후원할 계획을 세웠다.
(the, the, planned, support, government, elderly, to)
➡ _____

(4) 그는 부와 명예 둘 다 얻었다.
(gained, fame, both, he, and, wealth)
➡ _____

07 다음 영영풀이에 해당하는 말을 주어진 철자로 시작하여 쓰시오.

(1)
> not able to see anything

➡ b_____

(2)
> to continue to live after something bad happens

➡ s_____

(3)
> to treat someone with respect

➡ h_____

Conversation

① 도움 요청하고 답하기

A Can you help me move these books? 이 책들 옮기는 거 도와줄 수 있어?
B Sure. / I'm sorry, but I can't. 그럼. / 미안한데 못할 거 같아.

■ 상대방에게 도움을 요청할 때는 'Can you help me ~?'로 시작하는 문장으로 표현할 수 있다. help me 뒤에 동사원형이나 to부정사를 써서 구체적으로 어떤 도움이 필요한지를 밝힌다. 'Can I ask you a favor?'나 'Can you give me a hand?' 등의 표현도 쓸 수 있다.

■ 이에 대한 긍정의 대답으로는 'Sure.' 등을, 부정의 대답으로는 'I'm sorry, but I can't.'나 'I'm afraid, but I can't.' 등을 쓴다.

■ 도움을 요청할 때 can 대신 would나 could를 써서 'Could you help me ~?'나 'Would you help me ~?'라고 말하면 공손하고 정중한 느낌을 준다.

도움 요청하기

- Can[Could/Would/Will] you help me (to) 동사원형 ~? (내가 ~하는 거 도와줄 수 있어?)
- Could you please 동사원형 ~? (~해 줄 수 있니?)
- Can you give me a hand to 동사원형?
- Can[May] I ask you a favor? (부탁 좀 해도 될까요?)
- Can[Could] you do me a favor? (부탁 좀 들어 주겠니?)

도움 요청에 답하기

- 수락하기: Sure. / Okay. / Certainly. / No problem. / Go ahead. / All right.
- 거절하기: I'm sorry, but I can't. / No, I'm afraid not.

핵심 Check

1. 다음 우리말에 맞게 대화의 빈칸을 채우시오.

> A: Can you do me a _____? (부탁 좀 해도 될까요?)
> B: Okay. _____ _____. (문제없어요.)

2. 다음 주어진 단어를 이용하여 대화를 완성하시오.

> A: _____? (help, can, wash, you, the dishes, me, to)
> B: Sure.

2 제안하기

> Why don't we donate our clothes to the community center? 우리의 옷을 지역 문화 센터에 기부하는 게 어떨까?

■ 특정 행동을 함께 하자고 제안할 때는 'Why don't we ~?'로 시작하는 표현을 쓴다. 'How about ~?'이나 'What about ~?' 등의 표현도 쓸 수 있는데, 이때 동사 형태는 'How about donating our clothes?'처럼 전치사 about 뒤에 동명사를 쓰는 것에 유의한다.

■ 'Why don't you + 동사 ~?'는 함께 하자는 것은 아니고 상대방에게만 권유하는 것이다.

제안하기

- Why don't we + 동사원형 ~? (~하는 게 어떨까?)
- How[What] about (동)명사 ~?
- Let's 동사원형 ~. (~하자.)

■ 상대방의 제안에 응할 때는 'Sure, I'd love to.', 그렇지 않을 때는 'Sorry, but I can't.'로 대답할 수 있다. 허락을 요청하는 말에 거절하는 경우에는, 보통 간단히 이유를 덧붙인다.

핵심 Check

3. 다음 대화의 밑줄 친 부분과 같은 의미가 되도록, 주어진 단어를 이용해 문장을 만드시오.

> A: <u>How about having some ice cream?</u>
> B: Sure, I'd love to.

➡ (Why) _____
  (What) _____
  (Let's) _____

[4-5] 다음 주어진 어구를 배열하여 대화를 완성하시오.

4.
> A: _____? (the movies, we, tomorrow, why, to, don't, go)
> B: That sounds good.

5.
> A: _____? (school. about, after, how, soccer, playing)
> B: Okay.

Listen & Talk 1 B

B: Hey, Minji! ❶What's wrong with your leg?

G: I ❷broke it last week.

B: Really? What happened?

G: I ❸was in a hurry ❹to catch a train. But I ❺fell down in the street.

B: Oh, that's terrible! ❻Is there anything I can do for you?

G: Well, ❼can you help me carry this bag?

B: Sure.

B: 민지야! 너 다리에 무슨 문제가 있니?
G: 지난주에 부러졌어.
B: 그래? 무슨 일이야?
G: 기차를 타려고 서두르고 있었어. 그런데 길에 넘어졌어.
B: 오, 정말 끔찍하다! 내가 너를 위해 해줄 게 있니?
G: 음, 이 가방을 드는 걸 도와줄 수 있니?
B: 그럼.

❶ 'What's wrong with ~?'는 상대방의 안 좋은 일에 대해 묻는 표현으로 '너 ~에 문제가 있니?'의 뜻이다. 'What's the matter with ~?', 'Is there anything wrong with ~?', 'What happened to ~?' 등의 표현과 바꿔 쓸 수 있다.

❷ broke는 break(부러지다)의 과거형이다.

❸ be in a hurry: 서두르다

❹ to부정사의 부사적 용법 중 목적(~하기 위해서)의 의미로 사용되었다.

❺ fall down: 넘어지다

❻ Is there anything I can do for you?는 '내가 너를 위해 해줄 게 있니?'의 의미로 도움을 제안할 때 쓰는 표현이다. 'Can I give you a hand?', 'May I help you?', 'What can I do for you?', 'Do you need my help?' 등으로 바꿔 쓸 수 있다.

❼ 'Can you help me ~?'는 상대방에게 도움을 요청할 때 사용하는 표현이다. help me 뒤에 동사원형이나 to부정사를 써서 구체적으로 어떤 도움이 필요한지를 밝힌다.

Check(√) True or False

(1) Minji broke her leg last month. T ☐ F ☐

(2) The boy will help Minji to carry her bag. T ☐ F ☐

Listen & Talk 2 A

G: ❶What kinds of volunteer activities can we do?

B: ❷Why don't we clean up our town's streets?

G: All right! ❸Let's do it.

G: 우리 어떤 종류의 봉사 활동들을 할 수 있을까?
B: 우리 동네 길거리를 청소하는 게 어때?
G: 좋아! 그러자.

❶ What kinds of ~: 어떤 종류의 volunteer: 자원봉사의; 자원 봉사자

❷ Why don't we ~?: ~하는 게 어떨까? clean up: ~을 치우다, 청소하다

❸ 'Let's 동사원형 ~.'은 '~하자'의 뜻으로, 어떤 일을 제안할 때 사용한다. 'Let's 동사원형 ~.' 외에도 'Why don't we ~?'의 표현을 쓸 수 있다.

Check(√) True or False

(3) They talk about volunteer activities to do. T ☐ F ☐

(4) They will clean up their town's streets. T ☐ F ☐

Listen & Talk 1 A

B: Mia, ❶can you help me move these books?

G: Sure. ❷What are you going to do with them?

B: ❸I'm going to ❹donate them to a children's library.

❶ 상대방에게 도움을 요청할 때는 'Can you help me ~?'로 시작하는 문장으로 표현할 수 있다. help me 뒤에 동사원형이나 to부정사를 써서 구체적으로 어떤 도움이 필요한지를 밝힌다. 'Can I ask you a favor?'나 'Can you give me a hand?' 등의 표현도 쓸 수 있다.

❷ 상대방의 계획에 대하여 물을 때는 'What are you going to do ~?'로 물을 수 있다. (= What will you do ~? = What are you planning to do ~?)

❸ 'What are you going to+동사원형 ~?'에 대답할 때는 'I'm going to+동사원형'으로 말할 수 있다. 내용상 주어가 바뀔 경우 그에 따라 'be동사'를 바꾸어 써야 한다. be going to 동사원형: ~할 것이다

❹ donate: 기부하다

Listen & Talk 1 C

B1: Wow! These dogs are so dirty. Jay, can you ❶help me wash them?

B2: Allen, ❷I'm sorry, but I can't. ❸I have to feed the cats now. ❹Why don't you ask Nicky?

B1: Okay! Nicky, ❺can I ask you a favor?

G: Sure, Allen. What is it?

B1: Can you help me wash these dogs?

G: Sure. But I have to ❻walk these dogs first. After that, I will help you.

B1: All right! Thank you.

❶ help는 불완전 타동사로 '~이 …하는 것을 돕다'의 의미로 사용되었다. 목적격 보어로 to부정사와 동사원형을 쓰는 준사역동사이다. 그러므로 목적격 보어 자리의 wash 대신에 to wash도 가능하다.

❷ 상대방의 요청을 거절할 때 쓰는 표현이다. (=I'm afraid I can't.)

❸ have to 동사원형: ~해야 한다 feed: 먹이를 주다

❹ 상대방에게 함께 ~하자고 제안이나 권유할 때에는 'Why don't we+동사원형 ~?'을 사용할 수 있다. 'Why don't you+동사원형 ~?'은 함께 하자는 것이 아니고 상대방에게만 권유하는 것이다.

❺ 상대방에게 도움을 요청할 때 'Can you do me a favor?'(나 좀 도와줄 수 있니?)라고 말할 수 있다. 상대방이 도움을 주겠다고 하면 'Can you (please) help me ~?' 등의 표현을 통하여 구체적인 내용을 말할 수도 있다.

❻ walk: 산책시키다. (사람·동물을) 걷게 하다

Listen & Talk 2 B

G: Good morning, students! ❶As you know, there was a big fire in Mapletown. ❷Why don't we raise money and help the people there? Come to our special event ❸at the school grounds on May 3! Please ❹bring your items and donate them. We will sell your items. Then, we will ❺give all the money to Mapletown. Please ❻give a hand to people in need.

❶ as: (접) ~과 같이, ~하는 대로 as you know: 아시다시피 fire: 화재

❷ Why don't we ~?: ~하는 게 어떨까? raise money: 돈을 모금하다 raise와 help는 접속사 and로 연결되어 있다.

❸ at+장소: ~에, on+날짜: ~에

❹ bring과 donate는 접속사 and로 연결되어 있는 명령문이므로, 동사원형이 되어야 한다. them = the people in Mapletown

❺ give+간접목적어(~에게)+직접목적어(~을, ~를) = give+직접목적어+to+간접목적어

❻ give a hand: ~을 돕다 in need: 어려움에 처한

Listen & Talk 2 C

B1: Next Wednesday is Volunteer Day. We ❶cleaned up the park last time. ❷What are we going to do this time?

G: ❸Why don't we visit a nursing home and clean it up?

B2: That's not a bad idea. But I want to do something fun. Why don't we ❹hold a party for the people there?

G: That's a good idea. What can we do at the party?

B1: We can ❺serve some food.

B2: And ❻how about playing some music? I can play the piano.

G: And I can play the cello.

B1: It sounds like a good plan.

❶ clean up: ~을 치우다, 청소하다

❷ What are we going to do this time?: 이번엔 뭘 할까?

❸ Why don't we ~?: ~하는 게 어떨까? nursing home: 양로원 clean up은 구동사이다. 구동사는 동사+부사(up, on, off, over 등)로 이루어져 있다. '동사+부사+목적어'의 어순이나 '동사+목적어+부사'의 어순 둘 다 가능하다. 하지만 목적어 자리에 인칭대명사(it, them)가 올 때는 반드시 '동사+목적어+부사'의 어순으로 쓴다.

❹ hold a party: 파티를 열다

❺ serve: (음식을) 제공하다

❻ 'How about (동)명사 ~?'는 특정 행동을 제안할 때 사용할 수 있는 표현으로, '~하는 게 어때?'의 의미이다.

● 다음 우리말과 일치하도록 빈칸에 알맞은 말을 쓰시오.

Listen & Talk 1 A

B: Mia, _____ you _____ _____ move these books?

G: Sure. _____ _____ you _____ to do with them?

B: I'm _____ _____ _____ them to a children's library.

해석

B: Mia, 이 책들 옮기는 거 도와줄 수 있어?
G: 그럼. 너 이 책으로 뭐 할 거야?
B: 나는 이 책을 어린이 도서관에 기부할 거야.

Listen & Talk 1 B

B: Hey, Minji! What's wrong _____ your leg?

G: I _____ _____ last week.

B: Really? What happened?

G: I was in _____ _____ to catch a train. But I _____ _____ in the street.

B: Oh, that's terrible! _____ _____ anything I _____ _____ for you?

G: Well, _____ _____ _____ me carry this bag?

B: Sure.

B: 민지야! 너 다리에 무슨 문제가 있니?
G: 지난주에 부러졌어.
B: 그래? 무슨 일이야?
G: 기차를 타려고 서두르고 있었어. 그런데 길에 넘어졌어.
B: 오, 정말 끔찍하다! 내가 너를 위해 해 줄 게 있니?
G: 음, 이 가방을 드는 걸 도와줄 수 있니?
B: 그럼.

Listen & Talk 1 C

B1: Wow! These dogs are so dirty. Jay, _____ _____ _____ me _____ _____?

B2: Allen, I'm sorry, _____ I can't. I have _____ _____ the cats now. Why _____ _____ ask Nicky?

B1: Okay! Nicky, can I _____ _____ _____ _____ _____?

G: Sure, Allen. What is it?

B1: _____ _____ _____ me wash these dogs?

G: Sure. But I _____ _____ walk these dogs first. After that, I will help you.

B1: All right! Thank you.

B1: 와! 이 개들 정말 더럽다. Jay, 이 개들 씻기는 거 도와줄 수 있니?
B2: Allen, 미안한데 못할 거 같아. 지금 이 고양이들에게 밥 줘야 해. Nicky 한테 물어보는 게 어때?
B1: 알겠어! Nicky, 나 좀 도와줄 수 있니?
G: 물론이지, Allen. 뭔데?
B1: 이 개들 씻기는 거 도와줄 수 있니?
G: 그럼. 근데 나 이 개들 산책 먼저 시켜야 해. 끝나고 나서 도와줄게.
B1: 그래! 고마워.

Listen & Talk 2 A

G: What _____ _____ _____ activities can we do?

B: Why _____ _____ _____ _____ our town's streets?

G: All right! Let's do it.

G: 우리 어떤 종류의 봉사 활동을 할 수 있을까?
B: 우리 동네 길거리를 청소하는 게 어때?
G: 좋아! 그러자.

[01~02] 주어진 문장 뒤에 이어질 대화의 순서를 바르게 배열하시오.

01

> Hey, Minji! What's wrong with your leg?

> (A) I was in a hurry to catch a train. But I fell down in the street.
> (B) Really? What happened?
> (C) Oh, that's terrible!
> (D) I broke it last week.

➡ _____

02

> Next Wednesday is Volunteer Day. We cleaned up the park last time. What are we going to do this time?

> (A) Why don't we visit a nursing home and clean it up?
> (B) That's a good idea. What can we do at the party?
> (C) That's not a bad idea. But I want to do something fun. Why don't we hold a party for the people there?
> (D) We can serve some food.

➡ _____

[03~04] 다음 대화를 읽고 물음에 답하시오.

> G1: We have a class activity day next Friday. What do you want to do on that day?
> B: Why don't we ①do some volunteer activities? We can help others and ②make our community better.

> G1: That sounds great, but ③choosing a good place is not easy.
> B: We need someone ④which has volunteered a lot.
> G1: I know Sumin ⑤has volunteered a lot. Sumin, 우리가 좋은 장소들을 찾는 것을 도와 주겠니? (help, some, can, places, you, us, good, find, ?)
> G2: Sure. I usually search for information on the internet. Why don't we check the volunteering website for teens?
> B: That's a good idea.

03 위 대화의 ①~⑤ 중 어색한 것을 골라 고치시오.

➡ _____
_____

04 밑줄 친 우리말에 맞게 괄호 안에 주어진 단어를 알맞게 배열하시오

➡ _____

[05~06] 다음 대화를 읽고 물음에 답하시오.

> A: Why don't we (A)_____ volunteer work at the animal care center?
> B: Sounds good. What can we do there?
> A: We can take care (B)_____ the dogs and cats.

05 빈칸 (A)에 알맞은 말을 쓰시오.

➡ _____

06 빈칸 (B)에 알맞은 전치사를 쓰시오.

➡ _____

Grammar

① **목적격 관계대명사**

> The little black dress **which** she wore in a movie is famous even today. 그녀가 영화에서 입었던 아담한 검은 드레스는 오늘날까지도 유명하다.

- 관계대명사가 관계대명사절 내에서 목적어의 역할을 할 때 이것을 목적격 관계대명사라고 한다.

- 목적격 관계대명사는 선행사가 사람이면 who나 whom, that을, 사물이나 동물은 which나 that을 쓴다. 일반적으로 목적격 관계대명사는 생략할 수 있다.

선행사	사람	사물, 동물	사람, 사물, 동물
목적격 관계대명사	who/whom	which	that

- He was the man (**who/whom/that**) I saw on TV. (그는 내가 TV에서 본 남자였다.)

- He showed me the photos (**which/that**) he had taken. (그는 그가 찍은 사진들을 내게 보여주었다.)

- 목적격 관계대명사절에서는 앞에 있는 관계대명사가 동사의 목적어 역할을 하기 때문에 동사 뒤에 목적어가 없다는 것에 특히 주의해야 한다.
  - These are the boys. I like them(=the boys) most in my class.
    = These are the boys (**who/whom/that**) I like most in my class.

  - This is the book. I have to read it(=the book).
    = This is the book (**which/that**) I have to read.

- 목적격 관계대명사가 전치사의 목적어인 경우 전치사는 관계대명사절의 끝에 오거나 관계대명사 앞에 올 수 있다. 전치사가 관계대명사절의 끝에 올 경우에는 관계대명사를 생략할 수 있지만 전치사가 관계대명사 앞에 올 경우에는 관계대명사를 생략하지 않으며 관계대명사 that을 쓸 수 없다.
  - I need a chair (**which/that**) I can sit **on**. (나는 내가 앉을 수 있는 의자가 필요하다.)
    = I need a chair **on which** I can sit.
    = I need a chair on that I can sit. (✕)

핵심 Check

1. 다음 괄호 안에서 알맞은 말을 고르시오.

   (1) David is the boy with (whom / that) I often play soccer.

   (2) Tom is reading the book (whom / which) I gave to him.

2 감정을 나타내는 과거분사

• She was **shocked** because their lives were very difficult. 그녀는 그들의 삶이 매우 어려웠기 때문에 충격을 받았다.

■ 현재분사는 '능동'의 의미를 갖고, 과거분사는 '수동'의 의미를 갖는다.
  • Math is the most **interesting** subject to me. (능동: 수학이 흥미를 불러일으키는 과목이다.) (수학은 내게 가장 흥미로운 과목이다.)
  • I'm **interested** in math. (수동: 내가 흥미를 느끼게 되는 것이다.) (나는 수학에 흥미가 있다.)

■ 감정을 나타내는 타동사의 과거분사는 '~한 감정을 느끼는'이라는 의미로, 주로 사람을 주어로 하여 형용사로 쓰일 때가 많다.
  • I was very **disappointed** at my friends. (나는 내 친구들에게 무척 실망했다.)

■ 주로 사물을 주어로 하여 '~한 감정을 유발하는'의 의미를 나타내는 현재분사와 혼동하지 않도록 유의한다.
  • It can be very **disappointing** to lose important matches. (중요한 경기에서 패하는 것은 매우 실망스러울 수 있다.)

■ 주어가 사람일 때도 현재분사를 쓸 수 있으므로, 의미에 따라 구분하여 쓴다.
  • She was certainly not **boring**. (그녀는 분명히 따분하지 않다.)
  • She was **bored** with hearing about the work. (그녀는 그 일에 관련된 이야기를 듣는 것이 따분했다.)

핵심 Check

2. 다음 괄호 안에서 알맞은 말을 고르시오.
  (1) Look at the (sleeping / slept) dog.
  (2) It was an (exciting / excited) game.
  (3) He showed me a book (writing / written) in English.
  (4) I'm (exciting / excited) to get married.

01 다음 빈칸에 들어갈 말로 알맞지 <u>않은</u> 것을 <u>모두</u> 고르시오.

> The only food _____ they could find was grass.

① who   ② whose   ③ whom

④ that   ⑤ which

02 다음 우리말을 영어로 옮길 때, 빈칸에 알맞은 말이 순서대로 짝지어진 것은?

> • 그 게임은 재미있어 보였지만 나는 곧 내가 그 게임에 흥미가 없다는 것을 알아차렸다.
>
> → The game looked _____ but soon I noticed that I was not _____ in the game.

① interested – interesting

② interested – interested

③ interesting – interesting

④ interesting – interested

⑤ interest – interest

03 다음 문장에서 어법상 <u>어색한</u> 부분을 바르게 고쳐 쓰시오.

(1) He likes the dog who he adopted last month.

_____ ➡ _____

(2) Anna is the woman which I like most.

_____ ➡ _____

(3) I'm exciting at the thought of going skiing tomorrow.

_____ ➡ _____

> adopt: 입양하다
> at the thought of: ~을 생각하면, ~ 생각에

04 다음 우리말에 맞게 괄호 안에 주어진 단어를 빈칸에 바르게 배열하시오. (필요하면 어형을 바꿀 것)

> 우리 엄마가 만든 치킨 샐러드는 정말 맛있다. (my mom, is, made, delicious, the chicken salad, very, which)

➡ _____

01 다음 〈보기〉의 밑줄 친 부분과 용법이 다른 것은?

> ┤ 보기 ├
>
> Lee Jieun is a singer <u>that</u> my partner likes.

① Breakfast is the meal <u>that</u> people eat in the morning.

② People <u>that</u> respect her will come to help her.

③ I want to have a date with a girl <u>who</u> I love.

④ Kate will read the book <u>which</u> her friend wrote.

⑤ This is the TV program <u>that</u> I really wanted to watch.

02 ^{중요} 다음 빈칸에 들어갈 수 있는 말이 <u>다른</u> 하나는?

① *The Old Man and the Sea* is the book _____ I have read several times.

② This is the wallet _____ you were looking for.

③ Select the album _____ cover you'd like to change.

④ Billy is my roommate _____ I have lived with for five years.

⑤ This is the cat _____ I like.

03 다음 빈칸에 알맞은 것은?

> She was really _____ at the news.

① surprise   ② surprises

③ surprised   ④ surprising

⑤ to surprise

04 주어진 어휘를 이용하여 다음 우리말을 영어로 쓰시오.

> Alex가 나에게 보낸 박스에 드레스가 있다. (there, a dress, sent)

➡ _____

_____

05 다음 괄호 안에서 알맞은 말을 고르시오.

(1) *Tom and Jerry* is a cartoon (who / that) I often watch.

(2) Mike needs someone (who / which) he can trust.

(3) Jane is the girl with (that / whom) I had dinner at the restaurant.

(4) I am not (interested / interesting) in that sort of thing.

(5) The children found the game (interesting / interested).

06 다음 중 어법상 바르지 <u>않은</u> 것은?

① Well, I'm excited.

② The movie was exciting.

③ Mr. Sing said he was pleased with the outcome.

④ The children were frightening at the way their mom yelled.

⑤ I feel scared when I walk home alone.

07 다음 중 어법상 옳은 문장을 고르시오.

① This is the picture I took yesterday with my new camera.

② Seoul Grand Park is a park who my uncle often visits.

③ The book I read it yesterday was very interesting.

④ The student which I am very close with is Steve.

⑤ It is the building at that he has worked for over 5 years.

08 다음 밑줄 친 that의 성격이 나머지 넷과 다른 것은?

① Jiho is eating the fried rice that his sister made.

② The important thing is that we stay on schedule.

③ Ethan never eats food that is sold at a fast food store.

④ Audrey is the only woman that I love.

⑤ The movie that I watched last Sunday was *Alita*.

09 다음 〈보기〉에 주어진 단어를 변형하여 문맥에 맞게 빈칸에 쓰시오. (한 번씩만 쓸 것)

┌─── 보기 ───┐
embarrass   scare   shock
└──────────┘

(1) Do not be _____ of bees.

(2) He put me in a very _____ situation.

(3) The members of his team were _____ at the results.

10 다음 두 문장을 한 문장으로 바르게 바꾸지 않은 것을 모두 고르시오.

> • *Donald Duck* is a cartoon.
> • My partner often watches *Donald Duck*.

① *Donald Duck* is a cartoon which my partner often watches.

② *Donald Duck* is a cartoon that my partner often watches.

③ *Donald Duck* is a cartoon who my partner often watches.

④ *Donald Duck* is a cartoon my partner often watches.

⑤ *Donald Duck* is a cartoon which my partner often watches it.

서답형

11 다음 문장에서 생략할 수 있는 것을 찾아 쓰시오.

(1) I met the woman who you ate dinner with last Sunday.

(2) I received an email that my friend in Chicago had sent to me.

(3) Seoul is a city which is full of energy.

➡ (1) _____ (2) _____ (3) _____

12 다음 중 밑줄 친 부분의 쓰임이 잘못된 것은?

① Rina looked bored in the science class.

② Who was the girl that you met in front of the library?

③ The dog which I raise has a long tail.

④ Everyone feels depressing at some time or another.

⑤ Don't be disappointed about such a thing.

서답형

13 다음 두 문장을 관계대명사를 사용하여 한 문장으로 바꾸시오.

(1) • Audrey Hepburn is a person.
   • My partner respects her a lot.

➡ _____

_____

(2) • This is the ID.
   • The spy used the ID before.

➡ _____

(3) • The letter made me happy.
   • You sent the letter to me last week.

➡ _____

_____

(4) • Do you remember the girl?
   • I met her at the party.

➡ _____

_____

(5) • I like the music.
   • I often listen to the music.

➡ _____

_____

(6) • Do you know the girl?
   • Anne is talking to the girl.

➡ _____

_____

중요

14 다음 빈칸에 들어갈 말로 알맞은 것은?

I don't like English. It is difficult and _____.

① exciting   ② excited

③ boring   ④ bored

⑤ annoyed

15 다음 밑줄 친 부분의 쓰임이 어색한 것은?

① The chicken salad which Lee Yeonbok made is very delicious.

② Winter is the season that comes after autumn.

③ Here are some of the people whom I helped.

④ That man over there is the dentist about that I told you.

⑤ I want to call the boy who I met at the party.

서답형

16 우리말에 맞게 괄호 안의 어휘를 바르게 배열하시오.

(1) 그녀는 그들의 삶이 매우 어려웠기 때문에 충격을 받았다. (she, lives, because, was, were, difficult, shocked, their, very)

➡ _____

(2) 나는 사파리에서 보았던 호랑이를 잊을 수 없다. (I, I, the tiger, safari, saw, which, forget, can't, on)

➡ _____

(3) 여행 가이드로서의 직업에 만족하십니까? (you, your, are, satisfied, job, tour guide, as, a, with)

➡ _____

서답형

17 다음 빈칸에 amaze의 알맞은 형태를 쓰시오.

(1) People were _____ at the fire.

(2) It is _____ how the sea water looks different each season.

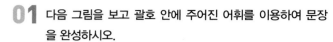
01 다음 그림을 보고 괄호 안에 주어진 어휘를 이용하여 문장을 완성하시오.

(play / excite)

_____ a basketball game makes me _____.

02 괄호 안에 주어진 말을 바르게 배열하여 문장을 완성하시오. (단어 하나를 문맥에 맞게 변형할 것.)

(1) (I, you, Latin dance, know, were, didn't, interest, in)

➡ _____

(2) (Emma, test score, her, disappoint, was, at)

➡ _____

(3) (I, highway signs, confuse, think, are, these, very)

➡ _____

(4) (I, a thing, one, no, that, knows, worry, such, am, about)

➡ _____

(5) (he, I, for me, was, was, not, not, bore, bore, so) (For me로 시작할 것)

➡ _____

03 다음 문장에서 어법상 틀린 부분을 찾아 바르게 고쳐 쓰시오.

This is the house in that he was born.

_____ ➡ _____

04 다음 두 문장을 관계대명사를 이용하여 한 문장으로 연결하여 쓰시오.

(1) • Jayu Park is a park.
  • My grandfather often visits the park.

➡ _____
_____

(2) • *Tom and Jerry* is a cartoon.
  • My little sister often watches *Tom and Jerry*.

➡ _____
_____

(3) • That is the girl.
  • I saw the girl this morning.

➡ _____

(4) • The girl did not participate in the meeting.
  • I wanted to meet the girl.

➡ _____
_____

(5) • The woman is Ms. Larson.
  • Mom is talking to Ms. Larson.

➡ _____
_____
_____

(6) • Mariel took pictures of Ben and his car.
  • Ben and his car were on the crime scene.

➡ _____
_____

05 잘못된 부분을 바르게 고쳐 문장을 다시 쓰시오.

(1) King Sejong is a person which my brother respects a lot.

➡ _____

_____

(2) This is the bridge who they built about 20 years ago.

➡ _____

_____

(3) The girl talked to a boy whom she met him at the party.

➡ _____

(4) I don't like the movie which I saw it yesterday.

➡ _____

(5) There are many subjects about that people feel little interest.

➡ _____

_____

_____

06 괄호 안에 주어진 어휘를 이용하여 우리말에 맞게 영작하시오.

(1) 나는 어젯밤 잠을 잘 자지 못했기 때문에 하루 종일 매우 피곤했다. (tire, all day, feel, well, because) (I로 시작할 것)

➡ _____

_____

(2) 나는 집에 홀로 남겨지는 것이 두려웠다. (home, to be, at, scare, leave, alone)

➡ _____

(3) 야구 경기를 보는 것은 나를 지루하게 한다. (watch, a baseball game, make, bore)

➡ _____

07 두 문장을 관계대명사를 사용하여 한 문장으로 썼을 때, 빈칸에 해당하는 문장을 쓰시오.

(1) • _____

• My partner often watches *The Smurfs*.

→ *The Smurfs* is a cartoon that my partner often watches.

(2) • _____

• I traveled with my friend.

→ Let me introduce my friend with whom I traveled.

(3) • The key was under the sofa.

• _____

→ The key that Laura was looking for all day long was under the sofa.

(4) • There is a certain reason.

• _____

→ There is a certain reason for which I cannot speak about it.

08 다음 문장을 어법에 맞게 고쳐 쓰시오.

(1) He put me in a very embarrassed situation.

➡ _____

(2) My mom was surprising at the news.

➡ _____

(3) It was shocked that he lied to me.

➡ _____

(4) We were all exciting because my brother made a goal in the soccer game.

➡ _____

The Spirit of Audrey

<u>During</u> World War II, a little girl and her mother were hungry and
during+특정 기간을 나타내는 명사

sick. The only food <u>that</u> they could find was grass. The little girl felt
선행사 The only food를 수식하는 목적격 관계대명사

<u>scared</u> all the time. Luckily, the girl survived, <u>thanks to</u> the help of
주어인 The little girl의 감정을 나타내는 형용사　　　　　　　~ 덕택에

others. One of the groups <u>that</u> helped her was UNICEF.
선행사 the groups를 수식하는 주격 관계대명사

<u>Later</u>, the girl became a worldwide movie star. Her name was Audrey
후에

Hepburn.

spirit 마음, 정신
grass 풀, 잔디
all the time 늘, 내내
luckily 운이 좋게도, 다행스럽게도
survive 살아남다, 생존하다
thanks to ~ 덕택에, ~ 때문에
worldwide 세계적인

 확인문제

● 다음 문장이 본문의 내용과 일치하면 T, 일치하지 <u>않으면</u> F를 쓰시오.

1　During World War II, Hepburn and her mother were hungry and sick. ☐

2　Hepburn survived World War II for herself. ☐

3　One of the groups that helped Hepburn was UNESCO. ☐

4　Hepburn became a worldwide movie star. ☐

<u>When</u> she grew up, Hepburn became a symbol of beauty. She was
접속사(~할 때)

very popular <u>because of</u> her hit movies, <u>such as</u> *My Fair Lady* and
~ 때문에　　　　　　~ 와 같은

Roman Holiday. The little black dress <u>which</u> she wore in a movie <u>is</u>
선행사 The little black dress를 수식하는 목적격 관계대명사　주어 The little black dress를 서술하는 동사

famous even today. Many people still love her style.

The autumn of 1987 was <u>a turning point</u> in Hepburn's life. She went
전환점

to <u>an international music festival</u> in Macau. Many people donated
국제 음악 축제

money at the festival, and the money went to UNICEF.
an international music festival

<u>Thanks to</u> her fame, UNICEF collected <u>more</u> money <u>than</u> ever before.
~ 덕택에　　　　　　　　　　　비교급 than: ~보다 더

Hepburn realized <u>that</u> her fame could help others, so she became a
목적어에 해당하는 명사절을 이끄는 접속사

UNICEF Goodwill Ambassador.

beauty 아름다움, 미(美)
turning point 전환점
international 국제적인, 국제의
donate 기부하다
fame 명성
collect 모으다, 수집하다
realize 깨닫다
goodwill ambassador 친선 대사

17 헵번은 자신의 명성이 다른 사람들을 도울 수 있다는 것을 깨닫고, 유니세프 친선 대사가 되었다.

➡ _____

18 먼저, 헵번은 1988년에 에티오피아로 갔다.

➡ _____

19 그곳에서, 그녀는 굶주린 아이들에게 음식을 가져다주었다.

➡ _____

20 그녀는 그들의 삶이 매우 어려웠기 때문에 충격을 받았다.

➡ _____

21 그 후, 그녀는 다른 나라들에서도 봉사하였다.

➡ _____

22 1990년, 그녀는 의약품을 나눠 주고 깨끗한 식수 프로그램을 지원하기 위하여 베트남을 방문하였다.

➡ _____

23 그녀의 마지막 여행은 1992년 소말리아에 간 것이었으며, 이듬해 그녀는 사망하였다.

➡ _____

24 많은 사람이 그녀의 아름다움과 스타일을 칭송했지만, 헵번의 진정한 아름다움은 그녀의 마음이었다.

➡ _____

25 그녀를 기리기 위해, 유니세프는 '오드리의 정신'이라는 동상을 만들었다.

➡ _____

26 그녀를 존경하는 사람들이 그녀의 사명을 이어 나가고 있다.

➡ _____

27 그녀가 가장 좋아했던 구절은 그녀의 사명을 보여 준다.

➡ _____

28 나이가 들어갈수록, 당신에게 손이 두 개가 있다는 것을 기억하라.

➡ _____

29 한 손은 자신을 돕기 위한 것이고, 다른 한 손은 타인을 돕기 위한 것이다.

➡ _____

[01~04] 다음 글을 읽고 물음에 답하시오.

(A)[During / While] World War II, a little girl and her mother were hungry and sick. The only food that ⓐthey could find (B)[being / was] grass. The little girl felt scared all the time. Luckily, the girl survived, ⓑthanks to the help of others. One of the groups that helped her (C)[was / were] UNICEF. ⓒLate, the girl became a worldwide movie star. Her name was Audrey Hepburn.

서답형
01 위 글의 괄호 (A)~(C)에서 어법상 알맞은 낱말을 골라 쓰시오.

➡ (A)＿＿＿ (B)＿＿＿ (C)＿＿＿

서답형
02 위 글의 밑줄 친 ⓐthey가 가리키는 것을 본문에서 찾아 쓰시오.

➡ ＿＿＿＿＿＿＿＿＿＿＿＿

03 위 글의 밑줄 친 ⓑthanks to와 뜻이 다른 말을 고르시오.

① due to   ② because of
③ instead of   ④ owing to
⑤ on account of

중요
04 위 글의 밑줄 친 ⓒ를 알맞은 어형으로 고치시오.

➡ ＿＿＿＿＿＿＿＿＿＿＿＿

[05~08] 다음 글을 읽고 물음에 답하시오.

When she grew up, Hepburn became a symbol of beauty. She was very popular because of her hit movies, ⓐsuch as *My Fair Lady* and *Roman Holiday*. The little black dress which she wore in a movie is famous even today. Many people still love her style.

The autumn of 1987 was a turning point in Hepburn's life. She went to an international music festival in Macau. Many people donated money at the festival, and the money went to UNICEF. Thanks to her ⓑ＿＿, UNICEF collected more money than ever before. Hepburn realized ⓒthat her ⓓ＿＿ could help others, so she became a UNICEF Goodwill Ambassador.

서답형
05 위 글의 밑줄 친 ⓐsuch as와 바꿔 쓸 수 있는 단어를 쓰시오.

➡ ＿＿＿＿＿＿＿＿＿＿＿＿

서답형
06 본문의 한 단어를 변형하여 위 글의 빈칸 ⓑ와 ⓓ에 공통으로 들어갈 알맞은 단어를 쓰시오.

➡ ＿＿＿＿＿＿＿＿＿＿＿＿

07 위 글의 밑줄 친 ⓒthat과 문법적 쓰임이 같은 것을 모두 고르시오.

① Kate knows that you like Mike.
② She is the girl that he loves.
③ Give me the pen that is on the desk.
④ He is the man that I met yesterday.
⑤ The point is that he is still careless.

8 위 글의 Hepburn에 관한 내용으로 적절하지 <u>않은</u> 것은?

① 그녀는 자랐을 때, 아름다움의 상징이 되었다.

② 그녀가 영화에서 입었던 아담한 검은 드레스는 오늘날까지도 유명하다.

③ 1987년 가을에 그녀는 배우로서 쇠퇴기에 들어섰다.

④ 1987년 가을에 그녀는 마카오의 한 국제 음악 축제에 갔다.

⑤ 자신의 명성이 다른 사람들을 도울 수 있다는 것을 깨닫고, 그녀는 유니세프 친선 대사가 되었다.

[09~12] 다음 글을 읽고 물음에 답하시오.

First, Hepburn went to Ethiopia in 1988. (①) There, she brought food to hungry children. (②) She was shocked because their lives were very difficult. (③) In 1990, she visited Vietnam to hand out medicine and support clean drinking water programs. (④) Her last trip was to Somalia in 1992, and she passed away the following year. (⑤)

Many people praised her beauty and style, but Hepburn's real beauty was her heart. To honor her, UNICEF made a statue, *The Spirit of Audrey*. People who respect her keep her mission alive. Her favorite saying shows her mission.

As you get older, remember you have two hands. One is for ⓐhelping yourself, and the other is for helping others.

09 위 글의 흐름으로 보아, 주어진 문장이 들어가기에 가장 적절한 곳은?

After that, she volunteered in other countries.

①   ②   ③   ④   ⑤

10 아래 〈보기〉에서 위 글의 밑줄 친 ⓐhelping과 문법적 쓰임이 <u>다른</u> 것의 개수를 고르시오.

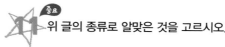

① I remember posting his letter.

② Would you mind calling back later?

③ He was watching TV in the room.

④ Thank you for visiting my website.

⑤ She smelled something burning.

① 1개   ② 2개   ③ 3개   ④ 4개   ⑤ 5개

11 위 글의 종류로 알맞은 것을 고르시오.

① article   ② diary   ③ book report

④ essay   ⑤ biography

12 위 글의 내용과 일치하지 <u>않는</u> 것은?

① 헵번은 1988년에 에티오피아로 갔다.

② 헵번은 에티오피아에서 의약품을 나눠 주었다.

③ 1990년, 헵번은 베트남을 방문하였다.

④ 헵번의 마지막 여행은 1992년 소말리아에 간 것이었다.

⑤ 헵번은 1993년에 사망하였다.

[13~15] 다음 인터뷰를 읽고 물음에 답하시오.

Reporter: ⓐ   was your life during World War II? Can you tell me about it?

Audrey: It was terrible. ⓑMy family and I was hungry and sick. We survived thanks to the help of others.

Reporter: ⓒ   did you begin to work for UNICEF?

Audrey: In 1987, a musical festival in Macau changed my life. I learned that my fame could help other people.

Reporter: After that, what did you do?

Audrey: I visited some countries in Africa and Asia and volunteered there.

13 위 인터뷰의 빈칸 ⓐ와 ⓒ에 공통으로 들어갈 알맞은 말을 고르시오.

① How   ② What   ③ When

④ Why   ⑤ Where

서답형
14 위 인터뷰의 밑줄 친 ⓑ에서 어법상 틀린 부분을 찾아 고치시오.

➡ _____

서답형
15 다음 문장에서 위 인터뷰의 내용과 다른 부분을 찾아서 고치시오.

> Audrey visited some countries in Africa and Asia and volunteered there before 1987.

➡ _____

[16~19] 다음 글을 읽고 물음에 답하시오.

First, Hepburn went to Ethiopia in 1988. There, she brought food ⓐ hungry children. She was shocked because their lives were very difficult. After that, she volunteered in other countries. In 1990, she visited Vietnam ⓑto hand out medicine and support clean drinking water programs. Her last trip was ⓐ Somalia in 1992, and she passed away the following year.

Many people praised her beauty and style, but Hepburn's real beauty was her heart. To honor her, UNICEF made a statue, *The Spirit of Audrey*. People who respect her keep her mission alive. Her favorite saying shows her mission.

As you get older, remember you have two hands. One is ⓒ helping yourself, and the other is ⓒ helping others.

16 위 글의 빈칸 ⓐ와 ⓒ에 들어갈 전치사가 바르게 짝지어진 것은?

① for – by   ② to – by

③ to – for   ④ for – to

⑤ at – for

17 위 글의 밑줄 친 ⓑto hand와 to부정사의 용법이 다른 것을 고르시오. (2개)

① He grew up to be a scientist.

② Do you know how to make it?

③ She was happy to solve the problem.

④ It's time to go to bed.

⑤ They ran fast to win the race.

18 위 글의 내용으로 보아 알 수 없는 것은?

① 헵번은 여러 나라들에서 봉사하였다.

② 많은 사람이 헵번의 아름다움과 스타일을 칭송했다.

③ 헵번은 배우로서는 성공하지 못했다.

④ 헵번을 기리기 위해, 유니세프는 '오드리의 정신'이라는 동상을 만들었다.

⑤ 헵번을 존경하는 사람들이 그녀의 사명을 이어 나가고 있다.

19 위 글을 읽고 대답할 수 없는 질문은?

① When did Hepburn go to Ethiopia?

② In Ethiopia, what did Hepburn bring to hungry children?

③ Why did Hepburn visit Vietnam?

④ When was Hepburn's last trip?

⑤ Where did UNICEF make a statue, *The Spirit of Audrey*?

[20~22] 다음 글을 읽고 물음에 답하시오.

My little big hero is my mom. She was born in 1972. She lives in Seoul.

She smiles a lot and tries to see the good in everything.

My mom had a serious car accident. She was in the hospital for six months. But she was very strong and ⓐfinally got better.

She always helps people in need. She donates money and does volunteer work. She is my big hero!

20 위 글의 밑줄 친 ⓐfinally와 뜻이 다른 것을 모두 고르시오.

① at last
② actually
③ in the end
④ at least
⑤ in the long run

21 글쓴이의 엄마의 성격으로 알맞지 않은 것을 고르시오.

① strong-willed
② selfish
③ friendly
④ charitable
⑤ generous

22 위 글을 읽고 답할 수 없는 질문은?

① Who is the writer's hero?
② What is the writer's mom like?
③ When does the writer's mom feel happy?
④ What was one of the most important moments in the writer's mom's life?
⑤ Why does the writer think that his or her mom is a hero?

[23~25] 다음 글을 읽고 물음에 답하시오.

First, Hepburn went to Ethiopia in 1988. There, she brought food to hungry children.

She was shocked because their lives were very difficult. After that, she volunteered in other countries. In 1990, she visited Vietnam to hand out medicine and support clean ⓐ drinking water programs. Her last trip was to Somalia in 1992, and she passed away the following year.

Many people praised her beauty and style, but Hepburn's real beauty was her heart. To honor her, UNICEF made a statue, *The Spirit of Audrey*. People who respect her keep her mission alive. Her favorite saying shows her mission.

As you get older, remember you have two hands. One is for helping yourself, and the other is for helping others.

23 위 글의 제목으로 알맞은 것을 고르시오.

① Hepburn Visited Ethiopia!
② Hepburn's Real Beauty Was Her Heart!
③ Why Was Hepburn Shocked?
④ People Praised Hepburn's Beauty!
⑤ Hepburn's Favorite Saying

24 위 글의 밑줄 친 ⓐdrinking과 문법적 쓰임이 같은 것을 모두 고르시오.

① I know the girl drinking water there.
② Who was drinking water in the room?
③ I saw a man drinking water in a bus.
④ She enjoys drinking water in summer.
⑤ He is fond of drinking water when he's tired.

서답형
25 다음 질문에 대한 알맞은 대답을 영어로 쓰시오.

Q: What did UNICEF do to honor Hepburn?

➡ _____

[01~03] 다음 글을 읽고 물음에 답하시오.

During ⓐWorld War II, a little girl and her mother were hungry and sick. The only food ⓑ _____ they could find was grass. The little girl felt scared all the time. Luckily, the girl survived, thanks to the help of others. One of the groups that helped her was UNICEF. Later, the girl became a worldwide movie star. Her name was Audrey Hepburn.

01 위 글의 밑줄 친 ⓐWorld War II를 영어로 읽는 법을 쓰시오.

➡ _____

02 위 글의 빈칸 ⓑ에 들어갈 알맞은 말을 쓰시오.

➡ _____

03 다음 빈칸 (A)와 (B)에 알맞은 단어를 넣어 Audrey Hepburn에 대한 소개를 완성하시오.

Audrey Hepburn survived World War II thanks to (A)_____ _____ of others and later became a worldwide (B)_____ _____.

[04~07] 다음 글을 읽고 물음에 답하시오.

When she grew up, Hepburn became a symbol of beauty. She was very popular because of her hit movies, such as *My Fair Lady* and *Roman Holiday*. The little black dress which she wore in a movie is famous even today. Many people still love her style.

The autumn of 1987 was ⓐa turning point in Hepburn's life. She went to an international music festival in Macau. Many people ⓑ _____ money at the festival, and the money went to UNICEF. (A)[In spite of / Thanks to] her fame, UNICEF (B)[collected / corrected] more money (C)[than / then] ever before. ⓒHepburn realized that her fame could help others, so she became a UNICEF Goodwill Ambassador.

04 다음 빈칸 (A)와 (B)에 알맞은 단어를 넣어 ⓐa turning point에 대한 서술을 완성하시오.

Hepburn who was a very popular actress went to an international (A)_____ _____ in Macau in the autumn of 1987. Then she realized that her fame could help others, so she became a (B)_____ _____ _____.

05 주어진 영영풀이를 참고하여 빈칸 ⓑ에 철자 d로 시작하는 단어를 시제에 맞춰 쓰시오.

give to a charity or good cause

➡ _____

06 위 글의 괄호 (A)~(C)에서 문맥이나 어법상 알맞은 것을 골라 쓰시오.

➡ (A)_____ (B)_____ (C)_____

07 위 글의 밑줄 친 ⓒ를 다음과 같이 바꿔 쓸 때 빈칸에 들어갈 알맞은 말을 쓰시오.

➡ _____ Hepburn realized that her fame could help others, she became a UNICEF Goodwill Ambassador.

[08~10] 다음 글을 읽고 물음에 답하시오.

First, Hepburn went to Ethiopia in 1988. There, she brought food to hungry children. She was (A)[shocking / shocked] because their lives were very difficult. After that, she volunteered in other countries. In 1990, she visited Vietnam to hand out medicine and support clean drinking water programs. Her last trip was to Somalia in 1992, and she ⓐpassed away the following year.

Many people praised her beauty and style, but Hepburn's real beauty was her heart. To honor her, UNICEF made a statue, *The Spirit of Audrey*. People who respect her (B)[keep / keeps] her mission alive. Her favorite saying shows her mission.

As you ⓑget older, remember you have two hands. One is for helping yourself, and (C) *[another / the other] is for helping others.*

08 위 글의 괄호 (A)~(C)에서 어법상 알맞은 낱말을 골라 쓰시오.

➡ (A)_____ (B)_____ (C)_____

09 위 글의 내용과 일치하도록 다음 빈칸 (A)와 (B)에 알맞은 단어를 본문에서 찾아 쓰시오.

Judging from the fact that Hepburn visited many countries and (A)_____ there, Hepburn's real beauty was (B)_____ _____.

10 위 글의 밑줄 친 ⓐpassed away, ⓑget과 바꿔 쓸 수 있는 단어를 각각 쓰시오.

➡ ⓐ _____ ⓑ _____

[11~13] 다음 인터뷰를 읽고 물음에 답하시오.

Reporter: How was your life during World War II? Can you tell me about ⓐit?
Audrey: It was terrible. My family and I were hungry and sick. We survived thanks to the help of others.
Reporter: How did you begin to work for UNICEF?
Audrey: In 1987, a musical festival in Macau changed my life. I learned that my fame could help ⓑother people.
Reporter: After that, what did you do?
Audrey: I visited some countries in Africa and Asia and volunteered there.

11 위 인터뷰의 밑줄 친 ⓐit가 가리키는 것을 본문에서 찾아 쓰시오.
➡ _____

12 위 인터뷰의 밑줄 친 ⓑother people과 바꿔 쓸 수 있는 단어를 본문에서 찾아 쓰시오.

➡ _____

13 다음 빈칸 (A)와 (B)에 공통으로 들어갈 알맞은 단어를 넣어, Audrey가 UNICEF를 위해 일하게 된 이유를 그녀의 어린 시절과 연결하여 완성하시오.

During World War II, Audrey's family and Audrey were hungry and sick. They survived thanks to the (A)_____ of others.

In 1987, after a musical festival in Macau, Audrey learned that her fame could (B)_____ other people, so she began to work for UNICEF.

Presentation Time

Lee Taeseok was a great person. He was a priest and also a doctor. He built
성직자   build(짓다)의 과거형

hospitals and schools for the people of Tonj. He took care of them and taught
돌보았다   수업을 했다

classes. From this person, I learned that I should help people in need.
learned의 목적어로 that절이 사용되었다.   어려움에 처한

이태석은 위대한 사람이었다. 그는 성직자이고 또한 의사였다. 그는 톤즈의 사람들을 위해 병원과 학교를 세웠다. 그는 그들을 돌보고 수업을 했다. 이 사람으로부터, 나는 어려움에 처한 사람들을 도와야 한다고 배웠다.

After You Read B

Reporter: How was your life during World War II? Can you tell me about it?
during+특정 기간을 나타내는 명사   your life during World War II

Audrey: It was terrible. My family and I were hungry and sick.
My life during World War II

    We survived thanks to the help of others.
      ~ 덕택에, ~ 때문에

Reporter: How did you begin to work for UNICEF?
     = working

Audrey: In 1987, a musical festival in Macau changed my life. I learned that
         목적어에 해당하는 명사절을 이끄는 접속사

    my fame could help other people.

Reporter: After that, what did you do?
    앞에 나온 문장을 받는 지시대명사

Audrey: I visited some countries in Africa and Asia and volunteered there.
          some countries in Africa and Asia를 가리킨다.

구문해설 • during: ~ 동안, ~ 중에 • terrible: 끔찍한 • survive 살아남다, 생존하다
• thanks to ~ 덕택에, ~ 때문에 • volunteer: 자원 봉사를 하다

리포터: 제2차 세계 대전 동안 당신의 삶은 어땠습니까? 그것에 대해 말해주실 수 있나요?

오드리: 끔찍했어요. 제 가족과 저는 굶주리고 아팠어요. 우리는 다른 사람들의 도움 덕분에 살아남았어요.

리포터: 당신은 어떻게 유니세프를 위해 일하게 되었나요?

오드리: 1987년에, 마카오의 한 음악 축제가 제 삶을 바꿨어요. 저는 제 명성이 다른 사람들을 도울 수 있다는 것을 알게 되었어요.

리포터: 그 다음에, 무엇을 했나요?

오드리: 아프리카와 아시아의 몇몇 나라들을 방문해서 그곳에서 자원 봉사를 했어요.

Culture Link

Talking Books Program

This is a program that makes audiobooks for blind people. It was started in
     주격 관계대명사   수동태

1931 in the United States. You just read books and record your voice. These
년도와 넓은 장소 앞에 쓴 전치사 in

audiobooks are given to blind people for free.
give는 'to+간접목적어'의 형태를 쓴다.   무료로

구문해설 • blind: 눈이 먼, 맹인인 • audiobook: 오디오북 (책의 내용을 녹음한 것)

말하는 책 프로그램

이것은 시각장애인을 위한 오디오북을 만드는 프로그램이다. 이것은 1931년 미국에서 시작되었다. 당신은 책을 읽고 당신의 목소리를 녹음하기만 하면 된다. 이러한 오디오북들은 시각장애인들에게 무료로 주어진다.

23 위 글의 밑줄 친 ⓑAs와 같은 의미로 쓰인 것을 고르시오

① She works as hard as her mother.

② Do as you would be done by.

③ He came up as I was speaking.

④ As he is honest, everyone likes him.

⑤ Her anger grew as she talked.

24 위 글을 읽고 Hepburn이 방문한 나라와 방문 연도를 순서대로 쓰시오. (나라 이름은 우리말로 쓰시오)

➡ (1) _____, (2) _____,

     (3) _____

[25~27] 다음 인터뷰를 읽고 물음에 답하시오.

Reporter: How was your life during World War II? Can you tell me about it?

Audrey: It was (A)[terrible / terrific]. My family and I were hungry and sick. We survived thanks to the help of others.

Reporter: ⓐHow did you begin to work for UNICEF?

Audrey: In 1987, a musical festival in Macau (B)[changed / exchanged] my life. I learned that my fame could help other people.

Reporter: After that, (C)[how / what] did you do?

Audrey: I visited some countries in Africa and Asia and volunteered there.

25 위 인터뷰의 괄호 (A)~(C)에서 문맥이나 어법상 알맞은 낱말을 골라 쓰시오.

➡ (A)_____ (B)_____ (C)_____

26 위 인터뷰의 밑줄 친 ⓐ를 다음과 같이 바꿔 쓸 때 빈칸에 들어갈 알맞은 말을 쓰시오.

➡ How did you begin _____ for UNICEF?

27 위 인터뷰를 읽고 답할 수 없는 질문은?

① How was Audrey's life during World War II?

② How did Audrey survive World War II?

③ How did Audrey begin to work for UNICEF?

④ Why did Audrey participate in a musical festival in Macau?

⑤ What countries did Audrey visit after she began to work for UNICEF?

[28~29] 다음 글을 읽고 물음에 답하시오.

For my volunteer work, I helped young students with math homework. I ⓐdid this at my community library. ⓑFrom this volunteer work, I learned that helping others are a great experience.

28 위 글의 밑줄 친 ⓐdid this가 가리키는 것을 본문에서 찾아 쓰시오.

➡ _____

29 위 글의 밑줄 친 ⓑ에서 어법상 틀린 부분을 찾아 고치시오.

➡ _____

01 출제율 90%

다음 짝지어진 두 단어의 관계가 같도록 빈칸에 알맞은 단어를 쓰시오.

> beauty : beautiful – _____ : favorable

02 출제율 95%

다음 〈보기〉에서 사람의 성격을 묘사할 때 쓸 수 있는 단어의 개수는?

┌─ 보기 ─────────────────
• beautiful   • friendly   • gentle
• curious   • polite   • careful
• outgoing   • patient
└─────────────────────────

① 4개   ② 5개   ③ 6개   ④ 7개   ⑤ 8개

03 출제율 100%

다음 빈칸에 공통으로 들어갈 말을 쓰시오.

> • _____ kinds of movies do you want to see this evening?
> • _____ about enjoying music at home without going outside?

04 출제율 90%

다음 밑줄 친 단어와 뜻이 같은 단어를 모두 고르시오.

> <u>Thanks to</u> you, I won the dancing contest.

① For   ② Because of
③ Without   ④ Despite
⑤ Due to

[05~06] 다음 대화의 순서를 바르게 배열한 것을 고르시오.

05 출제율 90%

> (A) I'm going to donate them to a children's library.
> (B) Mia, can you help me move these books?
> (C) Sure. What are you going to do with them?

① (A) – (C) – (B)   ② (B) – (A) – (C)
③ (B) – (C) – (A)   ④ (C) – (A) – (B)
⑤ (C) – (B) – (A)

06 출제율 90%

> (A) We can play music for the sick children
> (B) Sounds good. What can we do there?
> (C) Why don't we do volunteer work at the children's hospital?

① (A) – (C) – (B)   ② (B) – (A) – (C)
③ (B) – (C) – (A)   ④ (C) – (A) – (B)
⑤ (C) – (B) – (A)

[07~09] 다음 대화를 읽고 물음에 답하시오.

B1: Next Wednesday is Volunteer Day. We cleaned up the park last time. (①)
G: Why don't we ⓐ<u>visiting</u> a nursing home and ⓑ<u>clean up it</u>? (②)
B2: That's not a bad idea. But I want ⓒ<u>doing</u> ⓓ<u>fun something</u>. (③) Why don't we ⓔ<u>held</u> a party for the people there?
G: That's a good idea. (④) What can we do at the party?
B1: We can serve some food.
B2: And how about playing some music? I can play the piano. (⑤)
G: And I can play the cello.
B1: It sounds like a good plan.

07 위 대화의 ①~⑤ 중 주어진 문장이 들어갈 알맞은 곳은?

> What are we going to do this time?

① ② ③ ④ ⑤

출제율 95%

08 ⓐ~ⓔ 중 어법상 <u>어색한</u> 것의 개수를 고르시오.

① 1개 ② 2개 ③ 3개 ④ 4개 ⑤ 5개

출제율 90%

09 다음 영영풀이에 해당하는 단어를 위 대화에서 찾아 쓰시오.

> a place where people who are too old or sick to take care of themselves live

➡ _____

[10~12] 다음 대화를 읽고 물음에 답하시오.

G1: We have a class activity day next Friday. What do you want to do on that day? (①)

B: Why don't we (A)_____ some volunteer activities? (②)

G1: That sounds great, but choosing a good place is not easy.

B: We need someone who has volunteered a lot. (③)

G1: I know Sumin has volunteered a lot. Sumin, can you help us find some good places?

G2: Sure. (④) I usually search for information on the internet. (B)십대들을 위한 자원 봉사 웹 사이트를 확인해 보는 게 어떠니?

B: That's a good idea. (⑤)

출제율 85%

10 위 대화의 ①~⑤ 중 주어진 문장이 들어갈 알맞은 곳은?

> We can help others and make our community better.

① ② ③ ④ ⑤

출제율 100%

11 빈칸 (A)에 적절한 것을 고르시오.

① prepare ② join ③ do
④ keep ⑤ have

출제율 95%

12 밑줄 친 (B) 우리말을 주어진 어구를 이용해 영작하시오.

➡ _____

(check, for, why, teens, the volunteering website)

출제율 90%

13 어법상 <u>어색한</u> 것을 바르게 고쳐 문장을 다시 쓰시오.

(1) This is the cell phone who I broke yesterday.

➡ _____

(2) The speed at that everything moved felt strange.

➡ _____

(3) The girl who I met her the other day was very pretty.

➡ _____

(4) I was very worring about his health.

➡ _____

14 다음 두 문장의 의미가 같도록 빈칸에 알맞은 말을 쓰시오.

출제율 90%

(1) The game was exciting to me.
= I was _____ about the game.
(2) Jack thinks baseball is boring.
= Jack isn't _____ in baseball.

[15~16] 다음 글을 읽고 물음에 답하시오.

During World War II, a little girl and her mother were hungry and sick. ①The only food ⓐthat they could find was grass. The little girl felt ②excited all the time. ③Luckily, the girl survived, ④thanks to the help of others. One of the groups that helped her was UNICEF. Later, the girl became a ⑤worldwide movie star. Her name was Audrey Hepburn.

15 위 글의 밑줄 친 ①~⑤에서 흐름상 어색한 부분을 찾아 고치시오.

출제율 90%

➡ _____

16 위 글의 밑줄 친 ⓐthat과 문법적 쓰임이 다른 것을 모두 고르시오.

출제율 95%

① There's a man that wants to see you.
② Is this the farm that they talked about?
③ He said that the story was true.
④ These are the books that you lent me.
⑤ I was afraid that she might be late.

[17~19] 다음 글을 읽고 물음에 답하시오.

When she grew up, Hepburn became a symbol of beauty. She was very popular (A)[because / because of] her hit movies, such as *My Fair Lady* and *Roman Holiday*. The little black dress which she wore in a movie (B)[is / to be] famous even today. Many people still love her style.

(①) The autumn of 1987 was a (C)[turning / turned] point in Hepburn's life. (②) She went to an international music festival in Macau. (③) Many people donated money at the festival, and the money went to UNICEF. (④) Hepburn realized that her fame could help others, so she became a UNICEF Goodwill Ambassador. (⑤)

17 위 글의 괄호 (A)~(C)에서 어법상 알맞은 낱말을 골라 쓰시오.

출제율 100%

➡ (A)_____ (B)_____ (C)_____

18 위 글의 흐름으로 보아, 주어진 문장이 들어가기에 가장 적절한 곳은?

출제율 95%

Thanks to her fame, UNICEF collected more money than ever before.

① ② ③ ④ ⑤

19 다음 질문에 대한 알맞은 대답을 주어진 단어로 시작하여 쓰시오. (7~8 단어)

출제율 85%

Q: Why did Hepburn become a UNICEF Goodwill Ambassador?
A: Because _____.

[20~22] 다음 글을 읽고 물음에 답하시오.

First, Hepburn went to Ethiopia in 1988. There, she brought food to hungry children. She was shocked because their lives were very difficult. After that, she ⓐ_____ in other countries. In 1990, she visited Vietnam to hand out medicine and support clean drinking water programs. Her last trip was to Somalia in 1992, and she passed away the following year.

Many people praised her beauty and style, but Hepburn's real beauty was her heart. To honor her, UNICEF made a statue, *The Spirit of Audrey*. People who respect her keep her mission alive. Her favorite saying shows ⓑher mission.

As you get older, remember you have two hands. ⓒOne is for helping you, and the other is for helping others.

20 주어진 영영풀이를 참고하여 빈칸 ⓐ에 철자 v로 시작하는 단어를 시제에 맞춰 쓰시오.

to offer to do something without being forced to do it

➡ _____

21 위 글의 밑줄 친 ⓑher mission이 가리키는 것을 본문에서 찾아 쓰시오.

➡ _____

22 위 글의 밑줄 친 ⓒ에서 어법상 틀린 부분을 찾아 고치시오.

➡ _____

[23~25] 다음 인터뷰를 읽고 물음에 답하시오.

Reporter: How was your life during World War II? Can you tell me about it?

Audrey: It was terrible. My family and I were hungry and sick. ⓐ우리는 다른 사람들의 도움 덕분에 살아남았다.

Reporter: How did you begin to work for UNICEF?

Audrey: In 1987, a musical festival in Macau changed my life. I learned that my fame could help other people.

Reporter: After that, what did you do?

Audrey: I visited some countries in Africa and Asia and volunteered ⓑthere.

23 위 인터뷰의 밑줄 친 ⓐ의 우리말에 맞게 주어진 어휘를 이용하여 8 단어로 영작하시오.

thanks to

➡ _____

24 위 인터뷰의 밑줄 친 ⓑthere가 가리키는 것을 본문에서 찾아 쓰시오.

➡ _____

25 위 인터뷰의 내용과 일치하지 않는 것은?

① 제2차 세계 대전 동안 Audrey의 삶은 끔찍했다.

② 제2차 세계 대전 동안 Audrey의 가족과 Audrey는 굶주리고 아팠다.

③ Audrey가 유니세프를 위해 일하게 된 계기는 1987년 마카오의 한 음악 축제였다.

④ Audrey는 유니세프를 위해 일하면서 아프리카와 아시아의 몇몇 나라들을 방문했다.

⑤ Audrey는 아프리카와 아시아의 몇몇 나라들에서 영화배우로 일했다.

[01~02] 다음 대화를 읽고 물음에 답하시오.

> B: Hey, Minji! What's wrong ⓐ_____ your leg?
> G: I broke it last week.
> B: Really? What happened?
> G: I was ⓑ_____ a hurry ⓒ_____ catch a train. But I fell ⓓ____ in the street.
> B: Oh, that's terrible! <u>내가 너를 위해 해줄 게 있니?</u>
> G: Well, can you help me carry this bag?

01 빈칸 ⓐ~ⓓ에 들어갈 단어를 〈보기〉에서 찾아 쓰시오.

┌─ 보기 ┤
  to down of in for with
└─────────

➡ _____

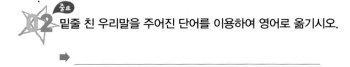 **02** 밑줄 친 우리말을 주어진 단어를 이용하여 영어로 옮기시오.

➡ _____
   (there, anything)

03 우리말에 맞게 주어진 단어를 이용해 영어로 옮기시오.

> G: Good morning, students! As you know, there was a big fire in Mapletown. (A)<u>우리가 돈을 모금해서 그곳 사람들을 도와주는 게 어떨까요?</u> Come to our special event at the school grounds on May 3! Please bring your items and donate them. We will sell your items. Then, we will give all the money to Mapletown. (B)<u>어려운 사람들에게 도움을 주십시오.</u>

➡ (A) _____
   (raise, help, why, there)
   (B) _____
   (in, please, give, people)

04 두 문장을 관계대명사를 사용하여 한 문장으로 썼을 때 빈칸에 알맞은 문장을 쓰시오.

(1) • This is my aunt.
    • _____
    ➡ This is my aunt about whom I told you.
(2) • This is the cake.
    • _____
    ➡ This is the cake which I made for my family.
(3) • _____
    • It was served at the restaurant.
    ➡ The food that was served at the restaurant was delicious.
(4) • I met the woman.
    • _____
    ➡ I met the woman you ate dinner with last Sunday.

05 다음 두 문장의 의미가 같도록 빈칸에 알맞은 말을 쓰시오.

(1) Nick thinks the result was disappointing.
  = Nick was _____ with the result.
(2) Richard thinks *Alita* is exciting.
  = Richard is _____ about *Alita*.

[06~08] 다음 글을 읽고 물음에 답하시오.

> When she grew up, Hepburn became a symbol of beauty. She was very popular because of her hit movies, such as *My Fair Lady* and *Roman Holiday*. ⓐ<u>그녀가 영화에서 입었던 아담한 검은 드레스는 심지어 오늘날까지도 유명하다.</u> Many people still love her style.

The autumn of 1987 was a turning point in Hepburn's life. She went to an international music festival in Macau. Many people donated money at the festival, and the money went to UNICEF. Thanks to her fame, UNICEF collected more money than ever before. Hepburn realized that her fame could help others, so she became a UNICEF Goodwill Ambassador.

06 다음 문장에서 위 글의 내용과 <u>다른</u> 부분을 찾아서 고치시오.

> Hepburn was very popular because she was a UNICEF Goodwill Ambassador.

➡ _____
_____
_____

07 위 글의 밑줄 친 ⓐ의 우리말에 맞게 한 단어를 보충하여, 주어진 어휘를 배열하시오.

> is / she / the little black dress / today / which / wore / famous / in a movie

➡ _____
_____

08 위 글의 내용과 일치하도록 다음 빈칸에 알맞은 단어를 쓰시오.

> The event which became _____ _____ _____ in Hepburn's life was an international music festival in Macau in the autumn of 1987.

[09~11] 다음 글을 읽고 물음에 답하시오.

First, Hepburn went to Ethiopia in 1988. There, she brought food to hungry children. She was (A)[pleased / shocked] because their lives were very ①difficult. After that, she volunteered in other countries. In 1990, she visited Vietnam to hand out medicine and support clean drinking water programs. Her (B)[last / latest] trip was ②from Somalia in 1992, and she passed away the ③following year.

Many people praised her beauty and style, but Hepburn's ④real beauty was her heart. To honor her, UNICEF made a statue, *The Spirit of Audrey*. People who respect her keep her mission (C)[alive / live]. Her ⑤favorite saying shows her mission.

As you get older, remember you have two hands. One is for helping yourself, and the other is for helping others.

09 위 글의 괄호 (A)~(C)에서 문맥상 알맞은 낱말을 골라 쓰시오.

➡ (A)_____ (B)_____ (C)_____

10 위 글의 밑줄 친 ①~⑤에서 흐름상 <u>어색한</u> 부분을 찾아 고치시오.

➡ _____

11 다음 질문에 대한 알맞은 대답을 영어로 쓰시오. (5 단어)

> Q: In what year did Hepburn pass away?

➡ _____

01 다음 대화의 흐름에 맞게 빈칸을 완성하시오. (제안하기의 표현을 사용할 것)

A: Are you interested in recycled art?

B: Yes, I am.

A: There is a recycled art festival in City Park. _____ go and see some works of recycled art?

B: That's good. _____ (1, how, meet)

A: _____ (afraid) _____ at 2? (meet, what)

B: OK. _____ meet in front of the front gate of City Park.

---

02 다음 정보를 바탕으로 자신의 영웅에 대한 이야기 카드를 만드시오.

Personal Information

• Who is your hero?: my mom

• When was he/she born?: in 1972

• Where does he/she live?: in Seoul

Personality

What is he/she like?

She smiles a lot and tries to see the good in everything.

Important Moments

What are some of the most important moments in his/her life?

She had a serious car accident.

Reason

Why is he/she your hero?

She always helps people in need.

My little big hero is (A)_____. She was born in 1972. She lives in Seoul. She smiles a lot and tries to see (B)_____ in everything. My mom had a serious (C)_____. She was in the hospital for six months. But she was very strong and finally got better. She always helps people (D)_____. She donates money and does volunteer work. She is my (E)_____!

단원별 모의고사

[01~02] 다음 빈칸에 알맞은 단어를 고르시오.

01

> She _____ music records as a hobby.

① breaks
② carries
③ honors
④ serves
⑤ collects

02

> They decided to _____ an essay contest.

① take
② do
③ hold
④ get
⑤ bring

03 다음 우리말과 일치하도록 빈칸을 채우시오. (주어진 철자가 있을 경우 그 철자로 시작할 것)

(1) 많은 사람들이 여왕에게 존경을 표하기 위해 왔다.
➡ Many people came to h_____ the queen.

(2) 나는 그 자동차 사고로 다리가 부러졌다.
➡ I _____ my leg in the car _____.

(3) 그들은 임무를 성공적으로 완수했다.
➡ They finished their _____ successfully.

(4) 광장에는 그 왕의 조각상이 서 있다.
➡ The _____ of the king stands in the square.

(5) 그 추락 사고에서 다섯 명만이 살아남았다.
➡ Only five people _____ the crash.

04 다음 주어진 문장과 같은 의미가 되도록 빈칸을 채우시오. (3 단어)

> My sister always listens to music.
> ➡ My sister listens to music _____.

[05~06] 다음 대화를 읽고 물음에 답하시오.

> B: Hey, Minji! ⓐWhat's wrong with your leg?
> G: ⓑI broke it last week.
> B: Really? What happened?
> G: ⓒI am in a hurry to catch a train. ⓓBut I fell down in the street.
> B: ⓔOh, that's terrific! Is there anything I can do for you?
> G: Well, 이 가방을 드는 걸 도와줄 수 있니?
> B: Sure.

05 ⓐ~ⓔ 중 문법상 또는 흐름상 어색한 부분을 찾아 고치시오. (2개)

➡ _____

06 밑줄 친 우리말을 영작하시오.

➡ _____

07 다음 대화의 빈칸 ⓐ~ⓔ에 들어갈 수 없는 표현을 고르시오.

> B: Mia, ⓐ_____ me ⓑ_____?
> G: ⓒ_____. ⓓ_____ to do with them?
> B: ⓔ_____ donate them to a children's library.

① What are you going
② move these books
③ Of course not
④ can you help
⑤ I'm going to

08 다음 대화의 밑줄 친 우리말을 영작하시오.

> A: 수학 문제 푸는 걸 도와줄 수 있니?
> B: I'm sorry, but I can't.

➡ _____

[09~12] 다음 대화를 읽고 물음에 답하시오.

> G1: ⓐWe have a class activity day next Friday. ⓑWhat do you want to do on that day?
>
> B: ⓒWhy don't we do some volunteer activities? ⓓWe can help others and make our community better.
>
> G1: That sounds great, ⓔbut choosing a good place are not easy.
>
> B: (need, we, who, a, someone, volunteered, lot, has)
>
> G1: I know Sumin has volunteered a lot. Sumin, can you help us find some good places?
>
> G2: Sure. I usually search (A)_____ information on the internet. Why don't we check the volunteering website (B)_____ teens?
>
> B: That's a good idea.

09 위 대화의 ⓐ~ⓔ 중에서 어법상 어색한 것을 고르시오.

① ⓐ   ② ⓑ   ③ ⓒ   ④ ⓓ   ⑤ ⓔ

10 괄호 안의 단어를 알맞게 배열하여 영작하시오.

➡ _____

11 빈칸 (A)와 (B)에 공통으로 들어갈 단어를 쓰시오.

➡ _____

12 위 대화의 내용과 일치하지 <u>않는</u> 것은?

① 봉사 활동을 많이 해 본 사람이 필요하다.
② 수민이는 봉사 활동을 위한 좋은 장소를 고르는 것이 쉽지 않다고 생각한다.
③ 남자아이는 봉사활동이 다른 사람들을 돕고 지역 사회를 더 좋게 만들 수 있다고 생각한다.
④ 다음 주 금요일에 학급 활동이 있다.
⑤ 그들은 대화 후에 십대들을 위한 자원 봉사 웹사이트를 확인할 것이다.

13 다음 중 어법상 바르지 <u>않은</u> 것은?

① The man is going to meet the students who he taught a long time ago.
② Everyone was surprised at the fact.
③ Andy bought the same bike that I wanted.
④ This is the backpack which I bought it yesterday.
⑤ I'm really interested in this book. I want to read it.

14 다음 〈보기〉에 주어진 단어를 변형하여 문맥에 맞게 문장을 완성하시오.

┌─── 보기 ───┐
relax   interest
└─────────────┘

(1) Watching movies makes me _____.
(2) They found the game _____.

15 다음 빈칸에 들어갈 알맞은 말을 <u>모두</u> 고르시오.

The man _____ you met yesterday is a spy.

① who   ② whose
③ whom   ④ that
⑤ which

16 괄호 안에 주어진 어휘를 이용하여 우리말을 영작하시오.

(1) 그녀가 읽고 있었던 책이 없어졌다. (missing)

➡ _____

(2) 내가 함께 점심을 먹고 있던 남자는 Yoojin이
었다. (the man, have)

➡ _____

_____

(3) 우리는 그 아름다운 풍경에 놀랐다. (amaze,
at, scenery)

➡ _____

(4) Dan은 재미있는 남자는 아니지만, 그와 있을
때 나는 지루하지 않다. (a funny guy, bore)

➡ _____

_____

17 다음 중 어법상 바르지 <u>않은</u> 것은?

① I am going to go on a trip tomorrow. I'm
so excited.

② I'll give you the butterflies which I
caught yesterday.

③ I met the girl in whom you are
interested.

④ The child was very scared of the
crocodile and began to cry.

⑤ Someone was following me, and I felt
scaring.

[18~19] 다음 글을 읽고 물음에 답하시오.

When she grew up, Hepburn became a
symbol of beauty. She was very popular
because of her hit movies, such as *My Fair
Lady* and *Roman Holiday*. The little black dress
which she wore in a movie is famous even
today. Many people still love her style.

The autumn of 1987 was a turning point in
Hepburn's life. She went to an international
music festival in Macau. Many people donated
money at the festival, and the money went
to UNICEF. Thanks to her fame, UNICEF
collected more money than ever before.
Hepburn realized that her fame could help
others, so she became a UNICEF Goodwill
Ambassador.

18 다음 질문에 대한 알맞은 대답을 빈칸에 쓰시오.

Q: For what reason could UNICEF
collect more money than ever before
in an international music festival in
Macau in the autumn of 1987?

A: It could do so _____ _____

_____ _____.

19 위 글의 주제로 알맞은 것을 고르시오.

① Hepburn's life as a symbol of beauty

② Hepburn's hit movies, such as *My Fair
Lady* and *Roman Holiday*

③ Hepburn's fame and a turning point in
her life

④ an international music festival in Macau

⑤ Hepburn's life as a UNICEF Goodwill
Ambassador

[20~22] 다음 글을 읽고 물음에 답하시오.

First, Hepburn went to Ethiopia in 1988. There, she brought food to hungry children. She was shocked because ⓐtheir lives were very difficult. After that, she volunteered in other countries. In 1990, she visited Vietnam to hand out medicine and support clean drinking water programs. Her last trip was to Somalia in 1992, and she passed away the following year.

Many people praised her beauty and style, but Hepburn's real beauty was her heart. To honor her, UNICEF made a statue, *The Spirit of Audrey*. People ⓑwho respect her keep her mission alive. Her favorite saying shows her mission.

As you get older, remember you have two hands. One is for helping yourself, and the other is for helping ⓒ .

20 다음 빈칸에 알맞은 단어를 넣어 밑줄 친 ⓐtheir lives가 가리키는 것을 설명하시오.

the lives of _____ _____ in Ethiopia

21 위 글의 밑줄 친 ⓑwho와 문법적 쓰임이 같은 것을 고르시오.

① Who is that woman?
② Who can jump farther, Tom or Bill?
③ Nobody knew who he was.
④ Who do you mean?
⑤ Anyone who wants to come is welcome.

22 위 글의 빈칸 ⓒ에 들어갈 알맞은 말을 고르시오.

① the other   ② others
③ one   ④ your family
⑤ another

[23~25] 다음 글을 읽고 물음에 답하시오.

My little big hero is my mom. She was born in 1972. She lives in Seoul.
She smiles a lot and tries to see the good in everything.
My mom had a serious car accident. She was in the hospital for six months. But she was very strong and finally got better.
She always helps people in need. She donates money and does volunteer work. She is my big hero!

23 위 글의 제목으로 알맞은 것을 고르시오.

① Mom Was Born in 1972!
② Try to See the Good in Everything
③ Mom Had a Serious Car Accident
④ My Little Big Hero
⑤ My Friendly Mom and Me

24 다음 질문에 대한 알맞은 대답을 완전한 문장으로 쓰시오.

Q: How long was the writer's mom in the hospital?

➡ _____

25 위 글의 글쓴이의 엄마에 관한 내용으로 적절하지 <u>않은</u> 것은?

① 서울에 산다.
② 많이 웃는다.
③ 자동차 사고로 몸이 불편하다.
④ 어려움에 처한 사람들을 항상 돕는다.
⑤ 자원 봉사를 한다.

INSIGHT
on the textbook

교과서 파헤치기

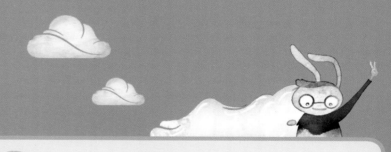

※ 다음 영어를 우리말로 쓰시오.

01	rude		22	sister school
02	last		23	scary
03	Chinese		24	shake
04	calendar		25	protect
05	evil		26	symbol
06	lock		27	valuable
07	face		28	good luck
08	colored		29	crow
09	full moon		30	pillow
10	try		31	remind
11	bow		32	traditional
12	separation		33	peace
13	represent		34	darkness
14	guard		35	talk about
15	international		36	blow one's nose
16	last year		37	watch over
17	Vietnamese		38	take off
18	guest		39	be afraid of
19	greet		40	have been to 장소
20	palm		41	be full of
21	spirit		42	go away
			43	remind A of B

※ 다음 우리말을 영어로 쓰시오.

01 해변, 바닷가 _____

02 가루, 분말 _____

03 옷, 의복 _____

04 (닭이) 울다 _____

05 경험 _____

06 축제 _____

07 박쥐 _____

08 우산 _____

09 선물 가게 _____

10 어둠, 암흑 _____

11 베개 _____

12 인도의, 인도 사람의 _____

13 자물쇠; 잠그다 _____

14 반달 _____

15 도착하다 _____

16 뮤지컬 _____

17 운 _____

18 전통의, 전통적인 _____

19 지불하다 _____

20 의미하다 _____

21 평화, 화해 _____

22 수탉 _____

23 생각나게 하다 _____

24 말하다, (정확히) 알다 _____

25 승리 _____

26 ~쪽으로 _____

27 영혼, 정신 _____

28 손바닥 _____

29 나타내다, 상징하다 _____

30 무례한 _____

31 보호하다 _____

32 채색된 _____

33 사악한, 악마의 _____

34 흔들다, 흔들리다 _____

35 사라지다, 떠나가다 _____

36 (옷 등을) 벗다 _____

37 A에게 B를 생각나게 하다 _____

38 ~을 가리키다 _____

39 ~에 대해 이야기하다 _____

40 ~으로 가득 차다 _____

41 ~을 듣다 _____

42 ~을 주시하다, 지키다 _____

43 ~을 두려워하다 _____

※ 다음 영영풀이에 알맞은 단어를 <보기>에서 골라 쓴 후, 우리말 뜻을 쓰시오.

1 _____ : a male chicken: _____

2 _____ : no light: _____

3 _____ : morally bad or wicked: _____

4 _____ : a soft thing to put your head on while you sleep: _____

5 _____ : to say hello or welcome: _____

6 _____ : to have the front part toward something: _____

7 _____ : to stand for something else: _____

8 _____ : to make the loud sound that a rooster makes: _____

9 _____ : success in defeating an opponent: _____

10 _____ : very important or expensive: _____

11 _____ : the inside part of the hand between the wrist and the fingers: _____

12 _____ : to keep something or someone safe from danger: _____

13 _____ : to make someone remember something: _____

14 _____ : making people feel afraid, frightening: _____

15 _____ : to lower your head or bend your body: _____

16 _____ : an object that represents something: _____

보기			
scary	greet	protect	bow
face	palm	evil	symbol
darkness	crow	represent	valuable
remind	victory	rooster	pillow

※ 다음 우리말과 일치하도록 빈칸에 알맞은 것을 골라 쓰시오.

1　_____ Korean _____
　　A. symbols　　　B. traditional

2　Peter is _____ Korea _____ meet a friend, Mina, _____ a sister school.
　　A. from　　　B. to　　　C. visiting

3　Peter is going to _____ _____ her grandfather's house _____ a week.
　　A. at　　　B. stay　　　C. for

4　When he _____, Mina _____ him the _____ room.
　　A. guest　　　B. shows　　　C. arrives

5　Peter, you will _____ _____.
　　A. here　　　B. stay

6　This _____ room is _____ of _____ Korean things.
　　A. traditional　　　B. full　　　C. guest

7　Look _____ this _____.
　　A. pillow　　　B. at

8　What _____ these _____?
　　A. things　　　B. are

9　_____ _____.
　　A. bats　　　B. they're

10　Bats _____ my _____? That's _____!
　　A. scary　　　B. pillow　　　C. on

11　Not really. In Korea, bats are _____ of _____ and a long _____.
　　A. life　　　B. symbols　　　C. luck

12　That's _____. In many Western countries, bats _____ people of _____ and scary things.
　　A. darkness　　　B. surprising　　　C. remind

13　Mina _____ Peter _____ _____ room.
　　A. grandfather's　　　B. her　　　C. shows

14　Peter and Mina's grandfather _____ and _____ each _____.
　　A. other　　　B. greet　　　C. meet

15　Hi, Peter! _____ you ever _____ this _____ of lock before?
　　A. kind　　　B. seen　　　C. have

16　No, I _____. It's _____ old _____ I can't really tell, but is it a fish?
　　A. that　　　B. haven't　　　C. so

17　Yes. _____ a long time, Koreans have _____ that fish are good _____.
　　A. guards　　　B. thought　　　C. for

1　전통적인 한국의 상징물

2　피터는 자매 학교 친구인 미나를 만나기 위해 한국을 방문 중이다.

3　피터는 일주일간 미나네 할아버지 댁에 머무를 것이다.

4　그가 도착하자, 미나가 그에게 손님방을 보여준다.

5　피터, 넌 여기에 머무르게 될 거야.

6　이 손님방은 한국의 전통 물건들로 가득 차 있어.

7　이 베개를 봐.

8　이것들은 뭐야?

9　그건 박쥐들이야.

10　내 베개 위에 박쥐가? 그거 겁나는데!

11　그렇지 않아. 한국에서는 박쥐가 행운과 장수의 상징이거든.

12　그거 놀라운 일인데. 서구의 많은 나라에서 박쥐는 사람들에게 어둠과 무서운 것들을 상기시키거든.

13　미나는 피터에게 할아버지의 방을 보여준다.

14　피터와 미나의 할아버지가 만나서 서로 인사한다.

15　안녕, 피터! 너는 이런 종류의 자물쇠를 전에 본 적 있니?

16　아니요, 본 적 없어요. 그 자물쇠는 너무 오래되어서 사실 알아볼 수가 없는데, 그건 물고기인가요?

17　맞아. 오랜 세월 동안, 한국인들은 물고기가 훌륭한 파수꾼이라고 생각해 왔단다.

18 Fish don't _____ their eyes, _____ when they _____ .
A. sleep   B. even   C. close

19 _____ _____ .
A. interesting   B. that's

20 We think fish can watch _____ valuable things. That's _____ this lock looks _____ a fish.
A. like   B. why   C. over

21 _____ I _____ .
A. understand   B. now

22 They go _____ and _____ _____ the garden.
A. around   B. walk   C. outside

23 What is _____ that _____ of paper ? It looks _____ .
A. piece   B. scary   C. on

24 Do you _____ this _____ of a rooster?
A. painting   B. mean

25 Oh, is _____ a _____ ?
A. rooster   B. it

26 Yes, it is. Roosters _____ _____ morning.
A. every   B. crow

27 Their _____ means _____ a new day is _____ .
A. beginning   B. that   C. crowing

28 For many years, Koreans have believed _____ spirits go _____ when a rooster _____ .
A. away   B. crows   C. evil

29 Really? I've _____ _____ that _____ .
A. before   B. heard   C. never

30 _____ , I'm _____ of darkness and evil _____ .
A. spirits   B. actually   C. afraid

31 Could you _____ a rooster _____ me, Mina?
A. for   B. draw

32 Sure. I'll _____ a big _____ for you!
A. rooster   B. draw

33 _____ the drawing _____ your door. Then it will _____ you.
A. protect   B. above   C. put

34 _____ , I _____ .
A. will   B. yes

35 I'm enjoying this trip _____ much _____ I want to stay _____ .
A. longer   B. that   C. so

36 I love _____ the _____ Korean symbols _____ this house.
A. in   B. traditional   C. all

37 Now I _____ a _____ of them.
A. lot   B. understand

38 I _____ to _____ Korea again _____ my family.
A. with   B. visit   C. want

18 물고기는 잘 때도 눈을 감지 않거든.

19 그거 재미있군요.

20 우리는 물고기가 귀중품을 지킬 수 있다고 생각해. 그것이 이 자물쇠가 물고기 모양으로 생긴 이유란다.

21 이제 이해가 되는군요.

22 그들은 밖에 나가서 정원을 걷는다.

23 저 종이에는 무엇이 그려져 있는 거죠? 무서워 보여요.

24 이 수탉 그림을 말하는 거니?

25 오, 그게 수탉이에요?

26 응, 그렇단다. 수탉은 매일 아침 울지.

27 수탉의 울음은 새로운 날이 시작하는 것을 의미해.

28 오랫동안 한국인들은 수탉이 울 때 악령이 물러간다고 믿어 왔단다.

29 정말요? 전 그런 말을 들어본 적이 없어요.

30 사실 전 어둠과 악령을 무서워해요.

31 미나야, 날 위해 수탉을 그려 줄 수 있니?

32 물론이지. 내가 널 위해 커다란 수탉을 그려줄게!

33 그 그림을 네 문 위에 걸어 놓으렴. 그러면 그게 널 지켜 줄 거야.

34 네. 그럴게요.

35 난 이번 여행이 매우 즐거워서 더 오래 머무르고 싶다.

36 난 이 집의 모든 전통적인 한국의 상징물들이 아주 마음에 든다.

37 나는 이제 그것들을 많이 알게 되었다.

38 난 우리 가족과 함께 한국을 다시 방문하고 싶다.

※ 다음 괄호 안의 단어들을 우리말에 맞도록 바르게 배열하시오.

1 (Symbols / Korean / Traditional)
➡ _____

2 (is / Peter / Korea / visiting / meet / to / friend, / a / Mina, / school. / a / from / sister)
➡ _____

3 (is / to / going / at / Peter / stay / grandfather's / her / house / week. / a / for)
➡ _____

4 (arrives, / he / when / Mina / the / shows / room. / him / guest)
➡ _____

5 (you / Peter, / here / will / stay)
➡ _____

6 (is / guest / this / room / of / full / things. / Korean / traditional)
➡ _____

7 (look / this / at / pillow.)
➡ _____

8 (are / things? / these / what)
➡ _____

9 (bats. / they're)
➡ _____

10 (my / bats / pillow? / on // scary! / that's)
➡ _____

11 (really. / not // Korea, / in / are / bats / of / symbols / luck / and / life. / long / a)
➡ _____

12 (surprising. / that's // many / countries, / in / Western / remind / bats / of / darkness / people / things. / and / scary)
➡ _____

13 (Peter / shows / Mina / room. / grandfather's / her)
➡ _____

14 (Mina's / and / Peter / grandfather / greet / and / other. / meet / each)
➡ _____

15 (Peter! / Hi, // you / have / seen / ever / this / lock / before? / of / kind)
➡ _____

16 (haven't. / no, / I // it's / that / old / so / I / really / can't / tell, / but / fish? / a / it / is)
➡ _____

17 (yes. // a / time, / for / long / Koreans / thought / have / that / are / guards. / good / fish)
➡ _____

1 전통적인 한국의 상징물

2 피터는 자매 학교 친구인 미나를 만나기 위해 한국을 방문 중이다.

3 피터는 일주일간 미나네 할아버지 댁에 머무를 것이다.

4 그가 도착하자, 미나가 그에게 손님방을 보여준다.

5 피터, 넌 여기에 머무르게 될 거야.

6 이 손님방은 한국의 전통 물건들로 가득 차 있어.

7 이 베개를 봐.

8 이것들은 뭐야?

9 그건 박쥐들이야.

10 내 베개 위에 박쥐가? 그거 겁나는데!

11 그렇지 않아. 한국에서는 박쥐가 행운과 장수의 상징이거든.

12 그거 놀라운 일인데. 서구의 많은 나라들에서 박쥐는 사람들에게 어둠과 무서운 것들을 상기시키거든.

13 미나는 피터에게 할아버지의 방을 보여준다.

14 피터와 미나의 할아버지가 만나서 서로 인사한다.

15 안녕, 피터! 너는 이런 종류의 자물쇠를 전에 본 적 있니?

16 아니요, 본 적 없어요. 그 자물쇠는 너무 오래되어서 사실 알아볼 수가 없는데, 그건 물고기인가요?

17 맞아. 오랜 세월 동안, 한국인들은 물고기가 훌륭한 파수꾼이라고 생각해 왔단다.

18 (don't / fish / eyes, / their / close / even / sleep. / they / when)
➡ _____

19 (interesting. / that's)
➡ _____

20 (we / fish / can / think / over / watch / things. / valuable // that's / this / why / lock / a / fish. / like / looks)
➡ _____
_____

21 (understand. / I / now)
➡ _____

22 (outside / go / they / and / around / garden. / the / walk)
➡ _____

23 (is / what / that / on / paper? / of / piece // scary. / looks / it)
➡ _____

24 (mean / you / do / painting / this / rooster? / a / of)
➡ _____

25 (it / is / oh, / rooster? / a)
➡ _____

26 (is. / it / yes, / roosters / morning. / every / crow)
➡ _____

27 (crowing / their / means / that / a / beginning. / is / day / new)
➡ _____

28 (years, / many / for / Koreans / believed / have / spirits / evil / away / when / go / crows. / rooster / a)
➡ _____
_____

29 (really? / never / I've / heard / before. / that)
➡ _____

30 (actually, / I'm / darkness / of / afraid / and / spirits. / evil)
➡ _____

31 (you / rooster / could / a / draw / Mina? / me, / for)
➡ _____

32 (sure. // draw / I'll / big / for / a / rooster / you!)
➡ _____

33 (the / put / above / drawing / door. / your // then / will / you. / it / protect)
➡ _____
_____

34 (will. / I / yes,)
➡ _____

35 (I'm / this / enjoying / trip / much / so / that / longer. / I / stay / to / want)
➡ _____

36 (all / love / I / the / Korean / traditional / symbols / house. / in / this)
➡ _____

37 (I / now / understand / a / them. / of / lot)
➡ _____

38 (I / visit / to / want / again / Korea / family. / my / with)
➡ _____

18 물고기는 잘 때도 눈을 감지 않거든.

19 그거 재미있군요.

20 우리는 물고기가 귀중품을 지킬 수 있다고 생각해. 그것이 이 자물쇠가 물고기 모양으로 생긴 이유란다.

21 이제 이해가 되는군요.

22 그들은 밖에 나가서 정원을 걷는다.

23 저 종이에는 무엇이 그려져 있는 거죠? 무서워 보여요.

24 이 수탉 그림을 말하는 거니?

25 오, 그게 수탉이에요?

26 응, 그렇단다. 수탉은 매일 아침 울지.

27 수탉의 울음은 새로운 날이 시작하는 것을 의미해.

28 오랫동안 한국인들은 수탉이 울 때 악령이 물러간다고 믿어 왔단다.

29 정말요? 전 그런 말을 들어본 적이 없어요.

30 사실 전 어둠과 악령을 무서워해요.

31 미나야, 날 위해 수탉을 그려 줄 수 있니?

32 물론이지. 내가 널 위해 커다란 수탉을 그려줄게!

33 그 그림을 네 문 위에 걸어 놓으렴. 그러면 그게 널 지켜 줄 거야.

34 네, 그럴게요.

35 난 이번 여행이 매우 즐거워서 더 오래 머무르고 싶다.

36 난 이 집의 모든 전통적인 한국의 상징물들이 아주 마음에 든다.

37 나는 이제 그것들을 많이 알게 되었다.

38 난 우리 가족과 함께 한국을 다시 방문하고 싶다.

※ 다음 우리말을 영어로 쓰시오.

1 전통적인 한국의 상징물
➡ _____

2 피터는 자매 학교 친구인 미나를 만나기 위해 한국을 방문 중이다.
➡ _____

3 피터는 일주일간 미나네 할아버지 댁에 머무를 것이다.
➡ _____

4 그가 도착하자, 미나가 그에게 손님방을 보여준다.
➡ _____

5 피터, 넌 여기에 머무르게 될 거야.
➡ _____

6 이 손님방은 한국의 전통 물건들로 가득 차 있어.
➡ _____

7 이 베개를 봐.
➡ _____

8 이것들은 뭐야?
➡ _____

9 그건 박쥐들이야.
➡ _____

10 내 베개 위에 박쥐가? 그거 겁나는데!
➡ _____

11 그렇지 않아. 한국에서는 박쥐가 행운과 장수의 상징이거든.
➡ _____

12 그거 놀라운 일인데. 서구의 많은 나라들에서 박쥐는 사람들에게 어둠과 무서운 것들을 상기시키거든.
➡ _____

13 미나는 피터에게 할아버지의 방을 보여준다.
➡ _____

14 피터와 미나의 할아버지가 만나서 서로 인사한다.
➡ _____

15 안녕, 피터! 너는 이런 종류의 자물쇠를 전에 본 적 있니?
➡ _____

16 아니요, 본 적 없어요. 그 자물쇠는 너무 오래되어서 사실 알아볼 수가 없는데, 그건 물고기인가요?
➡ _____

17 맞아. 오랜 세월 동안, 한국인들은 물고기가 훌륭한 파수꾼이라고 생각해 왔단다.
➡ _____

18 물고기는 잘 때도 눈을 감지 않거든.

➡ _____

19 그거 재미있군요.

➡ _____

20 우리는 물고기가 귀중품을 지킬 수 있다고 생각해. 그것이 이 자물쇠가 물고기 모양으로 생긴 이유란다.

➡ _____

21 이제 이해가 되는군요.

➡ _____

22 그들은 밖에 나가서 정원을 걷는다.

➡ _____

23 저 종이에는 무엇이 그려져 있는 거죠? 무서워 보여요.

➡ _____

24 이 수탉 그림을 말하는 거니?

➡ _____

25 오, 그게 수탉이에요?

➡ _____

26 응, 그렇단다. 수탉은 매일 아침 울지.

➡ _____

27 수탉의 울음은 새로운 날이 시작하는 것을 의미해.

➡ _____

28 오랫동안 한국인들은 수탉이 울 때 악령이 물러간다고 믿어 왔단다.

➡ _____

29 정말요? 전 그런 말을 들어본 적이 없어요.

➡ _____

30 사실 전 어둠과 악령을 무서워해요.

➡ _____

31 미나야, 날 위해 수탉을 그려 줄 수 있니?

➡ _____

32 물론이지. 내가 널 위해 커다란 수탉을 그려줄게!

➡ _____

33 그 그림을 네 문 위에 걸어 놓으렴. 그러면 그게 널 지켜 줄 거야.

➡ _____

34 네, 그럴게요.

➡ _____

35 난 이번 여행이 매우 즐거워서 더 오래 머무르고 싶다.

➡ _____

36 난 이 집의 모든 전통적인 한국의 상징물들이 아주 마음에 든다.

➡ _____

37 나는 이제 그것들을 많이 알게 되었다.

➡ _____

38 난 우리 가족과 함께 한국을 다시 방문하고 싶다.

➡ _____

※ 다음 우리말과 일치하도록 빈칸에 알맞은 말을 쓰시오.

Think and Write

1. Do you know about _____ _____ _____?

2. _____ _____ many kinds.

3. _____ _____, there _____ a lion dance, a _____ dance, and an umbrella dance.

4. _____ _____ the most famous _____ _____ the lion dance.

5. In this dance, two dancers _____ and _____ _____ lions.

6. They _____ dance _____ special days, _____ _____ New Year's Day.

7. I think their _____ _____ are _____.

8. I hope _____ _____ this dance _____.

1. 당신은 전통적인 중국 춤에 대해 아는가?
2. 많은 종류들이 있다.
3. 예를 들면, 사자춤, 부채춤, 그리고 우산 춤이 있다.
4. 가장 유명한 춤들 중의 하나가 사자춤이다.
5. 이 춤에서, 두 명의 댄서들이 사자처럼 옷을 입고 행동한다.
6. 사람들은 사자춤을 대개 설날과 같은 특별한 날에 춘다.
7. 나는 그들의 춤 동작들이 멋지다고 생각한다.
8. 나는 언젠가 이 춤을 연습하기를 바란다.

Presentation Time

1. Do you want to _____ _____ _____ _____ in Korea?

2. Then _____ these steps.

3. First, please _____ _____ your shoes _____ you _____ _____ people's homes.

4. Next, _____ when you greet _____.

5. Also, use two hands when you _____ _____ _____ _____ _____.

6. And do not _____ _____ _____ at the table and do not _____ _____ people.

7. _____, do not _____ older people _____ their _____ _____.

1. 한국에서 즐거운 시간을 보내고 싶은가요?
2. 그러면 다음 단계를 따르세요.
3. 먼저 사람들의 집에 들어갈 때는 신발을 벗으세요.
4. 다음에 다른 사람들에게 인사할 때 절을 하세요.
5. 또한 나이가 많은 사람들에게 무언가를 줄 때는 두 손을 사용하세요.
6. 그리고 식탁에서 코를 풀지 말고 사람들을 가리키지 마세요.
7. 마지막으로 나이가 많은 사람들을 이름으로 부르지 마세요.

구석구석 지문 Test

※ 다음 우리말을 영어로 쓰시오.

Think and Write

1. 당신은 전통적인 중국 춤에 대해 아는가?
➡ _____

2. 많은 종류들이 있다.
➡ _____

3. 예를 들면, 사자춤, 부채춤, 그리고 우산 춤이 있다.
➡ _____

4. 가장 유명한 춤들 중의 하나가 사자춤이다.
➡ _____

5. 이 춤에서, 두 명의 댄서들이 사자처럼 옷을 입고 행동한다.
➡ _____

6. 사람들은 사자춤을 대개 설날과 같은 특별한 날에 춘다.
➡ _____

7. 나는 그들의 춤 동작들이 멋지다고 생각한다.
➡ _____

8. 나는 언젠가 이 춤을 연습하기를 바란다.
➡ _____

Presentation Time

1. 한국에서 즐거운 시간을 보내고 싶은가요?
➡ _____

2. 그러면 다음 단계를 따르세요.
➡ _____

3. 먼저 사람들의 집에 들어갈 때는 신발을 벗으세요.
➡ _____

4. 다음에 다른 사람들에게 인사할 때 절을 하세요.
➡ _____

5. 또한 나이가 많은 사람들에게 무언가를 줄 때는 두 손을 사용하세요.
➡ _____

6. 그리고 식탁에서 코를 풀지 말고 사람들을 가리키지 마세요.
➡ _____

7. 마지막으로 나이가 많은 사람들을 이름으로 부르지 마세요.
➡ _____

※ 다음 영어를 우리말로 쓰시오.

01 warming	
02 waste	
03 terrible	
04 put	
05 global	
06 sea level	
07 disappear	
08 fan	
09 nervous	
10 environment	
11 soil	
12 enough	
13 instead	
14 process	
15 interesting	
16 pollution	
17 lid	
18 raise	
19 consume	
20 produce	
21 bottom	

22 fix	
23 water	
24 space	
25 gardening	
26 healthy	
27 connect	
28 helpful	
29 experiment	
30 solution	
31 article	
32 productive	
33 feed	
34 chemical	
35 get+비교급	
36 in place	
37 go up	
38 turn off	
39 run out	
40 in danger	
41 remind A of B	
42 turn A into B	
43 throw away	

※ 다음 우리말을 영어로 쓰시오.

01	접시	
02	문제	
03	바닥, 맨 아래	
04	다큐멘터리, 기록물	
05	온난화	
06	섬	
07	끔찍한	
08	에어컨	
09	말하기 대회	
10	해결책	
11	오염	
12	정보	
13	(신문) 기사	
14	점토	
15	놀라운	
16	바느질하다	
17	재배하다	
18	먹이를 주다, 먹이다	
19	과정	
20	어디든	
21	화분, 그릇	

22	실험	
23	화학 물질	
24	전통적인	
25	생산적인	
26	매달려 있다	
27	해결하다	
28	환경	
29	사라지다	
30	먹다, 소모하다	
31	도움이 되는, 유용한	
32	정원 가꾸기, 원예	
33	지구의	
34	연결하다	
35	A를 B로 채우다	
36	올라가다, 상승하다	
37	위험에 처한	
38	A를 B로 바꾸다	
39	A를 B로 자르다	
40	A에게 B를 상기시키다	
41	버리다	
42	(전기, 가스, 수도 등을) 켜다	
43	~에 관해 걱정하다	

Listen and Talk 2 A

G: _____

M: _____
　　_____

G: _____

Listen and Talk 2 B

B: _____

G: _____

B: _____

G: _____

B: _____

G: _____
　　_____

B: _____

Listen and Talk 2 C

G: _____

B: _____

G: _____

B: _____

G: _____
　　_____

B: _____

G: _____
　　_____

B: _____

Do It Yourself

G: _____

B: _____
　　_____

G: _____

B: _____

G: _____

B: _____

G: 이 공 좀 보세요. 어떻게 사용하는지 말해 주실래요?

M: 30분 동안 축구를 하면 전구가 켜질 거예요. 당신은 전구를 어디서든 이용할 수 있어요.

G: 와, 그거 참 재미있네요.

B: 네 가방 예쁘다, Jenny. 어디서 샀어?

G: 내가 만들었어.

B: 네가 만들었다고? 놀랍다.

G: 너도 하나 만들어 보는 게 어때? 안 어려워.

B: 그래? 어떻게 만드는지 알려 줄 수 있니?

G: 그럼. 오래된 청바지를 찾아. 그걸 작은 조각으로 잘라. 그런 다음 조각들을 함께 꿰매면 돼.

B: 쉬울 것 같아. 내 여동생 생일 선물로 하나 만들어야겠어.

G: 지구촌 전등 끄기 행사에 대해 들어 봤니?

B: 아니, 들어 본 적이 없어. 그게 뭔데?

G: 지구촌 환경 행사야. 사람들은 한 시간 동안 불을 끄지.

B: 그걸 왜 하는데?

G: 사람들에게 환경문제에 대해서 상기시키기 위해서지. 이런 작은 행동이 세상을 바꿀 수 있다고 생각하는 거야.

B: 아, 이제 알겠어. 그거 어떻게 참여하는지 말해 줄 수 있니?

G: 그럼. 그냥 3월의 마지막 토요일에 오후 8시 반부터 9시 반까지 불을 끄기만 하면 돼.

B: 쉽네. 다음 번 행사 때 참여해야겠어.

G: 너 기분이 안 좋아 보인다. 무슨 일 있니?

B: 나는 내 과학 숙제를 걱정하고 있어. 나는 환경 지키기에 대한 짧은 비디오를 만들어야 해. 그런데 영상 만드는 게 어려워.

G: 음, 이 앱을 사용해 보는 게 어때? 쉬워.

B: 어떻게 사용하는지 말해 주겠니?

G: 물론. 앱을 열어. 사진들을 추가하고 음악을 골라. 그러면 이 앱이 너의 사진들을 이용해서 영상을 만들 거야.

B: 와, 그거 쉽다. 지금 시도해 볼게. 고마워.

※ 다음 우리말과 일치하도록 빈칸에 알맞은 것을 골라 쓰시오.

1 My _____ _____ : _____ Aquaponics
　　A. Project　　　B. Science　　　C. Home

2 _____ are you _____?
　　A. reading　　　B. what

3 I'm _____ an _____ _____ aquaponics.
　　A. article　　　B. about　　　C. reading

4 It's a way of _____ plants _____ .
　　A. without　　　B. growing　　　C. soil

5 We can also _____ plants and _____ fish in just one _____.
　　A. raise　　　B. grow　　　C. system

6 _____ that _____?
　　A. possible　　　B. is

7 We'll _____ . I'm going to _____ it _____ home for my science project.
　　A. at　　　B. try　　　C. see

8 Fish, _____, and plants are the _____ of aquaponics.
　　A. main　　　B. bacteria　　　C. parts

9 _____ you _____ the fish, they produce _____.
　　A. waste　　　B. feed　　　C. after

10 The waste is _____ _____ food for the plants _____ bacteria.
　　A. turned　　　B. by　　　C. into

11 The plants _____ the water _____ _____ the food.
　　A. by　　　B. clean　　　C. consuming

12 This _____ is _____ again and _____ !
　　A. repeated　　　B. process　　　C. again

13 _____ Aquaponics _____ Eric Jackson
　　A. by　　　B. home

14 Questions: _____ can I _____ an aquaponics system _____ home?
　　A. make　　　B. at　　　C. how

15 _____ is aquaponics _____?
　　A. good　　　B. why

16 Period: _____ May 15 _____ August 15
　　A. to　　　B. from

17 Materials: a pot & small stones, a fish _____, a plastic _____, a water pump, plants, some fish, a box _____, _____
　　A. clay　　　B. tube　　　C. cutter　　　D. tank

18 Steps: I made _____ in the _____ of a _____ .
　　A. bottom　　　B. holes　　　C. pot

19 _____ I _____ small stones and plants _____ it.
　　A. put　　　B. in　　　C. then

20 I made a big hole in the _____ of the fish tank and _____ the pot _____ the hole.
　　A. put　　　B. in　　　C. lid

21 I _____ the pot _____ place _____ clay.
A. with   B. in   C. fixed

22 I made _____ _____ in the lid and put a tube _____ it.
A. hole   B. another   C. through

23 I _____ a water pump _____ the fish tank.
A. in   B. put

24 I _____ the tube to _____ the pump _____ the pot.
A. connect   B. to   C. used

25 I _____ the fish tank _____ water and _____ some fish in it.
A. with   B. filled   C. put

26 Then I _____ _____ the pump.
A. on   B. turned

27 Results: From this experiment, I _____ my plants and _____ fish _____ aquaponics.
A. raised   B. with   C. grew

28 I just _____ the fish, but the plants have _____ 17 centimeters _____ three months.
A. grown   B. in   C. fed

29 The fish _____ _____ and the water is clean _____ the _____.
A. time   B. stay   C. all   D. healthy

30 Conclusion: Some important _____ about aquaponics were _____ from this _____.
A. things   B. learned   C. experiment

31 First, water is _____ _____ the plants don't need _____.
A. because   B. watering   C. saved

32 Second, it is good _____ the environment _____ no chemicals are _____.
A. because   B. used   C. for

33 _____, you can do aquaponics _____ because it doesn't need much _____.
A. anywhere   B. space   C. finally

34 *I found* _____ ... Some farmers use aquaponics to _____ vegetables and _____ fish.
A. out   B. raise   C. produce

35 They _____ aquaponics because it is _____ than traditional _____.
A. gardening   B. choose   C. easier   D. far

36 Also, it is a _____ more _____ way of _____ food.
A. much   B. growing   C. productive

37 The plants grow _____ faster than plants in _____, and it _____ space.
A. soil   B. much   C. saves

38 I hope more food is _____ in this _____ in the future _____ it is _____ for us and the environment.
A. healthy   B. way   C. produced   D. because

21 찰흙으로 화분을 제자리에 고정하였다.

22 덮개에 또 다른 구멍을 하나 만들고 그 안에 관을 넣었다.

23 어항에 수중 펌프를 넣었다.

24 관을 이용하여 펌프를 화분에 연결하였다.

25 어항에 물을 채우고 물고기 몇 마리를 거기에 넣었다.

26 그러고 나서 펌프를 작동하였다.

27 결과: 이 실험으로 나는 아쿠아포닉스로 식물과 물고기를 키웠다.

28 나는 그저 물고기에 밥만 주었는데도 식물은 석 달 동안 17cm나 자랐다.

29 물고기는 건강을 유지하며 물은 항상 깨끗하다.

30 결론: 아쿠아포닉스에 관한 몇 가지 중요한 사항이 이 실험에서 발견되었다.

31 첫째, 식물에 물을 줄 필요가 없으므로 물이 절약된다.

32 둘째, 화학 물질이 사용되지 않으므로 아쿠아포닉스는 환경에 이롭다.

33 끝으로, 넓은 공간이 필요하지 않으므로 당신은 어디에서나 아쿠아포닉스를 쉽게 할 수 있다.

34 나는 알게 되었다... 몇몇 농부들은 채소를 생산하고 물고기를 키우는 데 아쿠아포닉스를 이용한다.

35 그들은 아쿠아포닉스가 전통 재배 방식보다 훨씬 더 쉽기 때문에 그것을 선택한다.

36 또한, 아쿠아포닉스는 식량을 재배하는 훨씬 더 생산적인 방법이다.

37 식물들이 흙에서 자라는 식물보다 훨씬 빠르게 자라고 공간도 절약한다.

38 그것은 우리와 환경에 훨씬 건강하기 때문에 나는 미래에 더 많은 식량이 이런 방식으로 생산되기를 희망한다.

※ 다음 우리말과 일치하도록 빈칸에 알맞은 말을 쓰시오.

1 My _____ _____ : Home Aquaponics

2 _____ are you _____ ?

3 I'm _____ an _____ _____ aquaponics.

4 It's a way of _____ plants _____ _____ .

5 We can also _____ plants and _____ fish in just one _____ .

6 _____ that _____ ?

7 We'll _____ . I'm going to _____ it _____ home for my science project.

8 Fish, _____ , and plants are the _____ _____ of aquaponics.

9 _____ you _____ the fish, they produce _____ .

10 The waste is _____ _____ food for the plants _____ bacteria.

11 The plants _____ the water _____ _____ the food.

12 This _____ is _____ again and _____ !

13 _____ Aquaponics _____ Eric Jackson

14 Questions: _____ can I _____ an aquaponics system _____ home?

15 _____ is aquaponics _____ ?

16 Period: _____ May 15 _____ August 15

17 Materials: a pot & small stones, a fish _____ , a plastic _____ , a water pump, plants, some fish, a box _____ , _____

18 Steps: I made _____ in the _____ of a _____ .

19 _____ I _____ small stones and plants _____ it.

20 I made a big hole in the _____ of the fish tank and _____ the pot _____ the hole.

1 나의 과학 프로젝트: 가정용 아쿠아포닉스

2 무엇을 읽고 있니?

3 아쿠아포닉스에 관한 기사를 읽고 있어.

4 흙 없이 식물을 재배할 수 있는 방법이야.

5 또 한 가지 장치만으로도 식물과 물고기를 동시에 키울 수 있어.

6 그게 가능하니?

7 곧 알게 될 거야. 내가 과학 프로젝트로 집에서 해 볼 예정이 거든.

8 물고기, 박테리아, 식물이 아쿠아포닉스의 주요 부분이다.

9 물고기에게 먹이를 주면, 그것들은 배설물을 만들어 낸다.

10 이 배설물은 박테리아에 의해 식물의 먹이로 바뀐다.

11 식물은 그 먹이를 먹음으로써 물을 정화한다.

12 이러한 과정이 계속해서 반복된다!

13 가정용 아쿠아포닉스 에릭 잭슨

14 질문: 집에서 아쿠아포닉스 장치를 어떻게 만들 수 있을까?

15 아쿠아포닉스가 왜 좋은가?

16 기간: 5월 15일부터 8월 15일까지

17 재료: 화분과 작은 돌들, 어항, 플라스틱 관, 수중 펌프, 식물, 물고기, 커터칼, 찰흙

18 절차: 화분 바닥에 구멍들을 뚫었다.

19 그런 후에 화분에 작은 돌들을 넣고 식물을 심었다.

20 어항 덮개에 큰 구멍을 내고 구멍에 그 화분을 넣었다.

21 I _____ the pot _____ place _____ clay.

22 I made _____ _____ in the lid and put a tube _____ it.

23 I _____ a water pump _____ the fish tank.

24 I _____ the tube to _____ the pump _____ the pot.

25 I _____ the fish tank _____ water and _____ some fish in it.

26 Then I _____ _____ the pump.

27 Results: From this experiment, I _____ my plants and _____ fish _____ aquaponics.

28 I just _____ the fish, but the plants have _____ 17 centimeters _____ three months.

29 The fish _____ _____ and the water is clean _____ the _____.

30 Conclusion: Some important _____ about aquaponics were _____ from this _____.

31 First, water is _____ _____ the plants don't need _____.

32 Second, it is good _____ the environment _____ no chemicals are _____.

33 _____, you can do aquaponics _____ because it doesn't need much _____.

34 *I found* _____ ... Some farmers use aquaponics to _____ vegetables and _____ fish.

35 They _____ aquaponics because it is _____ _____ than traditional _____.

36 Also, it is a _____ more _____ way of _____ food.

37 The plants grow _____ faster than plants in _____, and it _____ space.

38 I hope more food is _____ in this _____ in the future _____ it is _____ for us and the environment.

---

21 찰흙으로 화분을 제자리에 고정하였다.

22 덮개에 또 다른 구멍을 하나 만들고 그 안에 관을 넣었다.

23 어항에 수중 펌프를 넣었다.

24 관을 이용하여 펌프를 화분에 연결하였다.

25 어항에 물을 채우고 물고기 몇 마리를 거기에 넣었다.

26 그러고 나서 펌프를 작동하였다.

27 결과: 이 실험으로 나는 아쿠아포닉스로 식물과 물고기를 키웠다.

28 나는 그저 물고기에 밥만 주었는데도 식물은 석 달 동안 17cm나 자랐다.

29 물고기는 건강을 유지하며 물은 항상 깨끗하다.

30 결론: 아쿠아포닉스에 관한 몇 가지 중요한 사항이 이 실험에서 발견되었다.

31 첫째, 식물에 물을 줄 필요가 없으므로 물이 절약된다.

32 둘째, 화학 물질이 사용되지 않으므로 아쿠아포닉스는 환경에 이롭다.

33 끝으로, 넓은 공간이 필요하지 않으므로 당신은 어디에서나 아쿠아포닉스를 쉽게 할 수 있다.

34 나는 알게 되었다... 몇몇 농부들은 채소를 생산하고 물고기를 키우는 데 아쿠아포닉스를 이용한다.

35 그들은 아쿠아포닉스가 전통 재배 방식보다 훨씬 더 쉽기 때문에 그것을 선택한다.

36 또한, 아쿠아포닉스는 식량을 재배하는 훨씬 더 생산적인 방법이다.

37 식물들이 흙에서 자라는 식물보다 훨씬 빠르게 자라고 공간도 절약한다.

38 그것은 우리와 환경에 훨씬 건강하기 때문에 나는 미래에 더 많은 식량이 이런 방식으로 생산되기를 희망한다.

※ 다음 문장을 우리말로 쓰시오.

1 My Science Project: Home Aquaponics
➡ _____

2 What are you reading?
➡ _____

3 I'm reading an article about aquaponics.
➡ _____

4 It's a way of growing plants without soil.
➡ _____

5 We can also grow plants and raise fish in just one system.
➡ _____

6 Is that possible?
➡ _____

7 We'll see. I'm going to try it at home for my science project.
➡ _____

8 Fish, bacteria, and plants are the main parts of aquaponics.
➡ _____

9 After you feed the fish, they produce waste.
➡ _____

10 The waste is turned into food for the plants by bacteria.
➡ _____

11 The plants clean the water by consuming the food.
➡ _____

12 This process is repeated again and again!
➡ _____

13 Home Aquaponics   by Eric Jackson
➡ _____

14 Questions: How can I make an aquaponics system at home?
➡ _____

15 Why is aquaponics good?
➡ _____

16 Period: From May 15 to August 15
➡ _____

17 Materials: a pot & small stones, a fish tank, a plastic tube, a water pump, plants, some fish, a box cutter, clay
➡ _____

18 Steps: I made holes in the bottom of a pot.
➡ _____

19 Then I put small stones and plants in it.
➡ _____

20 I made a big hole in the lid of the fish tank and put the pot in the hole.
➡ _____

21 I fixed the pot in place with clay.
➡ _____

22 I made another hole in the lid and put a tube through it.
➡ _____

23 I put a water pump in the fish tank.
➡ _____

24 I used the tube to connect the pump to the pot.
➡ _____

25 I filled the fish tank with water and put some fish in it.
➡ _____

26 Then I turned on the pump.
➡ _____

27 Results: From this experiment, I grew my plants and raised fish with aquaponics.
➡ _____

28 I just fed the fish, but the plants have grown 17 centimeters in three months.
➡ _____

29 The fish stay healthy and the water is clean all the time.
➡ _____

30 Conclusion: Some important things about aquaponics were learned from this experiment.
➡ _____

31 First, water is saved because the plants don't need watering.
➡ _____

32 Second, it is good for the environment because no chemicals are used.
➡ _____

33 Finally, you can do aquaponics anywhere because it doesn't need much space.
➡ _____

34 I found out... Some farmers use aquaponics to produce vegetables and raise fish.
➡ _____

35 They choose aquaponics because it is far easier than traditional gardening.
➡ _____

36 Also, it is a much more productive way of growing food.
➡ _____

37 The plants grow much faster than plants in soil, and it saves space.
➡ _____

38 I hope more food is produced in this way in the future because it is healthy for us and the environment.
➡ _____

※ 다음 괄호 안의 단어들을 우리말에 맞도록 바르게 배열하시오.

1 (Science / My / Project: / Aquaponics / Home)
➡ _____

2 (are / reading? / what / you)
➡ _____

3 (reading / I'm / article / aquaponics. / about / an)
➡ _____

4 (way / it's / of / a / growing / soil. / without / plants)
➡ _____

5 (can / we / also / plants / grow / and / fish / in / raise / system. / one / just)
➡ _____

6 (that / is / possible?)
➡ _____

7 (see. / we'll / going / I'm / try / to / at / it / home / my / for / project. / science)
➡ _____

8 (bacteria, / fish / and / are / plants / main / the / parts / aquaponics. / of)
➡ _____

9 (you / after / the / feed / fish, / they / waste. / produce)
➡ _____

10 (waste / the / turned / is / food / into / the / for / bacteria. / by / plants)
➡ _____

11 (plants / the / clean / water / the / consuming / by / food. / the)
➡ _____

12 (process / this / repeated / again! / is / again / and)
➡ _____

13 (Aquaponics / Home // Eric / by / Jackson)
➡ _____

14 (questions: can / how / make / I / aquaponics / an / home? / at / system)
➡ _____

15 (is / why / good? / aquaponics)
➡ _____

16 (period: / May / 15 / from / 15 / to / August)
➡ _____

17 (materials: / pot / a / & / stones, / small / fish / a / tank, / tube, / plastic / a / water / a / pump, / some / plants, / fish, / box / a / clay / cutter,)
➡ _____

18 (steps: / made / I / holes / the / in / bottom / pot. / a / of)
➡ _____

19 (I / then / small / put / stones / and / it. / in / plants)
➡ _____

20 (made / I / big / a / hole / the / in / lid / of / fish / the / tank / and / the / pot / put / hole. / the / in)
➡ _____

1 나의 과학 프로젝트: 가정용 아쿠아포닉스

2 무엇을 읽고 있니?

3 아쿠아포닉스에 관한 기사를 읽고 있어.

4 흙 없이 식물을 재배할 수 있는 방법이야.

5 또 한 가지 장치만으로도 식물과 물고기를 동시에 키울 수 있어.

6 그게 가능하니?

7 곧 알게 될 거야. 내가 과학 프로젝트로 집에서 해 볼 예정이거든.

8 물고기, 박테리아, 식물이 아쿠아포닉스의 주요 부분이다.

9 물고기에게 먹이를 주면, 그것들은 배설물을 만들어 낸다.

10 이 배설물은 박테리아에 의해 식물의 먹이로 바뀐다.

11 식물은 그 먹이를 먹음으로써 물을 정화한다.

12 이러한 과정이 계속해서 반복된다!

13 가정용 아쿠아포닉스 에릭 잭슨

14 질문: 집에서 아쿠아포닉스 장치를 어떻게 만들 수 있을까?

15 아쿠아포닉스가 왜 좋은가?

16 기간: 5월 15일부터 8월 15일까지

17 재료: 화분과 작은 돌들, 어항, 플라스틱 관, 수중 펌프, 식물, 물고기, 커터칼, 찰흙

18 절차: 화분 바닥에 구멍들을 뚫었다.

19 그런 후에 화분에 작은 돌들을 넣고 식물을 심었다.

20 어항 덮개에 큰 구멍을 내고 구멍에 그 화분을 넣었다.

21 (fixed / I / pot / the / place / in / clay. / with)
➡ _____

22 (another / made / I / hole / the / in / lid / and / put / through / a / it. / tube)
➡ _____

23 (put / I / water / a / pump / the / in / tank. / fish)
➡ _____

24 (used / I / tube / the / connect / to / pump / the / pot. / to / the)
➡ _____

25 (filled / I / fish / the / with / tank / water / and / put / it. / in / fish / some)
➡ _____

26 (I / then / on / turned / pump. / the)
➡ _____

27 (results: / this / from / experiment, / grew / I / plants / my / raised / and / aquaponics. / with / fish)
➡ _____

28 (just / I / fed / fish, / the / but / plants / the / grown / have / centimeters / 17 / months. / three / in)
➡ _____

29 (fish / the / stay / healthy / and / water / the / clean / is / time. / the / all)
➡ _____

30 (conclusion: / important / some / about / things / aquaponics / learned / were / from / experiment. / this)
➡ _____

31 (water / first, / saved / is / because / plants / the / watering. / need / don't)
➡ _____

32 (second, / is / good / it / for / environment / the / no / because / used. / are / chemicals)
➡ _____

33 (finally, / can / you / do / anywhere / aquaponics / because / doesn't / it / need / space. / much)
➡ _____

34 (found / I / out... // farmers / some / aquaponics / use / produce / to / and / vegetables / fish. / raise)
➡ _____

35 (choose / they / aquaponics / it / because / is / easier / far / traditional / than / gardening.)
➡ _____

36 (it / also, / is / much / a / productive / more / of / way / food. / growing)
➡ _____

37 (planrs / the / much / grow / than / faster / plants / soil, / in / and / space. / saves / it)
➡ _____

38 (hope / I / food / more / produced / is / this / in / way / the / in / future / it / because / healthy / is / us / for / environment. / the / and)
➡ _____

21 찰흙으로 화분을 제자리에 고정하였다.

22 덮개에 또 다른 구멍을 하나 만들고 그 안에 관을 넣었다.

23 어항에 수중 펌프를 넣었다.

24 관을 이용하여 펌프를 화분에 연결하였다.

25 어항에 물을 채우고 물고기 몇 마리를 거기에 넣었다.

26 그러고 나서 펌프를 작동하였다.

27 결과: 이 실험으로 나는 아쿠아포닉스로 식물과 물고기를 키웠다.

28 나는 그저 물고기에 밥만 주었는데도 식물은 석 달 동안 17cm나 자랐다.

29 물고기는 건강을 유지하며 물은 항상 깨끗하다.

30 결론: 아쿠아포닉스에 관한 몇 가지 중요한 사항이 이 실험에서 발견되었다.

31 첫째, 식물에 물을 줄 필요가 없으므로 물이 절약된다.

32 둘째, 화학 물질이 사용되지 않으므로 아쿠아포닉스는 환경에 이롭다.

33 끝으로, 넓은 공간이 필요하지 않으므로 당신은 어디에서나 아쿠아포닉스를 쉽게 할 수 있다.

34 나는 알게 되었다... 몇몇 농부들은 채소를 생산하고 물고기를 키우는 데 아쿠아포닉스를 이용한다.

35 그들은 아쿠아포닉스가 전통 재배 방식보다 훨씬 더 쉽기 때문에 그것을 선택한다.

36 또한, 아쿠아포닉스는 식량을 재배하는 훨씬 더 생산적인 방법이다.

37 식물들이 흙에서 자라는 식물보다 훨씬 빠르게 자라고 공간도 절약한다.

38 그것은 우리와 환경에 훨씬 건강하기 때문에 나는 미래에 더 많은 식량이 이런 방식으로 생산되기를 희망한다.

※ 다음 우리말을 영어로 쓰시오.

1 나의 과학 프로젝트: 가정용 아쿠아포닉스

➡ _____

2 무엇을 읽고 있니?

➡ _____

3 아쿠아포닉스에 관한 기사를 읽고 있어.

➡ _____

4 흙 없이 식물을 재배할 수 있는 방법이야.

➡ _____

5 또 한 가지 장치만으로도 식물과 물고기를 동시에 키울 수 있어.

➡ _____

6 그게 가능하니?

➡ _____

7 곧 알게 될 거야. 내가 과학 프로젝트로 집에서 해 볼 예정이거든.

➡ _____

8 물고기, 박테리아, 식물이 아쿠아포닉스의 주요 부분이다.

➡ _____

9 물고기에게 먹이를 주면, 그것들은 배설물을 만들어 낸다.

➡ _____

10 이 배설물은 박테리아에 의해 식물의 먹이로 바뀐다.

➡ _____

11 식물은 그 먹이를 먹음으로써 물을 정화한다.

➡ _____

12 이러한 과정이 계속해서 반복된다!

➡ _____

13 가정용 아쿠아포닉스   에릭 잭슨

➡ _____

14 질문: 집에서 아쿠아포닉스 장치를 어떻게 만들 수 있을까?

➡ _____

15 아쿠아포닉스가 왜 좋은가?

➡ _____

16 기간: 5월 15일부터 8월 15일까지

➡ _____

17 재료: 화분과 작은 돌들, 어항, 플라스틱 관, 수중 펌프, 식물, 물고기, 커터칼, 찰흙

➡ _____

_____

18 절차: 화분 바닥에 구멍을 뚫었다.
➡ _____

19 그런 후에 화분에 작은 돌들을 넣고 식물을 심었다.
➡ _____

20 어항 덮개에 큰 구멍을 내고 구멍에 그 화분을 넣었다.
➡ _____

21 찰흙으로 화분을 제자리에 고정하였다.
➡ _____

22 덮개에 또 다른 구멍을 하나 만들고 그 안에 관을 넣었다.
➡ _____

23 어항에 수중 펌프를 넣었다.
➡ _____

24 관을 이용하여 펌프를 화분에 연결하였다.
➡ _____

25 어항에 물을 채우고 물고기 몇 마리를 거기에 넣었다.
➡ _____

26 그러고 나서 펌프를 작동하였다.
➡ _____

27 결과: 이 실험으로 나는 아쿠아포닉스로 식물과 물고기를 키웠다.
➡ _____

28 나는 그저 물고기에 밥만 주었는데도 식물은 석 달 동안 17cm나 자랐다.
➡ _____

29 물고기는 건강을 유지하며 물은 항상 깨끗하다.
➡ _____

30 결론: 아쿠아포닉스에 관한 몇 가지 중요한 사항이 이 실험에서 발견되었다.
➡ _____

31 첫째, 식물에 물을 줄 필요가 없으므로 물이 절약된다.
➡ _____

32 둘째, 화학 물질이 사용되지 않으므로 아쿠아포닉스는 환경에 이롭다.
➡ _____

33 끝으로, 넓은 공간이 필요하지 않으므로 당신은 어디에서나 아쿠아포닉스를 쉽게 할 수 있다.
➡ _____

34 나는 알게 되었다... 몇몇 농부들은 채소를 생산하고 물고기를 키우는 데 아쿠아포닉스를 이용한다.
➡ _____

35 그들은 아쿠아포닉스가 전통 재배 방식보다 훨씬 더 쉽기 때문에 그것을 선택한다.
➡ _____

36 또한, 아쿠아포닉스는 식량을 재배하는 훨씬 더 생산적인 방법이다.
➡ _____

37 식물들이 흙에서 자라는 식물보다 훨씬 빠르게 자라고 공간도 절약한다.
➡ _____

38 그것은 우리와 환경에 훨씬 건강하기 때문에 나는 미래에 더 많은 식량이 이런 방식으로 생산되기를 희망한다.
➡ _____

※ 다음 우리말과 일치하도록 빈칸에 알맞은 말을 쓰시오.

After You Read

1. Window _____

2. Do you _____ _____ _____ plants in your house?

3. Then _____ window _____!

4. You can do it _____ _____ a window _____ plastic bottles.

5. _____ bottle _____ _____ the one _____, so you _____ _____ much space.

1. 창문 농경
2. 집에서 식물을 기르고 싶나요?
3. 그렇다면 창문 농경을 해 보세요!
4. 플라스틱 병으로 창문 근처 어디에서나 그것을 할 수 있습니다.
5. 각각의 병은 위에 매달려 있어서 많은 공간을 필요로 하지 않아요.

Think and Write

1. _____ Make Our School _____!

2. _____ _____ energy is _____ _____ us.

3. _____ _____ this problem, _____ _____ these things.

4. First, we should _____ _____ the lights _____ we _____ our classrooms.

5. _____, we should turn off the classroom computers _____ we are _____ _____ them.

6. _____, we should _____ the doors and windows _____ _____ air conditioners.

7. _____ these things will _____ _____ to our school and the environment.

1. 우리 학교를 친환경적으로 만듭시다!
2. 우리 주변에서 많은 에너지가 낭비되고 있습니다.
3. 이 문제를 해결하기 위해, 다음과 같은 일들을 해 봅시다.
4. 먼저 우리가 교실을 나갈 때 전깃불을 꺼야 합니다.
5. 다음 우리가 교실 컴퓨터를 사용하지 않을 때 그것들을 꺼야 합니다.
6. 마지막으로 에어컨을 사용할 때 교실 문과 창문을 닫아야 합니다.
7. 이런 일들을 하는 것은 우리 학교와 환경에 도움이 될 것입니다.

Culture Link

1. This refrigerator _____ _____ electricity.

2. It _____ _____ _____ dirty water.

3. It _____ _____ _____ countries that have _____ electricity.

4. _____ you need water, just _____ this _____ _____!

5. It _____ the use of _____ _____.

6. This _____ _____ is the Warka Water Tower.

7. _____ this tower, people can _____ water _____ the air. It _____ water.

1. 이 냉장고는 전력 없이 작동된다.
2. 그것은 더러운 물에 의해 동력을 공급받는다.
3. 이것은 전력이 거의 없는 나라에 유용하다.
4. 당신이 물이 필요할 때, 그냥 이 물방울을 마셔라!
5. 이것은 플라스틱 병의 사용을 줄인다.
6. 이 특별한 탑은 와카 워터 타워이다.
7. 이 탑 덕분에 사람들은 공기로부터 물을 얻을 수 있다. 이것은 물을 절약한다.

※ 다음 우리말을 영어로 쓰시오.

After You Read

1. 창문 농경
   ➡ _____

2. 집에서 식물을 기르고 싶나요?
   ➡ _____

3. 그렇다면 창문 농경을 해 보세요!
   ➡ _____

4. 플라스틱 병으로 창문 근처 어디에서나 그것을 할 수 있습니다.
   ➡ _____

5. 각각의 병은 위에 매달려 있어서 많은 공간을 필요로 하지 않아요.
   ➡ _____

Think and Write

1. 우리 학교를 친환경적으로 만듭시다!
   ➡ _____

2. 우리 주변에서 많은 에너지가 낭비되고 있습니다.
   ➡ _____

3. 이 문제를 해결하기 위해, 다음과 같은 일들을 해봅시다.
   ➡ _____

4. 먼저 우리가 교실을 나갈 때 전깃불을 꺼야 합니다.
   ➡ _____

5. 다음 우리가 교실 컴퓨터를 사용하지 않을 때 그것들을 꺼야 합니다.
   ➡ _____

6. 마지막으로 에어컨을 사용할 때 교실 문과 창문을 닫아야 합니다.
   ➡ _____

7. 이런 일들을 하는 것은 우리 학교와 환경에 도움이 될 것입니다.
   ➡ _____

Culture Link

1. 이 냉장고는 전력 없이 작동된다.
   ➡ _____

2. 그것은 더러운 물에 의해 동력을 공급받는다.
   ➡ _____

3. 이것은 전력이 거의 없는 나라에 유용하다.
   ➡ _____

4. 당신이 물이 필요할 때, 그냥 이 물방울을 마셔라!
   ➡ _____

5. 이것은 플라스틱 병의 사용을 줄인다.
   ➡ _____

6. 이 특별한 탑은 와카 워터 타워이다.
   ➡ _____

7. 이 탑 덕분에 사람들은 공기로부터 물을 얻을 수 있다. 이것은 물을 절약한다.
   ➡ _____

※ 다음 영어를 우리말로 쓰시오.

01 accident	_____	22 luckily	_____
02 fame	_____	23 serve	_____
03 beauty	_____	24 nursing home	_____
04 moment	_____	25 volunteer	_____
05 spirit	_____	26 homeless	_____
06 collect	_____	27 praise	_____
07 elderly	_____	28 mission	_____
08 survive	_____	29 raise	_____
09 respect	_____	30 honor	_____
10 following	_____	31 turning point	_____
11 goodwill ambassador	_____	32 saying	_____
12 statue	_____	33 favor	_____
13 realize	_____	34 support	_____
14 blind	_____	35 all the time	_____
15 international	_____	36 fall down	_____
16 alive	_____	37 hand out	_____
17 worldwide	_____	38 pass away	_____
18 feed	_____	39 thanks to	_____
19 item	_____	40 clean up	_____
20 medicine	_____	41 give a hand	_____
21 donate	_____	42 search for	_____
		43 take care of	_____

※ 다음 우리말을 영어로 쓰시오.

01 존경하다	
02 눈 먼, 장님의	
03 속담, 격언	
04 (음식을) 제공하다	
05 세계적인	
06 아름다움, 미(美)	
07 임무, 사명	
08 순간, 잠깐	
09 친선 대사	
10 호의, 친절	
11 (그) 다음의	
12 조각상	
13 열다, 개최하다	
14 사고	
15 들어 올리다, (자금을) 모으다	
16 나이가 지긋한	
17 깨닫다, 알아차리다	
18 모으다, 수집하다	
19 양로원	
20 마음, 정신, 영혼	
21 명성	

22 예우하다, 존중하다	
23 살아 있는, 존속하는	
24 전환점	
25 지지하다, 원조하다	
26 칭찬하다	
27 운이 좋게도, 다행스럽게도	
28 풀, 잔디	
29 약	
30 살아남다, 생존하다	
31 기부하다	
32 집 없는, 노숙자의	
33 자원봉사의, 자원 봉사자	
34 먹이를 주다	
35 사망하다	
36 넘어지다	
37 ~을 돌보다	
38 나누어 주다	
39 ~ 덕분에	
40 ~을 돕다	
41 어려움에 처한	
42 ~을 치우다, 청소하다	
43 늘, 내내	

※ 다음 영영풀이에 알맞은 단어를 <보기>에서 골라 쓴 후, 우리말 뜻을 쓰시오.

1 _____ : the state of being famous: _____

2 _____ : not able to see anything: _____

3 _____ : a sudden event that causes damage: _____

4 _____ : to put things together in one place: _____

5 _____ : to say nice things about someone: _____

6 _____ : to suddenly know something: _____

7 _____ : to provide with assistance: _____

8 _____ : to admire or look up to somebody: _____

9 _____ : to give something to help people: _____

10 _____ : a time when a huge change takes place: _____

11 _____ : to treat someone with respect: _____

12 _____ : a special task to be accomplished: _____

13 _____ : a sculpture of a person made from stone or metal: _____

14 _____ : to continue to live after something bad happens: _____

15 _____ : someone who is willing to do a job without getting paid: _____

16 _____ : a place where people who are too old or sick to take care of themselves live:

_____

보기			
statue	fame	turning point	support
blind	nursing home	praise	volunteer
mission	collect	respect	realize
accident	survive	honor	donate

※ 다음 우리말과 일치하도록 빈칸에 알맞은 말을 쓰시오.

Listen & Talk 1 A

B: Mia, _____ you _____ _____ _____ these books?

G: Sure. _____ _____ you _____ _____ do with them?

B: I'm _____ _____ _____ them to a children's library.

B: Mia, 이 책들 옮기는 거 도와줄 수 있어?
G: 그럼. 너 이 책으로 뭐 할 거야?
B: 나는 이 책을 어린이 도서관에 기부할 거야.

Listen & Talk 1 B

B: Hey, Minji! What's _____ _____ your leg?

G: I _____ _____ last week.

B: Really? What _____?

G: I was in _____ _____ _____ _____ a train. But I _____ _____ in the street.

B: Oh, that's _____! _____ _____ anything I _____ _____ for you?

G: Well, _____ _____ _____ _____ _____ _____ this bag?

B: Sure.

B: 민지야! 너 다리에 무슨 문제가 있니?
G: 지난주에 부러졌어.
B: 그래? 무슨 일이야?
G: 기차를 타려고 서두르고 있었어. 그런데 길에 넘어졌어.
B: 오, 정말 끔찍하다! 내가 너를 위해 해 줄 게 있니?
G: 음, 이 가방을 드는 걸 도와줄 수 있니?
B: 그럼.

Listen & Talk 1 C

B1: Wow! These dogs are so dirty. Jay, _____ _____ _____ me _____ _____?

B2: Allen, I'm sorry, _____ I _____. I have _____ _____ the cats now. _____ _____ _____ _____ Nicky?

B1: Okay! Nicky, can I _____ _____ _____ _____?

G: Sure, Allen. _____ is it?

B1: _____ _____ _____ me _____ these dogs?

G: Sure. But I _____ _____ _____ these dogs first. After that, I will help you.

B1: All right! _____ _____.

B1: 와! 이 개들 정말 더럽다. Jay, 이 개들 씻기는 거 도와줄 수 있니?
B2: Allen, 미안한데 못할 거 같아. 지금 이 고양이들에게 밥 줘야 해. Nicky한테 물어보는 게 어때?
B1: 알겠어! Nicky, 나 좀 도와줄 수 있니?
G: 물론이지, Allen. 뭔데?
B1: 이 개들 씻기는 거 도와줄 수 있니?
G: 그럼. 근데 나 이 개들 산책 먼저 시켜야 해. 끝나고 나서 도와줄게.
B1: 그래! 고마워.

Listen & Talk 2 A

G: _____ _____ _____ _____ _____ activities can we do?

B: Why _____ _____ _____ _____ our town's streets?

G: All _____! _____ do it.

G: 우리 어떤 종류의 봉사 활동을 할 수 있을까?
B: 우리 동네 길거리를 청소하는 게 어때?
G: 좋아! 그러자.

Listen & talk 2 B

G: Good morning, students! _____ _____ _____, there _____ a big fire in Mapletown. _____ _____ _____ _____ money and help the people there? Come to our special event _____ the school grounds _____ _____ 3! Please _____ _____ and _____ them. We will sell your items. Then, we will _____ _____ _____ _____ _____ Mapletown. Please _____ _____ to people _____ _____.

Listen & Talk 2 C

B1: Next Wednesday is Volunteer Day. We _____ _____the park last time. What are _____ _____ _____ do this time?

G: Why _____ _____ _____ a _____ _____ and _____ _____ _____?

B2: That's not a _____ _____. But I want _____ _____ _____ _____. _____ _____ _____ _____ a party for the people there?

G: That's a good idea. _____ can we do at the party?

B1: We _____ _____ some food.

B2: And _____ _____ _____ some music? I can play the piano.

G: And I _____ _____ _____ _____.

B1: It _____ _____ a good plan.

Do It Yourself A

G1: We have a class activity day next Friday. What do you _____ _____ _____ _____ _____ _____?

B: _____ _____ we do some _____ _____? We can _____ _____ and _____ our community _____.

G1: That _____ _____, but choosing a good place _____ not easy.

B: We need someone _____ _____ _____ _____ _____ _____.

G1: I know Sumin _____ _____ a lot. Sumin, can you _____ _____ _____ some good places?

G2: Sure. I _____ _____ _____ information on the internet. Why _____ _____ _____ the volunteering website for teens?

B: That's a _____ _____.

G: 좋은 아침입니다, 학생 여러분! 아시다시피, Mapletown에 큰 화재가 있었습니다. 우리 돈을 모금해서 그 곳 사람들을 도와주는 게 어떨까요? 5월 3일 학교 운동장에서 열리는 특별 행사에 오세요! 물품들을 가져와서 그것들을 기부해 주세요. 우리는 여러분의 물품들을 팔 것입니다. 그리고, 모든 돈을 Mapletown에 기부할 것입니다. 어려운 사람들에게 도움을 줍시다.

B1: 다음 주 수요일이 봉사 활동 날이네. 우리 저번에는 공원을 청소했지. 이번엔 뭘 할까?
G: 양로원 가서 청소하는 건 어때?
B2: 나쁜 생각은 아니야. 근데 좀 재미있는 걸 하고 싶어. 거기 계신 분들을 위해 파티를 여는 게 어떨까?
G: 좋은 생각이야. 우리가 파티에서 뭘 할 수 있지?
B1: 음식을 대접할 수 있지.
B2: 그리고 연주를 하는 게 어때? 나 피아노 칠 수 있어.
G: 나는 첼로를 켤 수 있어.
B1: 아주 좋은 계획 같아.

G1: 우리 다음 주 금요일에 학급 활동이 있어. 그 날 어떤 것을 하고 싶니?
B: 우리 자원 봉사 활동들을 해 보는 게 어때? 우리가 다른 사람들을 도울 수 있고, 우리의 지역 사회를 더 좋게 만들 수 있어.
G1: 그거 좋다, 하지만 좋은 장소를 고르는 건 쉽지 않아.
B: 우리는 봉사 활동을 많이 해본 사람이 필요해.
G1: 나는 수민이가 봉사 활동을 많이 한 것을 알고 있어. 수민아, 우리가 좋은 장소들을 찾는 것을 도와주겠니?
G2: 물론. 나는 주로 인터넷에서 정보를 찾아. 십대들을 위한 자원 봉사 웹사이트를 확인해 보는 게 어떠니?
B: 좋은 생각이다.

※ 다음 우리말에 맞도록 대화를 영어로 쓰시오.

Listen & Talk 1 A

B: _____

G: _____

B: _____

해석

B: Mia, 이 책들 옮기는 거 도와줄 수 있어?

G: 그럼. 너 이 책으로 뭐 할 거야?

B: 나는 이 책을 어린이 도서관에 기부할 거야.

Listen & Talk 1 B

B: _____

G: _____

B: _____

G: _____

B: _____

G: _____

B: _____

B: 민지야! 너 다리에 무슨 문제가 있니?

G: 지난주에 부러졌어.

B: 그래? 무슨 일이야?

G: 기차를 타려고 서두르고 있었어. 그런데 길에 넘어졌어.

B: 오, 정말 끔찍하다! 내가 너를 위해 해줄 게 있니?

G: 음, 이 가방을 드는 걸 도와줄 수 있니?

B: 그럼.

Listen & Talk 1 C

B1: _____

B2: _____

B1: _____

G: _____

B1: _____

G: _____

B1: _____

B1: 와! 이 개들 정말 더럽다. Jay, 이 개들 씻기는 거 도와줄 수 있니?

B2: Allen, 미안한데 못할 거 같아. 지금 이 고양이들에게 밥 줘야 해. Nicky 한테 물어보는 게 어때?

B1: 알겠어! Nicky, 나 좀 도와줄 수 있니?

G: 물론이지, Allen. 뭔데?

B1: 이 개들 씻기는 거 도와줄 수 있니?

G: 그럼. 근데 나 이 개들 산책 먼저 시켜야 해. 끝나고 나서 도와줄게.

B1: 그래! 고마워.

Listen & Talk 2 A

G: _____

B: _____

G: _____

G: 우리 어떤 종류의 봉사 활동을 할 수 있을까?

B: 우리 동네 길거리를 청소하는 게 어때?

G: 좋아! 그러자.

Listen & talk 2 B

G: _____

_____

_____

_____

_____

Listen & Talk 2 C

B1: _____

_____

G: _____

B2: _____

_____

G: _____

B1: _____

B2: _____

G: _____

B1: _____

Do It Yourself A

G1: _____

B: _____

_____

G1: _____

B: _____

G1: _____

_____

G2: _____

_____

B: _____

G: 좋은 아침입니다, 학생 여러분! 아시다시피, Mapletown에 큰 화재가 있었습니다. 우리 돈을 모금해서 그 곳 사람들을 도와주는 게 어떨까요? 5월 3일 학교 운동장에서 열리는 특별 행사에 오세요! 물품들을 가져와서 그것들을 기부해 주세요. 우리는 여러분의 물품들을 팔 것입니다. 그리고, 모든 돈을 Mapletown에 기부할 것입니다. 어려운 사람들에게 도움을 줍시다.

B1: 다음 주 수요일이 봉사 활동 날이네. 우리 저번에는 공원을 청소했지. 이번엔 뭘 할까?
G: 양로원 가서 청소하는 건 어때?
B2: 나쁜 생각은 아니야. 근데 좀 재미있는 걸 하고 싶어. 거기 계신 분들을 위해 파티를 여는 게 어떨까?
G: 좋은 생각이야. 우리가 파티에서 뭘 할 수 있지?
B1: 음식을 대접할 수 있지.
B2: 그리고 연주를 하는 게 어때? 나 피아노 칠 수 있어.
G: 나는 첼로를 켤 수 있어.
B1: 아주 좋은 계획 같아.

G1: 우리 다음 주 금요일에 학급 활동이 있어. 그 날 어떤 것을 하고 싶니?
B: 우리 자원 봉사 활동들을 해 보는 게 어때? 우리가 다른 사람들을 도울 수 있고, 우리의 지역 사회를 더 좋게 만들 수 있어.
G1: 그거 좋다, 하지만 좋은 장소를 고르는 건 쉽지 않아.
B: 우리는 봉사 활동을 많이 해본 사람이 필요해.
G1: 나는 수민이가 봉사 활동을 많이 한 것을 알고 있어. 수민아, 우리가 좋은 장소들을 찾는 것을 도와주겠니?
G2: 물론. 나는 주로 인터넷에서 정보를 찾아. 십대들을 위한 자원 봉사 웹사이트를 확인해 보는 게 어떠니?
B: 좋은 생각이다.

※ 다음 우리말과 일치하도록 빈칸에 알맞은 것을 골라 쓰시오.

1 The _____ of _____

    A. Audrey   B. Spirit

2 _____ World War II, a _____ girl and her mother _____ hungry and sick.

    A. little   B. during   C. were

3 The only food _____ they could _____ _____ grass.

    A. that   B. was   C. find

4 The little girl _____ _____ all the _____.

    A. scared   B. felt   C. time

5 _____, the girl survived, _____ _____ the help of others.

    A. to   B. luckily   C. thanks

6 One of the _____ that _____ her _____ UNICEF.

    A. helped   B. was   C. groups

7 _____, the girl _____ a _____ movie star.

    A. worldwide   B. became   C. later

8 _____ _____ was Audrey Hepburn.

    A. name   B. her

9 _____ she grew _____, Hepburn became a symbol of _____.

    A. beauty   B. up   C. when

10 She was very popular _____ _____ her hit movies, _____ _____ *My Fair Lady* and *Roman Holiday*.

    A. of   B. as   C. such   D. because

11 The little black dress _____ she _____ in a movie is famous _____ today.

    A. wore   B. even   C. which

12 Many people _____ _____ her _____.

    A. style   B. love   C. still

13 The autumn of 1987 was a _____ _____ in Hepburn's _____.

    A. life   B. point   C. turning

14 She _____ to an _____ music _____ in Macau.

    A. went   B. festival   C. international

15 Many people _____ _____ at the festival, and the money _____ to UNICEF.

    A. money   B. went   C. donated

---

1 오드리의 정신

2 제2차 세계 대전 동안, 한 어린 소녀와 그녀의 어머니는 굶주리고 아팠다.

3 그들이 찾을 수 있었던 유일한 음식은 풀뿐이었다.

4 어린 소녀는 내내 겁에 질려 있었다.

5 다행히도, 소녀는 다른 사람들의 도움 덕분에 살아남았다.

6 그녀를 도왔던 단체 중 하나는 유니세프(국제 연합 아동 기금)였다.

7 후에, 소녀는 세계적인 영화배우가 되었다.

8 그녀의 이름은 오드리 헵번이었다.

9 그녀가 자랐을 때, 헵번은 아름다움의 상징이 되었다.

10 그녀는 〈마이 페어 레이디〉와 〈로마의 휴일〉과 같은 흥행 영화들로 인해 매우 인기가 있었다.

11 그녀가 영화에서 입었던 아담한 검은 드레스는 심지어 오늘날까지도 유명하다.

12 많은 사람이 여전히 그녀의 스타일을 사랑한다.

13 1987년 가을은 헵번의 인생 전환점이었다.

14 그녀는 마카오의 한 국제 음악 축제에 갔다.

15 많은 사람이 축제에서 돈을 기부했고, 그 돈은 유니세프로 보내졌다.

16 _____ _____ her fame, UNICEF collected _____ money
_____ ever before.

    A. than   B. to   C. more   D. thanks

17 Hepburn _____ that her _____ could help _____, so she
became a UNICEF Goodwill Ambassador.

    A. realized   B. others   C. fame

18 First, Hepburn _____ _____ Ethiopia _____ 1988.

    A. to   B. in   C. went

19 _____, she _____ food _____ hungry children.

    A. brought   B. to   C. there

20 She was _____ _____ their _____ were very difficult.

    A. lives   B. because   C. shocked

21 _____ that, she _____ in _____ countries.

    A. after   B. other   C. volunteered

22 In 1990, she _____ Vietnam to _____ _____ medicine
and _____ clean drinking water programs.

    A. out   B. visited   C. support   D. hand

23 Her last trip was _____ Somalia in 1992, and she _____
_____ the _____ year.

    A. away   B. to   C. following   D. passed

24 Many people _____ her _____ and style, but Hepburn's
_____ was her _____.

    A. beauty   B. heart   C. real   D. praised

25 _____ _____ her, UNICEF made a _____, *The Spirit of
Audrey*.

    A. honor   B. statue   C. to

26 People who _____ her _____ her mission _____.

    A. alive   B. keep   C. respect

27 Her _____ _____ shows her _____.

    A. saying   B. favorite   C. mission

28 _____ *you* _____ *older,* _____ *you have two hands.*

    A. remember   B. get   C. as

29 _____ *is for helping* _____, *and the* _____ *is for helping*
_____.

    A. other   B. one   C. others   D. yourself

16 그녀의 명성 덕분에, 유니세프는 어느 때보다도 더 많은 돈을 모았다.

17 헵번은 자신의 명성이 다른 사람들을 도울 수 있다는 것을 깨닫고, 유니세프 친선 대사가 되었다.

18 먼저, 헵번은 1988년에 에티오피아로 갔다.

19 그곳에서, 그녀는 굶주린 아이들에게 음식을 가져다주었다.

20 그녀는 그들의 삶이 매우 어려웠기 때문에 충격을 받았다.

21 그 후, 그녀는 다른 나라들에서도 봉사하였다.

22 1990년, 그녀는 의약품을 나눠 주고 깨끗한 식수 프로그램을 지원하기 위하여 베트남을 방문하였다.

23 그녀의 마지막 여행은 1992년 소말리아에 간 것이었으며, 이듬해 그녀는 사망하였다.

24 많은 사람이 그녀의 아름다움과 스타일을 칭송했지만, 헵번의 진정한 아름다움은 그녀의 마음이었다.

25 그녀를 기리기 위해, 유니세프는 '오드리의 정신'이라는 동상을 만들었다.

26 그녀를 존경하는 사람들이 그녀의 사명을 이어 나가고 있다.

27 그녀가 가장 좋아했던 구절은 그녀의 사명을 보여 준다.

28 나이가 들어갈수록, 당신에게 손이 두 개가 있다는 것을 기억하라.

29 한 손은 자신을 돕기 위한 것이고, 다른 한 손은 타인을 돕기 위한 것이다.

※ 다음 괄호 안의 단어들을 우리말에 맞도록 바르게 배열하시오.

1 (Spirit / The / Audrey / of)
➡ _____

2 (World / II, / During / War / little / a / girl / and / mother / her / were / sick. / and / hungry)
➡ _____

3 (only / the / that / food / they / find / could / grass. / was)
➡ _____

4 (little / the / girl / scared / felt / time. / the / all)
➡ _____

5 (the / luckily / girl / survived, / to / thanks / the / of / others. / help)
➡ _____

6 (of / one / groups / the / helped / that / UNICEF. / was / her)
➡ _____

7 (the / later, / girl / became / worldwide / a / star. / movie)
➡ _____

8 (name / her / Hepburn. / Audrey / was)
➡ _____

9 (she / when / up, / grew / became / Hepburn / symbol / a / beauty. / of)
➡ _____

10 (was / she / popular / very / of / because / her / movies, / hit / as / such / *Lady* / *Fair* / *My* / and / *Holiday*. / *Roman*)
➡ _____

11 (little / the / dress / black / she / which / wore / a / in / movie / is / today. / even / famous)
➡ _____

12 (people / many / love / still / style. / her)
➡ _____

13 (autumn / the / 1987 / of / was / turning / a / point / life. / Hepburn's / in)
➡ _____

14 (went / she / to / international / an / festival / music / Macau. / in)
➡ _____

15 (people / many / money / donated / the / at / festival, / and / money / the / UNICEF. / to / went)
➡ _____

1 오드리의 정신

2 제2차 세계 대전 동안, 한 어린 소녀와 그녀의 어머니는 굶주리고 아팠다.

3 그들이 찾을 수 있었던 유일한 음식은 풀뿐이었다.

4 어린 소녀는 내내 겁에 질려 있었다.

5 다행히도, 소녀는 다른 사람들의 도움 덕분에 살아남았다.

6 그녀를 도왔던 단체 중 하나는 유니세프(국제 연합 아동 기금)였다.

7 후에, 소녀는 세계적인 영화배우가 되었다.

8 그녀의 이름은 오드리 헵번이었다.

9 그녀가 자랐을 때, 헵번은 아름다움의 상징이 되었다.

10 그녀는 〈마이 페어 레이디〉와 〈로마의 휴일〉과 같은 흥행 영화들로 인해 매우 인기가 있었다.

11 그녀가 영화에서 입었던 아담한 검은 드레스는 심지어 오늘날까지도 유명하다.

12 많은 사람이 여전히 그녀의 스타일을 사랑한다.

13 1987년 가을은 헵번의 인생 전환점이었다.

14 그녀는 마카오의 한 국제 음악 축제에 갔다.

15 많은 사람이 축제에서 돈을 기부했고, 그 돈은 유니세프로 보내졌다.

16 (to / thanks / fame, / her / UNICEF / more / collected / money / ever / before. / than)
➡ _____

17 (realized / Hepburn / that / fame / her / help / could / others, / she / so / became / UNICEF / a / Ambassador. / Goodwill)
➡ _____
_____

18 (Hepburn / first, / to / went / 1988 / in / Ethiopia)
➡ _____

19 (she / there, / brought / to / food / children. / hungry)
➡ _____

20 (was / she / because / shocked / lives / their / difficult. / very / were)
➡ _____

21 (that, / after / volunteered / she / countries. / other / in)
➡ _____

22 (1990, / in / visited / she / Vietnam / hand / to / medicine / out / and / clean / support / drinking / programs. / water)
➡ _____
_____

23 (last / her / trip / to / was / Somalia / 1992, / in / she / and / away / passed / year. / following / the)
➡ _____
_____

24 (people / many / her / praised / beauty / and / style, / but / real / Hepburn's / beauty / heart. / her / was)
➡ _____
_____

25 (honor / to / her, / made / UNICEF / statue, / a / of / Spirit / Audrey. / The)
➡ _____

26 (who / people / her / respect / keep / alive. / mission / her)
➡ _____

27 (favorite / her / shows / mission. / her / saying)
➡ _____

28 (you / as / older, / get / you / remember / hands. / two / have)
➡ _____

29 (is / one / helping / for / yourself, / the / and / other / for / is / others. / helping)
➡ _____

16 그녀의 명성 덕분에, 유니세프는 어느 때보다도 더 많은 돈을 모았다.

17 헵번은 자신의 명성이 다른 사람들을 도울 수 있다는 것을 깨닫고, 유니세프 친선 대사가 되었다.

18 먼저, 헵번은 1988년에 에티오피아로 갔다.

19 그곳에서, 그녀는 굶주린 아이들에게 음식을 가져다주었다.

20 그녀는 그들의 삶이 매우 어려웠기 때문에 충격을 받았다.

21 그 후, 그녀는 다른 나라들에서도 봉사하였다.

22 1990년, 그녀는 의약품을 나눠 주고 깨끗한 식수 프로그램을 지원하기 위하여 베트남을 방문하였다.

23 그녀의 마지막 여행은 1992년 소말리아에 간 것이었으며, 이듬해 그녀는 사망하였다.

24 많은 사람이 그녀의 아름다움과 스타일을 칭송했지만, 헵번의 진정한 아름다움은 그녀의 마음이었다.

25 그녀를 기리기 위해, 유니세프는 '오드리의 정신'이라는 동상을 만들었다.

26 그녀를 존경하는 사람들이 그녀의 사명을 이어 나가고 있다.

27 그녀가 가장 좋아했던 구절은 그녀의 사명을 보여 준다.

28 나이가 들어갈수록, 당신에게 손이 두 개가 있다는 것을 기억하라.

29 한 손은 자신을 돕기 위한 것이고, 다른 한 손은 타인을 돕기 위한 것이다.

※ 다음 우리말을 영어로 쓰시오.

1 오드리의 정신

➡ _____

2 제2차 세계 대전 동안, 한 어린 소녀와 그녀의 어머니는 굶주리고 아팠다.

➡ _____

3 그들이 찾을 수 있었던 유일한 음식은 풀뿐이었다.

➡ _____

4 어린 소녀는 내내 겁에 질려 있었다.

➡ _____

5 다행히도, 소녀는 다른 사람들의 도움 덕분에 살아남았다.

➡ _____

6 그녀를 도왔던 단체 중 하나는 유니세프(국제 연합 아동 기금)였다.

➡ _____

7 후에, 소녀는 세계적인 영화배우가 되었다.

➡ _____

8 그녀의 이름은 오드리 헵번이었다.

➡ _____

9 그녀가 자랐을 때, 헵번은 아름다움의 상징이 되었다.

➡ _____

10 그녀는 〈마이 페어 레이디〉와 〈로마의 휴일〉과 같은 흥행 영화들로 인해 매우 인기가 있었다.

➡ _____

11 그녀가 영화에서 입었던 아담한 검은 드레스는 심지어 오늘날까지도 유명하다.

➡ _____

12 많은 사람이 여전히 그녀의 스타일을 사랑한다.

➡ _____

13 1987년 가을은 헵번의 인생 전환점이었다.

➡ _____

14 그녀는 마카오의 한 국제 음악 축제에 갔다.

➡ _____

15 많은 사람이 축제에서 돈을 기부했고, 그 돈은 유니세프로 보내졌다.

➡ _____

16 그녀의 명성 덕분에, 유니세프는 어느 때보다도 더 많은 돈을 모았다.

➡ _____

17 헵번은 자신의 명성이 다른 사람들을 도울 수 있다는 것을 깨닫고, 유니세프 친선 대사가 되었다.

➡ _____

18 먼저, 헵번은 1988년에 에티오피아로 갔다.

➡ _____

19 그곳에서, 그녀는 굶주린 아이들에게 음식을 가져다주었다.

➡ _____

20 그녀는 그들의 삶이 매우 어려웠기 때문에 충격을 받았다.

➡ _____

21 그 후, 그녀는 다른 나라들에서도 봉사하였다.

➡ _____

22 1990년, 그녀는 의약품을 나눠 주고 깨끗한 식수 프로그램을 지원하기 위하여 베트남을 방문하였다.

➡ _____

23 그녀의 마지막 여행은 1992년 소말리아에 간 것이었으며, 이듬해 그녀는 사망하였다.

➡ _____

24 많은 사람이 그녀의 아름다움과 스타일을 칭송했지만, 헵번의 진정한 아름다움은 그녀의 마음이었다.

➡ _____

25 그녀를 기리기 위해, 유니세프는 '오드리의 정신'이라는 동상을 만들었다.

➡ _____

26 그녀를 존경하는 사람들이 그녀의 사명을 이어 나가고 있다.

➡ _____

27 그녀가 가장 좋아했던 구절은 그녀의 사명을 보여 준다.

➡ _____

28 나이가 들어갈수록, 당신에게 손이 두 개가 있다는 것을 기억하라.

➡ _____

29 한 손은 자신을 돕기 위한 것이고, 다른 한 손은 타인을 돕기 위한 것이다.

➡ _____

영어 기출 문제집

적중100

1학기

정답 및 해설

능률 | 김성곤

중 2

영어 기출 문제집

1학기

정답 및 해설

능률 | 김성곤

중 2

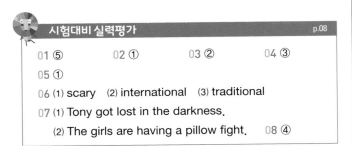

Understand the World

시험대비 실력평가   p.08

01 ⑤   02 ①   03 ②   04 ③

05 ①

06 (1) scary   (2) international   (3) traditional

07 (1) Tony got lost in the darkness.

    (2) The girls are having a pillow fight.   08 ④

01 last: 계속되다, 지속되다

02 greet: 맞이하다, 환영하다 welcome: 환영하다

03 represent: 나타내다, 상징하다 wreath: 화환, 화관

04 ③ try -ing: (시험삼아) ~해 보다 pray: 기도하다 ease: 편안
하게 하다 ④ meditation: 명상

05 lock: 자물쇠; 잠그다

06 (1) scary: 무서운, 두려운, 겁나는/그녀는 내게 무서운 이야기
들을 해 주었다. (2) international: 국제적인, 세계적인/수출
법규가 국제 통상에서 중요한 요인이 되었다. (3) traditional:
전통의, 전통적인/그녀는 한국 전통 의상을 입고 있다.

07 (1) darkness: 어둠, 암흑 (2) pillow: 베개

08 toward: ~ 쪽으로

서술형 시험대비   p.09

01 (1) (r)ude   (2) (t)ry   (3) (e)vil   (4) (v)ictory

02 (1) experience   (2) mean   (3) arrive   (4) celebrate

03 (1) face   (2) separation, able

04 colored

05 (1) at   (2) of

06 (1) She greeted us with a kind smile.

    (2) The meeting lasted three hours.

    (3) I put the coin in her palm.

    (4) A red flag represents danger.

01 보기는 동의어 관계이다. good: 좋은 nice: 좋은 (1) impolite:
버릇없는, 무례한 rude: 무례한 (2) attempt: 시도하다 try: 한
번 해 보다 (3) wicked: 못된, 사악한 evil: 사악한, 악마의 (4)
success: 성공, 성과 victory: 승리, 성공

02 (1) experience: 경험하다/호기심을 지키는 것이 내가 지속적

으로 새로운 것을 배우는 즐거움을 경험하도록 할 것이다. (2)
mean: 의미하다/그것이 내가 게으르다는 것을 의미하는 것은
아니다. (3) arrive: 도착하다/다음 기차는 언제 도착하나요?
(4) celebrate: 축하하다/그들은 크리스마스와 새해를 같이 축
하한다.

03 (1) face: ~을 향하다 (2) separation: 분리, 이별 be able to 동
사원형: ~할 수 있다

04 color: ~에 색칠하다 colored: 채색된, 색깔이 있는

05 (1) stay at: ~에서 머무르다 point at: ~을 가리키다 (2) be
afraid of: ~을 두려워하다 remind A of B: A에게 B를 생각
나게 하다

06 (1) greet: 맞이하다, 환영하다 (2) last: 계속되다, 지속되다
(3) palm: 손바닥 (4) represent: 나타내다, 상징하다

교과서

Conversation

핵심 Check   p.10~11

1 (C) → (A) → (B)   2 explain what, means

3 I'd like to know what that means.
   It means you should think carefully

4 Have you watched / have, Have

5 (C) → (A) → (D) → (B)

6 Have you had *gimchi* before?

교과서 대화문 익히기

Check(√) True or False   p.12

[1] T   [2] T   [3] F   [4] T

교과서 확인학습   p.14~15

Listen & Talk 1 A

Have you, been / haven't, Have / have, last year, was
/ sounds, to go, someday

Listen & Talk 1 B

to, Festival, many different traditional games / looks,
Which, should / Have you ever / No, I haven't / from /
How / on, throw, at / sounds fun

시험대비 기본평가   p.16

01 ①　　02 ②　　03 ③　　04 ④
05 ①

01 경험 유무를 물을 때 "Have you (ever) 과거분사 ~?"로 말한다.

02 mean: 의미하다 in Korea: 한국에서

03 'Have you 과거분사 ~?'는 경험을 묻는 표현이다.

04 (C) 고로드키 게임을 해 봤는지 묻자, (A) 안 해봤다고 대답하고 무엇인지 질문한다. (B) 상대방은 고로드키 게임이 러시아 전통 게임이라고 설명해 준다.

05 'have been to 장소'는 '~에 가 본 경험이 있다'의 의미이고, 'have gone to 장소'는 '~에 갔다(그래서 지금 없다)'는 의미이므로 gone을 been으로 바꿔야 적절하다.

시험대비 실력평가   p.17~18

01 ③　　02 ②　　03 ②　　04 What does an umbrella mean in China?　　05 ②
06 ②, ④　　07 (A) What is that? (B) Have you ever been to a Holi festival? (C) When is the festival? (D) Should I bring anything?　　08 ④　　09 ③
10 exciting　　11 ①　　12 a traditional game from, play, putting five sticks, throwing a bat

01 (A) give+me(간접목적어)+Yeot(직접목적어): 나에게 엿을 주다 (B) What does that mean (in Korea)?: (한국에서는) 이게 어떤 의미니? mean: 의미하다

02 브라질에 가 본 경험을 묻는 질문에, (B) 없다고 대답하며 상대방의 경험을 묻고 (A) 작년에 갔었는데 삼바 축제가 있었다고 답하자 (C) 삼바 축제에 흥미를 가지며 가고 싶다고 말한다.

03 'What about you?'는 상대방의 생각이나 의견을 묻는 표현이다. 여자아이는 상대방의 질문에 답하면서 상대방은 무엇을 살지 'What about you?'로 물어보고 있다.

04 What does ~ mean?: ~이 어떤 의미니?

05 ⓓ bad something → something bad, -thing으로 끝나는 부정대명사(something, anything, nothing 등)는 형용사가 뒤에서 수식한다. ⓔ sounds → sound, 주어가 the words로 복수 명사이므로 동사에 s를 붙이지 않는다.

06 ① 여자아이는 책을 Ling의 선물로 살 것이다. ② 중국에서 책의 의미는 대화에서 나와 있지 않다. ③ 이번 주 수요일이 Ling의 생일이다. ④ 초콜릿을 사러 갈 장소는 나와 있지 않다. ⑤ 중국인에게 우산은 이별을 의미하므로, 좋은 선물이 아니다.

07 (A) 다음에 Holi festival에 대해 설명하고 있다. (B) 다음에 'No, I haven't.'라고 답하고 있다. (C) 다음에 언제인지 답하고 있다. (D) 다음에 하얀 옷을 입어야 한다고 답하고 있다.

08 ④ 색깔이 있는 옷이 아니라 하얀 옷을 입어야 한다.

09 상대방의 경험에 대해 물어볼 때는, 현재완료 시제를 사용하여 'Have you 과거분사 ~?'라고 묻는다. 경험을 묻는 말에 'Yes, I have.'나 'No, I haven't.'로 대답할 수 있다.

10 exciting: 흥미로운

11 ⓑ~ⓔ는 gorodki를 가리키지만 ⓐ는 여러 가지 전통적인 게임을 하는 것을 가리킨다.

12 traditional: 전통적인 from: (출처·기원) … 출신의[에서 온] the way to 동사원형: ~하는 방법 throw: ~을 던지다 at: (방향) ~으로

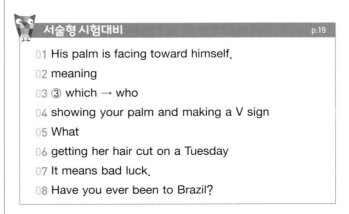

서술형 시험대비   p.19

01 His palm is facing toward himself.
02 meaning
03 ③ which → who
04 showing your palm and making a V sign
05 What
06 getting her hair cut on a Tuesday
07 It means bad luck.
08 Have you ever been to Brazil?

01 palm: 손바닥 face: ~을 향하다 toward: ~쪽으로

02 mean: 의미하다 meaning: 의미

03 사람(The boy)이 선행사이므로 주격 관계대명사 who를 사용해야 한다. The boy who is making the V sign: V사인을 하고 있는 소년

04 (C)가 가리키는 것은 여자아이가 말한 손바닥을 보여 주면서 V사인을 만드는 것을 의미한다..

05 What do you see in this picture?: 이 그림에서 무엇이 보이니? What does that mean?: 이게 어떤 의미니?

06 get+목적어+목적격보어(p.p): 목적어가 ~되도록 시키다 on+요일: ~요일에

07 mean: 의미하다 bad luck: 불운

08 Have you ever been to 장소?: ~에 가 본 적 있니? Brazil: 브라질

Grammar

핵심 Check   p.20~21

1 (1) have gone (2) have, visited (3) Have, read

2 (1) so busy that (2) so big that

시험대비 기본평가   p.22

01 (1) visit → visited (2) has finished → finished
   (3) Do you have → Have you (4) what → that
   (5) very → so (6) for → since (7) have → has

02 ③   03 ①

---

01 (1) 현재완료는 'have[has]+과거분사'의 형태이다. (2) 현재완료는 과거를 나타내는 어구와 함께 쓸 수 없다. (3) 현재완료의 의문문은 have 동사를 주어 앞으로 보낸다. (4), (5) 'so+형용사[부사]+that+주어+동사'의 형태로 '매우 …해서 ~하다'는 의미를 나타낸다. (6) 현재완료에서 'since+시간 명사', 'for+기간 명사'를 쓴다. (7) 주어가 3인칭 단수이므로 has를 써야 한다.

02 ③ Joel has worked for 6 hours straight.

03 so ... that ~: 너무 …해서 ~하다

시험대비 실력평가   p.23~25

01 ④   02 ①   03 ⑤   04 ③
05 (1) visited (2) has (3) gone (4) before (5) hasn't
06 ①   07 ⑤   08 (1) so (2) that

---

(3) such (4) couldn't   09 ④   10 ②

11 ②

12 (1) Julia got too angry to speak.
   (2) Sean is rich enough to buy the expensive car.
   (3) The panda is too cute for me to take my eyes off him.
   (4) The house was nice enough for Melanie to want to live there.

13 ④   14 ④

15 (1) Suyeon has just arrived at Busan Station. 또는 Suyeon arrived at Busan Station an hour ago.
   (2) Ron and his sisters have gone to England.
   (3) Grace was too fat to wear the beautiful dress. Grace was so fat that she couldn't wear the beautiful dress.
   (4) The drama was so boring that I turned off the TV.
   (5) He has lived in Busan since 2010.

16 ⓐ visited ⓑ been

17 (1) for → since (2) gone → been (3) too → so
   (4) poor enough → so poor (5) has lost → lost

18 ②

---

01 현재완료 의문문은 'Have+주어+과거분사~?'이다. 'have gone to ~'는 '~에 가버리고 없다'는 뜻이므로 1인칭 주어를 쓸 수 없다.

02 '…해서 ~하다'의 의미인 'so ... that ~' 구문이다.

03 현재완료형의 질문에 대한 답은 have[has] 동사를 이용해 답한다.

04 so ... that ~'은 '너무[매우] ~해서 …하다'의 의미로 원인과 결과를 나타낸다.

05 (1) 현재완료는 'have[has]+과거분사'의 형태이다. (2) 주어가 3인칭 단수이므로 has가 적절하다. (3) have[has] gone to는 '~에 가고 없다'는 결과를 나타낸다. (4) ago는 단독으로 쓸 수 없다. (5) 현재완료의 부정형은 'have[has] not+과거분사'이다.

06 ① Dad's explanation was so clear that we could understand it easily.

07 현재완료의 부정은 have 다음에 not이나 never를 붙인다.

08 (1), (2) '매우 …해서 ~하다'의 의미인 'so ... that ~' 구문이다. (3) 'so ... that' 구문에서 that 앞에 형용사나 부사 대신 명사가 오면 so 대신 such를 쓴다. (4) so+형용사/부사+that+주어+couldn't+동사원형: 너무 ~하여 …할 수 없었다

09 현재완료에서 'since+시간 명사', 'for+기간 명사'

10 'so ... that ~'은 so 뒤의 형용사나 부사가 원인을 나타내며, 접속사 that 뒤에는 그에 따른 결과를 나타낸다.

11 ②번은 경험 용법으로 쓰였고 나머지는 다 완료 용법으로 쓰였다.

12 (1) so ... that 주어 can't ~ = too ... to ~ (2) so ... that 주어 can ~ = ... enough to ~ (3), (4) 'so ... that ~' 구문에서 주어가 서로 다를 경우 'too ... to ~'나 '... enough to ~'로 바꿔 쓸 때 'for+목적격'으로 주어를 나타낸다.

13 현재완료의 결과적 용법(…해서 (그 결과) 지금 ~하다)을 이용하여 과거에 러시아로 가서 아직도 그곳에 머무르고 있다는 현재의 결과를 나타내도록 한다.

14 so ... that ~: 너무 …해서 ~하다

15 (1) 현재완료는 과거를 나타내는 어구와 함께 쓸 수 없다. (2) have[has] been to는 '~에 가 본적이 있다'는 경험을 나타내고, have[has] gone to는 '~에 가고 없다'는 결과를 나타내므로 have gone to로 고쳐야 한다. (3), (4) 'so ... that ~'이나 'too ... to ~'로 나타내는 것이 적절하다. (5) 현재완료에서 'since+시간 명사', 'for+기간 명사'

16 ⓐ last week이라는 과거를 나타내는 부사구가 있으므로 과거형으로 써야 한다. ⓑ 'have gone to'는 결과를 나타내는 말로 1인칭을 주어로 쓸 수 없다. 여기서 there는 to Vietnam을 대신하고 있다.

17 (1) 현재완료에서 'since+시간 명사', 'for+기간 명사' (2) have[has] been to는 '~에 가 본 적이 있다'는 경험을 나타내고, have[has] gone to는 '~에 가고 없다'는 결과를 나타낸다. (3), (4) so ... that ~: 너무 …해서 ~하다 (5) 현재완료는 과거를 나타내는 어구와 함께 쓸 수 없다.

18 too ... to ~ = so ... that 주어 can't ~, ... enough to ~ = so ... that 주어 can

---

서술형 시험대비   p.26~27

01 (1) Laura has lived in Chicago since 1998.
   (2) Dan has lost his cell phone.

02 (1) Kate is so young that she can't drive a car.
   (2) Stefanie is so wise that she can give advice to her friends.

03 (1) James has played soccer since he was a child.
   (2) It rains so heavily that we can't go outside.
   (3) Charlie has studied Korean for six months.

04 (1) Mr. Brown has lived in New York since 2015.
   (2) We have been to Sydney.
   (3) Elle didn't take a walk yesterday.
   (4) My long padding coat is warm enough for me to endure the winter.
   (5) Lylian was so afraid that she couldn't open her eyes.

---

05 (1) Mike was too sick to go to work yesterday.
   (2) The *samgyetang* was so hot that Amy could not eat it.
   (3) His essay was nice enough for his teacher to be satisfied.
   (4) Tom ran so fast that he could catch the last bus.

06 (1) His neighbor's party was so noisy that he couldn't sleep at all.
   (2) Rose has not arrived at the library yet.
   (3) The man was so kind that he helped me right away.
   (4) I have been to Paris once.
   (5) Andrew has left his smartphone in the train.

07 (1) Bella has never(not) driven a car before.
   (2) Bella has visited Angkor Wat before.
   (3) Bella has never[not] tasted Vietnamese food before.
   (4) Bella has practiced yoga before.

08 (1) The flowers are so beautiful that many people come to see them.
   (2) The house was so expensive that we decided not to buy it.
   (3) This dish is so spicy that I need to drink a lot of milk.
   (4) The movie was so sad that I cried a lot.
   (5) You are so smart that you always get A's.

09 has gone

---

01 (1) 1998년에 살기 시작해서 지금도 살고 있는 것이므로 현재완료의 '계속'을 이용한다. (2) cell phone을 잃어버려서 지금 없는 것이므로 현재완료의 '결과'를 이용한다.

02 too ... to ~ = so ... that 주어 can't ~, ... enough to ~ = so ... that 주어 can

03 (1), (3) 현재완료의 계속적 용법을 이용한다. (2) so ... that 주어 can't ~: 너무 …해서 ~할 수 없다

04 (1) 현재완료에서 'since+시간 명사', 'for+기간 명사' (2) have gone to는 3인칭만 주어가 될 수 있다. (3) 현재완료는 과거를 나타내는 부사와 함께 쓸 수 없다. (4) enough 는 형용사 다음에 와서 '... enough to ~'의 형식으로 쓰인다. (5) so ... that 주어 can't ~ = too ... to ~: 너무 …해서 ~할 수 없다

05 too ... to ~ = so ... that 주어 can't ~, ... enough to부정사 = so ... that 주어 can ~ / 이때 to부정사 앞에 for 목적격으로 쓰인 것은 to부정사의 의미상의 주어로 that 이하의 절로 바꿀 때는 주격으로 바꿔야 하며, to부정사로 썼을 때 생략된 동사의 목적어는 써 주어야 한다.

06 (1), (3) so+형용사[부사]+that+주어+동사: 매우 …해서 ~하

다 (2) 현재완료의 '완료' 용법 (4) 현재완료의 '경험' 용법 (5) 현재완료의 '결과' 용법

07 현재완료의 '경험' 용법을 이용한다.

08 'so+형용사[부사]+that+주어+동사'의 형태로 '매우 …해서 ~하다'라는 의미이다. so 뒤의 형용사나 부사는 원인을 나타내며, 접속사 that 뒤에 나오는 내용은 그에 따른 결과를 나타낸다.

09 현재완료의 '결과' 용법을 이용한다.

Reading

확인문제 p.28

1 T 2 F 3 T 4 F 5 T

확인문제 p.29

1 T 2 F 3 F 4 T 5 T 6 F

교과서 확인학습 A p.30~31

01 Traditional   02 from a sister school
03 stay at, for a week   04 him the guest room   05 stay here   06 is full of
07 Look at   08 these things   09 They're
10 on my pillow, scary   11 Not really, symbols of   12 surprising, remind, of
13 shows   14 meet, greet each other
15 Have you ever seen
16 haven't, so, that   17 For a long time, good guards   18 close their eyes   19 interesting   20 watch over, That's why, like   21 understand   22 walk around
23 that piece of paper   24 Do you mean
25 a rooster   26 crow   27 a new day
28 go away, crows   29 I've never heard   30 Actually, afraid
31 for me   32 draw a big rooster
33 Put, above, protect   34 will
35 so much that 36 traditional Korean symbols
37 a lot of them 38 with my family

교과서 확인학습 B p.32~33

1 Traditional Korean Symbols
2 Peter is visiting Korea to meet a friend, Mina, from a sister school.
3 Peter is going to stay at her grandfather's house for a week.
4 When he arrives, Mina shows him the guest room.
5 Peter, you will stay here.
6 This guest room is full of traditional Korean things.
7 Look at this pillow.
8 What are these things?
9 They're bats.
10 Bats on my pillow? That's scary!
11 Not really. In Korea, bats are symbols of luck and a long life.
12 That's surprising. In many Western countries, bats remind people of darkness and scary things.
13 Mina shows Peter her grandfather's room.
14 Peter and Mina's grandfather meet and greet each other.
15 Hi, Peter! Have you ever seen this kind of lock before?
16 No, I haven't. It's so old that I can't really tell, but is it a fish?
17 Yes. For a long time, Koreans have thought that fish are good guards.
18 Fish don't close their eyes, even when they sleep.
19 That's interesting.
20 We think fish can watch over valuable things. That's why this lock looks like a fish.
21 Now I understand.
22 They go outside and walk around the garden.
23 What is on that piece of paper? It looks scary.
24 Do you mean this painting of a rooster?
25 Oh, is it a rooster?
26 Yes, it is. Roosters crow every morning.
27 Their crowing means that a new day is beginning.
28 For many years, Koreans have believed evil spirits go away when a rooster crows.
29 Really? I've never heard that before.
30 Actually, I'm afraid of darkness and evil spirits.
31 Could you draw a rooster for me, Mina?
32 Sure. I'll draw a big rooster for you!
33 Put the drawing above your door. Then it will protect you.
34 Yes, I will.
35 I'm enjoying this trip so much that I want to stay

longer.

36 I love all the traditional Korean symbols in this house.

37 Now I understand a lot of them.

38 I want to visit Korea again with my family.

---

01 내 베개 위에 박쥐가 있는 것

02 한국에서는 박쥐가 행운과 장수의 상징이기 때문이다.

03 ②   04 ④   05 ③, ⑤

06 No, I haven't.   07 sister school   08 ⑤

09 ④   10 ③   11 lock

12 That's why this lock looks like a fish.

13 looks like → looks   14 ③   15 ⑤

16 (A) As   (B) so   17 ④   18 ⑤

19 (1) at any time → on special days, such as New Year's Day

    (2) three → two

20 (A) During   (B) a lot   (C) interesting

21 ②   22 (A) beginning   (B) protect   (C) will

23 ②, ⑤   24 (A) afraid   (B) go away

---

01 that은 지시대명사로 앞 문장의 내용을 받는다.

02 바로 뒤에 그 이유를 설명하고 있다.

03 ② 피터는 '일주일'간 미나네 할아버지 댁에 머무를 것이다.

04 ④ watch over: ~을 보살피다[보호하다/지켜보다], ~을 지키다, ① ~에게 (~을) 둘러보도록 안내하다[구경시켜 주다], ② ~을 기다리다, ③ ~을 조사하다, ⑤ ~을 기대하다, 즐거운 마음으로 기다리다

05 ⓐ와 ③과 ⑤는 경험 용법, ① 결과 용법, ② 계속 용법, ④ 완료 용법

06 현재완료로 물었기 때문에 No, I haven't.로 답하는 것이 적절하다.

07 sister school: 자매학교, 재정적으로, 역사적으로 혹은 사회적으로 다른 학교에 연결되어 있는 학교

08 베개에 박쥐 디자인이 있다는 것에 대해 Peter가 '무섭다'고 하니까 미나는 한국에서 박쥐는 행운과 장수의 상징이라고 말하고 있으므로 빈칸에는 동의하지 않는 말이 들어가야 한다. 그러므로 ⑤번의 '사실은 그렇지 않아.'가 적절하다. 나머지는 다 동의를 나타낼 때 쓰는 말이다. ② Why not?: (동의를 나타내어) 왜 아니겠어?

09 베개에 박쥐가 있는 것에 '무서워'하다가 한국에서 박쥐는 행운과 장수의 상징이라는 말에 '놀라워'했다. disappointed: 실망한, scared: 무서워하는, ashamed: 부끄러운, ⑤ depressed: 우울한

10 ⓐ와 ③은 '종류(명사)', 나머지는 다 '친절한(형용사)'

---

11 미나의 할아버지가 Peter에게 보여주신 '자물쇠'를 가리킨다.

12 'why'를 보충하면 된다.

13 look + 형용사, look like + 명사: ~처럼 보이다

14 위 글은 수탉 그림의 의미를 설명하는 글이므로, 제목으로는 ③번 '수탉 그림이 무엇을 의미하는가?'가 적절하다.

15 ⑤ 할아버지가 피터에게 그 그림을 그의 문 아래가 아닌 문 위에 걸어 놓으라고 한 이유는 대답할 수 없다. ① Peter, Mina's grandfather, and Mina. ② No, he doesn't. ③ It means that a new day is beginning. ④ A big rooster.

16 문장 앞에 As를 쓰거나 문장 중간에 so를 써서 고치는 것이 적절하다. For는 부가적인 이유를 나타낼 때 쓸 수 있으므로 (A)에 들어가기에는 적절하지 않다.

17 ④ '피터가 전통적인 한국의 상징물들에 대해 계속 공부하고 싶어 한다'는 내용은 본문에 없다.

18 앞의 내용의 예가 나오고 있으므로 For example이 가장 적절하다. ① 그러나, ② 다시 말해, ③ 그러므로, ④ 게다가

19 (1) 사람들은 사자춤을 '설날과 같은 특별한 날에' 춘다. (2) '두 명'의 댄서들이 사자처럼 옷을 입고 행동한다.

20 (A) 'during+특정 기간을 나타내는 명사', 'for+숫자가 붙은 기간'이므로 During이 적절하다. (B) 뒤에 명사가 없으므로 a lot이 적절하다. a lot of+명사 (C) 감정을 나타내는 말은 사람을 수식할 때는 보통 과거분사로, 사물을 수식할 때는 보통 현재분사로 쓰기 때문에 interesting이 적절하다.

21 ② 여행 기간은 알 수 없다. ① 한국, ③ 미나와 미나의 할아버지, ④ 전통적인 한국의 상징물들, ⑤ 재미있었다.

22 (A) 수탉이 매일 아침 운다고 했으므로, 수탉의 울음은 새로운 날이 '시작하는(beginning)' 것을 의미한다고 하는 것이 적절하다. (B) 그것이 너를 '지켜줄' 거라고 해야 하므로 protect가 적절하다. prevent: 막다[예방/방지하다], (C) '네, 그럴게요.' 라고 해야 하므로 will이 적절하다.

23 Actually = In fact = As a matter of fact: 사실, ① 그 결과, ③ 무엇보다도, 특히, ④ 다시 말해서

24 피터는 어둠과 악령들을 '무서워하고,' 수탉 그림 덕분에 그것들이 '물러가기를' 원하기 때문이다.

---

01 Mina shows the guest room to him.

02 luck and a long life

03 happiness and pleasant → darkness and scary

04 greet to → greet

05 Have you ever seen this kind of lock before?

06 fish don't close their eyes, even when they sleep

07 a fish

01 show는 to를 사용하여 3형식으로 고친다.

02 한국에서 박쥐는 '행운과 장수'를 상징한다.

03 서구의 많은 나라들에서, 박쥐는 사람들에게 '어둠과 무서운 것들'을 상기시켜 준다.

04 greet: ~에게 인사하다(타동사)

05 'before'를 보충하면 된다.

06 물고기는 잘 때도 눈을 감지 않기 때문이다.

07 미나의 할아버지가 피터에게 보여주는 자물쇠는 '물고기'처럼 생겼다.

08 피터가 가리키고 있는 종이 위에는 '수탉 그림'이 있다.

09 수탉의 울음은 '새로운 날이 시작하는 것을 의미'하고, 여러 해 동안, 한국 사람들은 '수탉이 울 때 악령이 물러간다.'고 믿어 왔다.

10 5단어로 영작하기 위하여 I have를 I've로 축약하면 된다.

11 be full of = be filled with: ~로 가득 차 있다

12 피터는 서구의 많은 나라들에서 박쥐는 사람들에게 어둠과 무서운 것들을 상기시켜 준다고 말하고 있기 때문에, 한국에서 박쥐가 행운과 장수의 상징이라는 미나의 말에 대한 응답으로는 'reasonable'이 아니라 'surprising'과 같이 '놀랍다'는 뜻의 단어로 고치는 것이 적절하다. reasonable: 타당한, 사리에 맞는, 합리적인

13 한국에서 박쥐는 사람들에게 '행운'과 '장수'와 같은 긍정적인 것들을 상기시켜 준다. 반면에, 서구의 많은 나라들에서, 박쥐는 어둠과 무서운 것들과 같은 '부정적인' 것들의 상징이다.

영역별 핵심문제　　　　p.41~45

01 ③ try는 '한번 해 보다'의 뜻으로 여기서는 '한번 먹어 보다'의 의미로 사용되었다.

02 face: ~을 향하다 ① 손바닥은 천장을 향해 있어야 됩니다. ④ 스캔할 사진 면이 위로 향하도록 해야 합니다. ⑤ 정원은 남쪽을 향해 있습니다. ②, ③ face: 얼굴 wrinkle: 주름

03 crow: 까마귀; (닭이) 울다/까마귀 날자 배 떨어진다./ 그들은 해가 뜨는 매일 아침 같은 시간에 웁니다.

04 palm: 손바닥; 야자나무 / 그가 손바닥으로 그녀의 턱을 괴었다. / 그들은 야자나무에 쉽게 올라갈 수 있다.

05 완료 시제를 사용할 때는 ~ ago, yesterday, when 등과 같이 명백한 과거를 나타내는 말과 함께 사용하지 않는다.

06 ⓒ와 ⓕ를 제외한 나머지 보기는 대화의 내용과 일치한다.

07 ④ have been to: ~에 가 본 적이 있다.

08 'What brings you here today?'가 어떤 일로 여기 왔는지 질문을 하는 것이므로, 주어진 문장이 이에 대한 대답이 될 수 있다.

09 mean: 의미하다

10 Have you ever been to~?: ~에 가 본 적 있니? Spanish: 스페인의 festival: 축제

11 ④ 무대에 큰 글씨 gracias가 있다.

12 (A) welcome to ~: ~에 오신 걸 환영합니다 (B) from: (출처·기원) ~ 출신의[에서 온] (C) on: ~ 위에 on the ground: 바닥에 (D) throw: ~을 던지다 at: (방향) ~으로

13 traditional: 전통적인

14 <보기>의 문장과 ③, ④번은 현재완료의 '경험'이다. ① 계속 ② 완료 ⑤ 결과

15 'so ... that ~'은 '너무[매우] ~해서 …하다'의 의미로 원인과 결과를 나타낸다.

16 현재완료는 특정한 과거를 나타내는 when과 함께 쓸 수 없다. When did you visit London?으로 써야 한다.

17 'so ... that ~'은 '너무[매우] ~해서 …하다'의 의미로 원인과 결과를 나타낸다.

18 so ... that ~: 너무[매우] ~해서 …하다

19 have[has] been to는 '~에 가 본 적이 있다'는 경험을, have[has] gone to는 '~에 가고 없다'는 결과를 나타낸다.

20 ② Nicole was so tired that she couldn't go shopping.

21 'so ... that ~'은 '너무[매우] ~해서 …하다'의 의미로 원인과 결과를 나타낸다.

22 현재완료의 '결과' 용법과 '계속' 용법을 이용한다.

23 ⓐ와 ①, ⑤ 부사적 용법, ②, ③ 명사적 용법, ④ 형용사적 용법

24 (A) 이 손님방은 한국의 '전통' 물건들로 가득 차 있다고 해야 하므로 traditional이 적절하다. modern: 현대의, (B) 뒷부분에 서구의 많은 나라들에서 박쥐는 사람들에게 어둠과 무서운 것들을 상기시켜 준다는 말이 나오기 때문에, 베개에 박쥐 디자인이 있다는 것에 대해 피터는 '겁난다'고 해야 하므로 scary가 적절하다. terrific 아주 좋은, 멋진, 훌륭한, (C) 어둠과 무서운 것들을 '상기시켜 준다'고 해야 하므로 remind가 적절하다. remain: 계속[여전히] …이다

25 so ~ that ...: 너무 ~해서 …하다

26 물고기는 잘 때도 눈을 감지 않는다는 것을 가리킨다.

27 이 글은 자물쇠가 물고기처럼 생긴 이유를 설명하는 글이므로, 주제로는 ⑤ '자물쇠가 물고기처럼 생긴 이유'가 가장 적절하다.

28 수탉의 울음은 새로운 날이 시작하는 것을 의미한다고 했기 때문에, 수탉이 울 때 '악령이 물러간다.'고 믿어왔다고 하는 것이 적절하다.

29 ⓑ be afraid of: ~을 두려워하다, ⓒ draw A for B: B를 위해 A를 그려 주다

30 피터는 '저 종이에는 무엇이 그려져 있는 거죠?' '오, 그게 수탉이에요?'라고 물어보고 있으므로, 종이 위에 수탉 그림이 있는 것을 모르고 있었다.

31 ⓐ, ②, ⑤ 명사적 용법, ① 형용사적 용법(It은 비인칭주어), ③ 부사적 용법(목적), ④ 형용사적 용법

32 이 집의 모든 전통적인 한국의 상징물들을 가리키므로 'them'이 적절하다.

단원별 예상문제 p.46~49

01 (C) → (B) → (A) → (D) **02** (D) → (F) → (A) → (B) → (E) → (C) **03** (A) haven't (B) Have (C) have

04 ④ **05** ④ **06** Chinese

07 separation **08** about

09 (b)ow, (c)row, (l)ast
  (1) lasted (2) crows (3) bow

10 (A) listened (B) Spanish

11 It means good luck for 12 months **12** ①, ⑤

13 (1) He is so fat that there is hardly any shirt that fits him.
  (2) His voice was so small that I couldn't hear him talk.
  (3) Jenny has waited for Sunny for an hour.

14 ①

15 (1) It has rained for a week.
  (2) Elvis has gone to Wien.

16 ④ **17** of

18 This guest room is full of traditional Korean things.

19 (A) haven't (B) are (C) why

20 그것은 너무 오래되어서 사실 알아볼 수가 없어요.

21 ④ **22** sheet **23** the drawing above your door **24** ③

25 he is enjoying this trip so much

26 visiting → to visit

01 Holi Festival이 있다는 말에 (C)에서 Holi가 무엇인지 질문하고 (B)에서 대답한다. (A)에서 축제에 흥미를 보이며, Holi Festival에 가 본 경험을 묻고 (D)에서 대답한다.

02 주어진 글의 무례하다는 말에, (D) 누가 무례한지 묻고 (F) 남자애가 하는 행동을 설명하며 언급하고 (A) 무엇이 잘못 되었는지 묻자 (B) 손바닥이 자기 쪽을 향하는 것은 나쁜 뜻을 가지고 있고, 손바닥을 보여 주면서 브이 사인을 만드는 것은 괜찮다고 대답한다. (E) 마지막으로, 손바닥을 보여주면서 브이 사인을 만드는 것의 의미를 묻고 (C) 대답한다.

03 상대방의 경험에 대해 물어볼 때는, 현재완료 시제를 사용하여 'Have you 과거분사 ~?'라고 묻는다. 경험을 묻는 말에 긍정으로 대답할 경우에는 'Yes, I have.', 부정으로 대답할 때는 'No, I haven't.'로 대답한다. (B)의 Have you? 다음에는 'ever been to Brazil'이 생략되어 있다.

04 (D) 작년에 있었다는 내용이므로 과거형을 사용해야 한다. 또한 a big samba festival이 단수명사이므로 was가 적절하다. (E) sound+형용사: ~하게 들리다 sound like + 명사: ~하게 들리다 (F) hope+to 동사: ~하기를 희망하다

05 It이 가리키는 것이 an umbrella이므로, What does an umbrella mean in China?(중국에서 우산이 뭘 의미하는데?)의 대답으로 나와야 적절하다.

06 Chinese: 중국의; 중국어

07 separation: 분리, 이별

08 hear about: ~에 대해서 듣다 / 넌 꽃박람회에 대해 들어 본 적이 있니? think about: ~에 대해 생각[고려]하다 / 나는 그녀에게 우산을 사주려고 생각하고 있어. talk about: ~에 대해 말하다 / 사람들은 여가 시간에 관해서 말하기를 좋아한다.

09 (1) last: 계속되다, 지속되다 / 그 회의는 어제 세 시간 동안 계속되었다. (2) crow: (닭이) 울다 / 수탉은 약 한 시간에 한 번씩 운다. (3) bow: (인사를 위해) 머리를 숙이다, 절하다 / 나는 항상 선생님께 고개 숙여 인사한다.

10 Have you 과거분사 ~?: ~해 본 경험이 있니? Spanish: 스페인의

11 mean: 의미하다 good luck: 행운 for+기간: ~ 동안

12 ② Mary has lived here for 10 years. ③ Have you ever been to Malaysia? ④ Scarlet moved to Los Angeles 5 years ago.

13 (1), (2) 'so ... that ~' 구문과 (3) 현재완료의 '계속' 용법을 이용한다.

14 'so ... that ~' 구문은 맞지만 현재완료가 아니라 과거시제이므로 ate이 알맞다.

15 (1) 현재완료의 '계속', (2) '결과' 용법을 이용한다.

16 ④ 한국에서 박쥐는 행운과 장수의 '상징'이라고 하는 것이 적절하다. ① (논의 등의) 주제[대상/화제], 과목 ② 전통, ③ 의견, ⑤ 문화

17 remind A of B: A에게 B를 상기시켜 주다, A에게 B가 생각나게 하다

18 'of'를 보충하면 된다.

19 (A) 현재완료로 물었기 때문에 대답에도 haven't가 적절하다. (B) fish는 단수와 복수의 형태가 같은데 물고기 한 마리는 a fish라고 하므로, fish 다음에는 are가 적절하다. (C) That's why = For that reason으로 why 다음에는 앞의 내용의 결과에 해당하는 말이 나온다. because 다음에는 이유를 나타내는 말이 나온다.

20 so ~ that 주어 can't ... : 너무나 ~해서 …할 수 없다

21 ④ 물고기는 잘 때도 눈을 감지 않는다.

22 종이는 'piece'나 'sheet'를 사용하여 셀 수 있다.

23 '문 위에 붙여 놓은 그림'을 가리킨다.

24 ③ 이 글은 '한국인들이 문 위에 수탉 그림을 걸어놓은 이유'를 설명하는 글이다.

25 '이번 여행이 매우 즐거워서' 더 오래 머무르고 싶어 한다.

26 want는 목적어로 to부정사를 써야 한다.

서술형 실전문제
p.50~51

01 (A) to buy   (B) buying
02 ① that's a good → that's not a good
03 umbrella
04 (1) Charlie has studied Korean for six months.
   (2) I have lost my umbrella.
05 (1) My uncle has worked for the company since 2007.
   (2) I have never seen such a beautiful bridge.
   (3) The mountain is so high that I can't walk to the top.
   (4) My parents are so wise that I usually follow their advice.
06 (1) The dogs are so cute that I can't take my eyes off them.

   (2) The weather was so nice that they went on a picnic.
07 (A) for   (B) him   (C) surprising
08 In Korea, bats are symbols of luck and a long life.
09 행운과 장수의 상징이다. / 사람들에게 어둠과 무서운 것들을 상기시켜 준다.
10 Do you mean this painting of a rooster?
11 the sun is setting → a new day is beginning
12 For many years, Koreans have believed evil spirits go away when a rooster crows.

01 (A) be going to 동사원형: ~할 것이다, ~할 예정이다 (B) 전치사 다음에는 명사나 동명사가 나올 수 있다.

02 우산이 중국에서 나쁜 것을 뜻한다고 말했기 때문에, 우산이 중국 사람들에게 좋은 선물이라고 말하는 것은 어색하므로 not을 붙여서 부정문으로 바꿔야 적절하다.

03 one은 앞에 이미 언급했거나 상대방이 알고 있는 사물을 가리킬 때 명사의 반복을 피하기 위해 사용하는데, 여기서는 umbrella를 가리킨다.

04 (1) 현재완료의 '계속', (2) '결과' 용법을 이용한다.

05 (1) 현재완료의 '계속' (2) 현재완료의 '경험' (3), (4) so ... that ~: 너무[매우] ~해서 …하다

06 'so+형용사[부사]+that+주어+동사'의 형태로 '매우 …해서 ~하다'라는 의미이다.

07 (A) 'for+숫자가 붙은 기간', 'during+특정 기간을 나타내는 명사'이므로 for가 적절하다. (B) 4형식 문장이므로 간접목적어로 him을 쓰는 것이 적절하다. show는 3형식으로 고칠 때 to를 사용한다. (C) 감정을 나타내는 말은 사람을 수식할 때는 보통 과거분사로, 사물을 수식할 때는 보통 현재분사로 쓰기 때문에 surprising이 적절하다.

08 한국에서 박쥐가 행운과 장수의 상징이라는 것을 가리킨다.

09 한국에서 박쥐는 행운과 장수의 상징이지만, 서구의 많은 나라들에서, 박쥐는 사람에게 어둠과 무서운 것들을 상기시켜 준다.

10 'of'를 보충하면 된다.

11 수탉이 매일 아침 우는 울음은 '새로운 날이 시작하는 것'을 의미한다.

12 '오랫동안 한국인들은 수탉이 울 때 악령이 물러간다고 믿어 왔다.'는 것을 가리킨다.

창의사고력 서술형 문제
p.52

|모범답안|

01 A: been to Spain

   B: I haven't.

   A: visited Spain

   A: a traditional Spanish, throw tomatoes at each other

   B: When is the festival?

02 (A) traditional   (B) is   (C) like   (D) special

   (E) to practice

단원별 모의고사
p.53~56

01 ④   02 ④   03 (1) palm (2) face

04 ③   05 What does that mean?

06 (1) Do you? → Have you?

   (2) Yes, I do. → Yes, I have.

07 (A) Which (B) What (C) How

08 Have you ever played *gorodki*?

09 ⑤ Putting → Put   10 ②   11 ③

12 a traditional Indian festival, Busan, throw colored powder and water at each other, white clothes, look more beautiful

13 ⑤

14 (1) The soup smelled too bad for me to have.

   (2) Einstein was clever enough to understand the theory.

15 (1) When did you go there?

   (2) I have studied English for 5 years.

   (3) I was so busy that I couldn't help her. 또는 I was too busy to help her.

   (4) The bunjee jump was so scary that we screamed a lot.

16 (1) for (2) since

17 Phillip has lived in China for such a long time that he can speak Chinese very well.

18 ②

19 bats remind people of darkness and scary things

20 ④   21 guards 22 ④

23 (A) don't close (B) watch over   24 ④

25 If 또는 When

01 접속사 But 앞에서 잘못된 이유를 이야기하고 손바닥을 보여 주면서 브이 사인을 만드는 것이 괜찮다고 말하는 것이 적절하다.

02 ⓐ What a nice picture! ⓑ Which boy? ⓒ The boy who is making the V sign. ⓓ His palm is facing toward himself.

03 (1) palm: 손바닥 (2) face: ~을 향하다

04 ③ in Spanish: 스페인어로

05 mean: 의미하다

06 브라질에 다녀온 경험에 대해 계속 이야기하고 있으므로 do동사가 아니라 have를 이용해서 질문과 대답을 해야 한다.

07 (A) 많은 다른 전통적인 게임들 중에서 하나를 선택하는 것이므로 Which가 어울린다. (B) 고로드키 게임이 무엇인지 질문하고 있다. (C) 게임을 하는 방법에 대해 설명하고 있으므로, 게임을 어떻게 하는지 질문해야 한다.

08 상대방의 경험에 대해 물어볼 때는, 현재완료 시제를 사용하여 'Have you ever 과거분사 ~?'라고 묻는다.

09 게임 방법을 명령문으로 설명하고 있다.

10 주어진 문장은 Holi festival이 무엇인지에 대한 대답이므로 ②가 어울린다.

11 ⓒ '가 본 적이 있어 하지만 인도 친구가 그것에 대해 내게 많이 이야기해 줬어.'는 어색하므로, 'No, I haven't.'가 어울린다.

12 traditional: 전통적인 Indian: 인도의 festival: 축제 be held: 개최되다 in+장소: ~에서 throw: ~을 던지다 at: (방향) ~으로 colored: 채색된, 색깔이 있는 clothes: 옷, 의복

13 <보기>와 ⑤번은 경험 용법 ①, ③ 완료 용법 ② 계속 용법 ④ 결과 용법

14 (1) so ... that 주어 can't ~ = too ... (의미상의 주어: for+목적격) to ~ (2) so ... that 주어 can ~ = ... enough to ~

15 (1) 현재완료는 과거의 특정 시점을 나타내는 when과는 함께 쓰이지 않는다. (2) 현재완료에서 'since+시간 명사', 'for+기간 명사' (3) so ... that 주어 can't ~ = too ... to ~ (4) 'so+형용사[부사]+that+주어+동사'의 형태로 '매우 …해서 ~하다' 'so that ~'은 '~하도록'의 의미로 쓰인다.

16 현재완료에서 'since+시간 명사', 'for+ 기간 명사'

17 'so+형용사[부사]+that+주어+동사' 구문에서 that 앞에 형용사나 부사 대신 명사가 오면 so 대신 such를 쓴다.

18 '내 베개 위에 박쥐가? 그거 겁나는데!'라고 했기 때문에 ②번의 'grateful'은 알맞지 않다. grateful: 고마워하는, 감사하는, 나머지는 다 '무서워[두려워]하는', '겁이 난'이라는 뜻이다.

19 remind A of B: A에게 B를 상기시켜 주다, A에게 B가 생각나게 하다

20 이 글은 '전통적인 한국의 상징물들 중 박쥐의 의미를 소개'하기 위한 글이다.

21 guard: 경비[감시/수비] 요원, 파수꾼, 어떤 것이나 사람을 지키는 사람들

22 ⓑ와 ④는 '~처럼', '~와 비슷한', 나머지는 다 '좋아하다'는 뜻이다.

23 물고기는 잘 때도 눈을 '감지 않기' 때문에, 사람들은 물고기가 귀중품을 '지킬 수' 있다고 생각한다. 그런 이유로 이 자물쇠가 물고기처럼 생겼다.

24 ⓐ와 ②번은 계속 용법, ① 결과 용법, ③ 완료 용법, ④ 경험용법, ⑤ 완료 용법

25 '그러면'은 '그 그림을 네 문 위에 걸어놓으면[놓을 때]'이라는 뜻이다.

Go Green Together

끄다 (3) get+비교급: 점점 ~해지다 / be동사와 결합되어 현재진행형(be+동사원형-ing)이 되어야 한다.

05 (1) 완전히 자랄 때까지 사람이나 동물 또는 식물을 돌보다 (2) 더 이상 보는 것이 불가능해지다

시험대비 실력평가 p.60

01 (c)onsume 02 ② 03 ① 04 ③
05 ④ 06 how to use 07 ⑤ 08 ③

01 둘은 동의어 관계이다. 초조한 – 먹다, 먹어 치우다

02 remind A of B: A에게 B를 상기시키다

03 Why don't you+동사원형은 ~? '~하는 게 어때?'라고 권유하는 말이다.

04 한 번 이상 일어나거나 어떤 것을 하다

05 움직이지 못하도록 무언가를 자리에 고정시키다

06 how(의문사) to+동사원형: '~하는 방법'

07 cut A into B: A를 B로 자르다, put A on B: A를 B에 놓다[두다]

08 '식물을 재배하다'는 grow가 일반적이고, raise를 사용하기도 한다. '물고기나 가축을 기르다'는 주로 raise를 사용하고, rear를 사용할 수 있다.

서술형 시험대비 p.61

01 (1) consuming (2) article (3) productive (4) turned

02 (1) feed (2) solutions (3) connect (4) bottom

03 (1) worried about (2) turn off (3) getting hotter

04 (1) (g)lobal warming (2) (t)hrow away
   (3) in (d)anger (4) (h)ang

05 (1) raise (2) disappear

01 (1) 식물은 먹이를 먹음으로써 물을 정화한다. 전치사 by 뒤에 동명사가 와야 한다. (2) 아쿠아포닉스에 관한 기사를 읽고 있어. (3) 아쿠아포닉스는 식량을 재배하는 훨씬 더 생산적인 방식이다. 명사 way를 수식하는 형용사 형태가 적절하다. (4) 이 배설물은 박테리아에 의해 식물의 먹이로 바뀐다. 주어인 waste가 음식으로 바뀌는 수동의 의미이므로 수동태로 'be+과거분사' 형태가 적절하다.

02 (1) 물고기에게 먹이를 주면, 그것들은 배설물을 만들어 낸다. (2) 그 연설은 환경문제와 그 해결책에 관한 것이다. (3) 나는 관을 이용하여 펌프를 화분에 연결하였다. (4) 나는 화분 바닥에 구멍을 뚫었다.

03 (1) be worried about ~: ~에 관해 걱정하다 (2) turn off: ~을

교과서 Conversation

핵심 Check p.62~63

1 ②
2 worried about wasting
3 ④
4 ⑤
5 how to draw

교과서 대화문 익히기

Check(√) True or False p.64

(1) T (2) F (3) F (4) T

교과서 확인학습 p.66~67

Listen & Talk 1 A
leave, on, worried about wasting / put, on / shouldn't

Listen & Talk 1 B
What, about / was about, getting hotter, going up, worried / about, before, disappearing, losing / terrible / to stop / turn off, them, instead of / try to

Listen & Talk 1 C
nervous / worried, about, solutions / talk about / enough information / instead, said, have to / isn't / in danger because, near / talk about, for, advice

Listen and Talk 2 A
how to use / turn, on / anywhere / interesting.

Listen and Talk 2 B
get / myself / amazing / Why don't you / how to make / Cut, into, sew, together / easy

Listen and Talk 2 C
Have, heard of / turn off, for / to remind, of, such / how to join / turn off, from, to, on, in

Do It Yourself
look upset / am worried about, saving, making / how about using / to use / Add / sounds easy

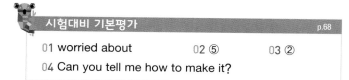

시험대비 기본평가

p.68

01 worried about   02 ⑤   03 ②
04 Can you tell me how to make it?

01 'be worried about ~'은 '~에 관해 걱정하다'라는 뜻이다.
02 남자의 대답이 '단지 30분 동안 축구를 하면 전구가 켜질 것이다.'라고 방법을 말해 주고 있기 때문에 빈칸에는 방법을 물어보는 말이 오는 것이 자연스럽다.
03 상대방에게 권유나 제안하는 표현으로 Why don't you+동사원형 ~? = How[What] about+-ing ~? = What do you say to+ -ing ~?를 사용한다. 동사원형 make가 있기 때문에 Why don't you가 적절하다.
04 조동사 can으로 시작하는 의문문으로, '~에게 …을 말하다'는 'tell+간접목적어(~에게)+직접목적어(…을/를)' 어순을 취한다. 직접목적어 자리에 '의문사+to부정사' 형태로 '어떻게 ~하는지'를 쓴다.

시험대비 실력평가

p.69~70

01 ③	02 how I should use it	03 ①, ④
04 ⑤	05 a bag	06 ①	07 ②
08 ④	09 ⑤	10 turn off	11 to
remind, of	12 ④		

01 '무슨 일이니?'라는 질문에 대한 답으로 글의 내용상 숙제를 하는 것에 대해 걱정하는 내용이 자연스럽다.
02 '의문사+to부정사'는 '의문사+주어+should+동사원형'으로 바꾸어 쓸 수 있다.
03 재귀대명사의 강조 용법으로 재귀대명사는 강조하는 말 뒤나 문장의 끝에 온다.
04 소녀가 가방을 만드는 방법에 대해 말하고 있으므로 how to 부정사가 적절하다.
05 one은 앞에 나온 명사를 가리키는 부정대명사로 a bag을 가리킨다.
06 '그것은 무엇에 관한 것이었니?' '그것은 지구 온난화에 관한 것이었어.' '~에 관한'은 about이다.
07 B의 첫 대화에서 학생들이 음식을 너무 많이 남긴다고 했기 때문에 B는 음식을 낭비하는 것에 대해 걱정하고 있다는 것을 알 수 있다.
08 We shouldn't는 We shouldn't put too much food on our plates.의 의미이므로 먹을 수 있는 만큼 음식을 식판에 담자는 의도다.
09 ⑤번의 A는 초콜릿 하루 생산량을 물었는데 B는 로봇이 초콜릿을 생산한다고 말하는 것은 어색하다.
10 버튼을 누름으로써 기계, TV, 엔진이나 전등이 작동하는 것을

멈추도록 하다
11 '~하기 위해'는 부정사를 이용하여 나타낸다. '~에게 …을 상기시키다'는 remind A of B 형태를 사용한다.
12 ④ Earth Hour 행사는 3월 마지막 토요일에 1시간 동안 불을 끔으로써 참여 가능하다고 했다.

서술형 시험대비

p.71

01 Can you tell me how to make it?
02 (1) how to make   (2) old   (3) Cut, into   (4) Sew
03 I'm worried about the Earth.
04 getting hotter, going up, disappearing / Turn off, don't need, use, instead of
05 We shouldn't put too much food on our plates.

01 'how to+동사원형': '~하는 방법, 어떻게 ~하는지'
02 가방을 만드는 방법은 소녀의 마지막 말에 언급되어 있다.
03 be worried about: ~에 관해 걱정하다
05 We shouldn't.는 음식을 식판에 너무 많이 담아서는 안 된다는 의미다.

[교과서]
Grammar

핵심 Check

p.72~73

1 (1) was found   (2) to   (3) with
2 (1) far   (2) even   (3) much

시험대비 기본평가

p.74

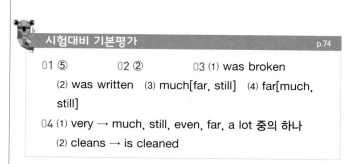

01 ⑤   02 ②   03 (1) was broken
(2) was written   (3) much[far, still]   (4) far[much, still]
04 (1) very → much, still, even, far, a lot 중의 하나
(2) cleans → is cleaned

01 동사를 'be+pp'로 바꾸고 수동태 문장의 주어 자리에는 능동태 문장의 목적어가 오고, by 다음에는 능동태 문장의 주어를 목적격으로 쓴다.
02 very는 원급의 형용사[부사]를 수식하며, 비교급은 수식하지 않는다.
03 (1) 수동태는 'be+pp'의 형태이다. (2) 책 이름은 단수로 취급한다. (3), (4) 비교급을 강조할 때는 비교급 앞에 much, still,

even, far, a lot 등의 부사(구)를 쓰므로 much, still, far 중의 하나를 쓰면 정답이다.

04 (1) 비교급을 강조할 때는 비교급 앞에 much, still, even, far, a lot 등의 부사를 쓴다. (2) 방이 청소되는 것이므로 수동태가 적절하다.

시험대비 실력평가 p.75~77

01 ⑤	02 ③	03 ④	04 ②
05 ①	06 (1) to (2) for (3) of		07 ③
08 ④	09 ③	10 ⑤	11 ②
12 ⑤	13 ②		

14 (1) *Sunflower* was painted by Van Gogh.
   (2) The pictures were not taken by Mel.
   (3) The building was made of stone.
   (4) Health is far more important than money.
   (5) The computer I wanted to buy was a lot cheaper than the old one. 15 bigger
16 is cleaned / are made / faster / more important
17 ⑤ 18 ④ 19 (1) was happened → happened (2) invented → was invented (3) many → much

01 *The Kiss*가 그려진 것이므로 수동태가 적절하다.

02 very는 원급의 형용사[부사]를 수식하며, 비교급은 수식하지 않는다.

03 ④ send는 간접목적어 앞에 to를 붙여야 한다. for me → to me

04 4형식의 직접목적어를 주어로 하는 수동태에서 buy는 간접목적어 앞에 for를 쓰는 동사이다.

05 비교급을 강조할 때는 비교급 앞에 much, still, even, far, a lot 등의 부사를 쓴다.

06 직접목적어를 주어로 한 수동태에서 간접목적어 앞에 (1) show는 전치사 to를, (2) make는 전치사 for를, (3) ask는 전치사 of를 쓴다.

07 ③번은 명사를 수식하고 있지만 나머지는 비교급을 강조하고 있다.

08 비교급을 강조할 때는 비교급 앞에 much, still, even, far, a lot 등의 부사를 쓰며, 첫 문장은 의미상 much가 적절하다.

09 <보기>와 ③ (비교급을 강조하여) 한층, 훨씬 ① …조차(도) ② 짝수의 ④ (수량·득점 따위가) 같은, 동일한 ⑤ (표면·판자 따위가) 평평한

10 ⑤ 목적격보어가 원형부정사인 경우, 수동태 문장에서는 to부정사로 바뀐다. Dan was made to finish the work by next Monday by them.

11 be satisfied with: ~에 만족하다 be filled with: ~로 가득 차다

12 throw away는 구동사로 하나의 단어처럼 취급하여 be thrown away로 나타낸다. away나 by를 빠뜨리지 않도록 주의한다.

13 조동사가 있는 문장의 수동태는 '조동사+be+p.p.' 형식을 갖는다.

14 (1), (2) *Sunflower*가 그려지고, 사진들이 찍히지 않은 것이므로 수동태가 적절하다. (3) be made of: ~로 만들어지다(물리적 변화) (4), (5) far와 a lot으로 비교급을 강조한다.

15 much로 수식받으면서 than이 뒤에 나오므로 비교급이 적절하다.

16 교실이 청소되어지고 차가 만들어지는 것이므로 수동태가 적절하다. even과 a lot으로 수식받고 있고 than이 이어지고 있으므로 비교급이 적절하다.

17 choose는 직접목적어를 주어로 한 수동태에서는 간접목적어 앞에 for를 쓴다.

18 시제가 saw로 과거형이므로 was seen으로 쓰고, 목적격보어 flying은 그대로 쓴다. (원형부정사일 경우에는 to부정사로 써야 한다.)

19 (1) happen은 자동사이므로 수동태로 쓰이지 않는다. (2) 냉장고가 발명된 것이므로 수동태가 적절하다. (3) 비교급 강조는 many가 아니라 much로 한다.

서술형 시험대비 p.78~79

01 (1) Our scientists discovered solutions to this problem.
   (2) I will sing this song.
   (3) The cookies were made for her by Dan.
   (4) Something must be done to help him by us.
   (5) By whom was the telephone invented in 1876?

02 (1) Cars are far more expensive than bicycles.
   (2) It was still more beautiful than I had imagined.
   (3) Manchester United is hoping to do even better this year.
   (4) It'll be a lot cheaper than buying a new jacket.
   (5) Jane is much cleverer than her twin brother.

03 (1) When we waste paper, so many trees are destroyed. 또는 When we waste paper, we destroy so many trees.
   (2) How much chocolate is produced in a day?
   (3) Wine is made from grapes.
   (4) Matt was seen to dance on the stage by his friends.
   (5) *Bibimbap* will be cooked for Mariel by Minjun tomorrow.
   (6) Robert will read a storybook to his little brother. 또는 A storybook will be read to his

little brother by Robert.

04 nicer

05 (1) This dress was designed by my friend.

   (2) *Charlie* and the *Chocolate Factory* was notwritten by William Shakespeare.

   (3) The interview was carried out in both Korean and English.

   (4) These items were asked of each respondent.

   (5) A long letter was written (to) her by him.

   (6) Annabel was satisfied with her life in Seoul.

06 (1) many, (2) too, (3) ever, (4) very, (5) lots를 much, still, even, far, a lot 등으로 **바꾸면 정답.**

07 (1) This tower is a lot higher than that (one).

   (2) My brother jumps even higher than I.

   (3) She is much more active than her brother.

   (4) Brenda is far kinder than before.

   (5) Democracy is still better than communism.

08 (1) I was taught math by Amanda last year., Mathwas taught (to) me by Amanda last year.

   (2) A chocolate cake was chosen for us by Teresa.

   (3) A question was asked of me by Ann.

09 Sumi runs much faster than Yuri.

01 (2) 미래시제의 수동태는 'will be+과거분사'이다. (3) make는 직접목적어를 주어로 하는 수동태만 가능하다. (4) 조동사가 있는 문장의 수동태는 '조동사+be+p.p.' 형식을 갖는다. (5) 의문사 who가 whom으로 바뀌는 것에 주의한다.

02 비교급을 강조할 때는 비교급 앞에 much, still, even, far, a lot 등의 부사(구)를 쓰므로 much, still, even, far, a lot 등을 비교급 앞에 쓰면 된다.

03 (1) tree를 주어로 하면 수동태가, we를 주어로 하면 능동태가 적절하다. (2) 초콜릿이 무엇을 생산하는 것이 아니므로 진행형이 아닌 수동태 'be+과거분사' (3) be made of: ~로 만들어지다(물리적 변화), be made from: ~로 만들어지다(화학적 변화) (4) 목적격보어가 원형부정사인 경우 수동태 문장에서는 to부정사로 바뀐다. (5) cook은 직접목적어를 주어로 한 수동태에서는 간접목적어 앞에 for를 쓴다. (6) read는 직접목적어를 주어로 하는 수동태만 가능하다.

04 much로 수식을 받으며 뒤에 than이 있으므로 비교급이 적절하다.

05 (1) 수동태는 '주어+be동사+과거분사+by+행위자'의 형식이다. (2) 수동태의 부정은 'be+not+과거분사'이다. (3) carry out을 하나의 단위처럼 생각해서 'be carried out'으로 써야 한다. (4) ask는 직접목적어를 주어로 한 수동태에서는 간접목적어 앞에 전치사 of를 써야 한다. (5) write는 직접목적어를 주어로 하는 수동태만 가능하다. (6) be satisfied with: ~에 만족하다

06 비교급 앞에 much, still, even, far, a lot 등의 부사로 비교급을 강조한다.

07 비교급 앞에 much, still, even, far, a lot 등의 부사(구)로 비교급을 강조한다.

08 직접목적어를 주어로 한 수동태에서 간접목적어 앞에 (1) teach는 전치사 to를, (2) choose는 for를, (3) ask는 of를 쓴다.

09 비교급 앞에 much를 써서 비교급을 강조한다.

교과서 Reading

확인문제 p.80

1 T 2 F 3 T 4 F

확인문제 p.81

1 T 2 F 3 T

확인문제 p.81

1 T 2 F 3 F

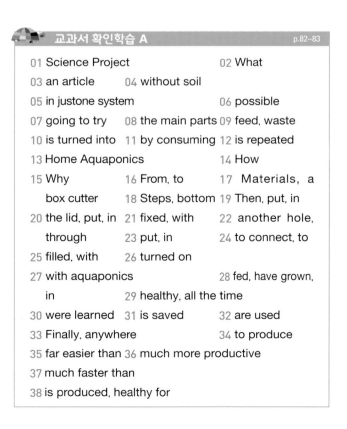

교과서 확인학습 A p.82~83

01 Science Project   02 What

03 an article   04 without soil

05 in justone system   06 possible

07 going to try   08 the main parts   09 feed, waste

10 is turned into   11 by consuming   12 is repeated

13 Home Aquaponics   14 How

15 Why   16 From, to   17 Materials, a box cutter   18 Steps, bottom   19 Then, put, in

20 the lid, put, in   21 fixed, with   22 another hole, through   23 put, in   24 to connect, to

25 filled, with   26 turned on

27 with aquaponics   28 fed, have grown, in   29 healthy, all the time

30 were learned   31 is saved   32 are used

33 Finally, anywhere   34 to produce

35 far easier than   36 much more productive

37 much faster than

38 is produced, healthy for

1 My Science Project: Home Aquaponics

2 What are you reading?

3 I'm reading an article about aquaponics.

4 It's a way of growing plants without soil.

5 We can also grow plants and raise fish in just one system.

6 Is that possible?

7 We'll see. I'm going to try it at home for my science project.

8 Fish, bacteria, and plants are the main parts of aquaponics.

9 After you feed the fish, they produce waste.

10 The waste is turned into food for the plants by bacteria.

11 The plants clean the water by consuming the food.

12 This process is repeated again and again!

13 Home Aquaponics / by Eric Jackson

14 Questions: How can I make an aquaponics system at home?

15 Why is aquaponics good?

16 Period: From May 15 to August 15

17 Materials: a pot & small stones, a fish tank, a plastic tube, a water pump, plants, some fish, a box cutter, clay

18 Steps: I made holes in the bottom of a pot.

19 Then I put small stones and plants in it.

20 I made a big hole in the lid of the fish tank and put the pot in the hole.

21 I fixed the pot in place with clay.

22 I made another hole in the lid and put a tube through it.

23 I put a water pump in the fish tank.

24 I used the tube to connect the pump to the pot.

25 I filled the fish tank with water and put some fish in it.

26 Then I turned on the pump.

27 Results: From this experiment, I grew my plants and raised fish with aquaponics.

28 I just fed the fish, but the plants have grown 17 centimeters in three months.

29 The fish stay healthy and the water is clean all the time.

30 Conclusion: Some important things about aquaponics were learned from this experiment.

31 First, water is saved because the plants don't need watering.

32 Second, it is good for the environment because no chemicals are used.

33 Finally, you can do aquaponics anywhere because it doesn't need much space.

34 I found out... Some farmers use aquaponics to produce vegetables and raise fish.

35 They choose aquaponics because it is far easier than traditional gardening.

36 Also, it is a much more productive way of growing food.

37 The plants grow much faster than plants in soil, and it saves space.

38 I hope more food is produced in this way in the future because it is healthy for us and the environment.

01 ②, ③ / ①, ④, ⑤   02 aquaponics

03 ③   04 (A)bacteria (B)into (C) consuming

05 (A)fish (B)bacteria (C)plants   06 ③

07 ④   08 ⓐ hole, ⓑ tube   09 ⑤

10 ③   11 ⑤   12 ②   13 ③

14 ①   15 ②   16 ②, ⑤

17 ⓐ Questions ⓑ Period ⓒ Materials ⓓ Steps

18 ⑤   19 ②   20 ④   21 ①

22 ⓐ Lots of energy is wasted around us. ⓑ the classroom computers   23 To do   24 ⑤

01 ⓐ: 현재분사, ⓒ: 동명사

02 '아쿠아포닉스(수경 식물과 수중 생물을 기르는 것을 합친 시스템)'를 가리킨다.

03 ③ '아쿠아포닉스'는 '한 가지' 장치만으로도 식물과 물고기를 동시에 키울 수 있다.

04 (A) bacteria가 복수이고 단수는 bacterium이다. (B) '먹이로 바뀐다'고 해야 하므로 into가 적절하다. be turned into: ~로 바뀌다, (C) 그 먹이를 '먹음으로써'라고 해야 하므로 consuming이 적절하다. consume: 먹다, 소모하다, save: 절약하다, 저축하다

05 아쿠아포닉스의 주요 부분은 '물고기', '박테리아', '식물'이다.

06 ③ '비교적', ⓐ와 나머지는 다 '몇 번이고', '되풀이해서'라는 뜻이다.

07 ④ 위 글은 '실험 보고서'이다. ① 요약, 개요, ② (특히 기계 등을 사면 따라 나오는) 설명서. ③ (책·연극·영화 등에 대한) 논평[비평], 감상문, 전기, ⑤ 독후감

08 덮개에 또 다른 '구멍'을 하나 만들고 그 안에 '관'을 넣었다.

Lesson 5

Give a Helping Hand

시험대비 실력평가
p.112

01 ④	02 ①	03 ①	04 ③
05 ②	06 ③	07 ⑤	08 ①
09 ③			

01 ④ lucky(운이 좋은) 이외의 단어들은 사람의 성격을 묘사할 때 사용할 수 있는 단어이다. ① creative: 창의적인 ② generous: 관대한 ③ lively: 쾌활한 ⑤ passionate: 열정적인

02 feed: 먹이를 주다

03 carry: 나르다, 운반하다

04 item: 항목, 물품 goods: 상품, 물품

05 die: 죽다 pass away: 죽다, 사망하다

06 all over the world: 전 세계에 worldwide: 세계적인; 세계적으로 ① nationally: 전국적으로 ② internationally: 국제적으로 ④ global: 세계적인 ⑤ variously: 여러 가지로

07 raise money: 돈을 모금하다

08 turning point: 전환점 / 큰 변화가 발생하는 때

09 moment: 순간, 잠깐 / 시간 상의 특정한 시점

서술형 시험대비
p.113

01 (a)live

02 (s)pirit

03 in

04 gave

05 (1) take (2) broke (3) handed (4) search

06 (1) I feel better thanks to your advice.

　(2) She passed away last month.

　(3) The government planned to support the elderly.

　(4) He gained both wealth and fame.

07 (1) (b)lind (2) (s)urvive (3) (h)onor

01 둘은 반의어 관계이다. luckily: 운이 좋게도 unluckily: 불행히도 alive: 살아 있는 dead: 죽은

02 soul: 영혼, 넋, 정신, 마음 spirit: 마음, 정신

03 be in a hurry: 급하다 in need: 어려움에 처한

04 give: 주다 give a hand: 돕다

05 (1) take care of: ~을 돌보다 (2) break one's arm: 팔이 부러지다 (3) hand out: 나누어 주다 (4) search for: ~을 찾다

06 (1) thanks to ~: ~ 덕분에 (2) pass away: 사망하다 (3) support: 지지하다, 원조하다 (4) fame: 명성

07 (1) blind: 눈 먼, 장님의 / 어떤 것도 볼 수 없는 (2) survive: 살아남다, 생존하다 / 나쁜 일이 일어난 후에 계속 살다 (3) honor: 예우하다, 존중하다 / 존경심을 가지고 누군가를 대하다

교과서 Conversation

핵심 Check
p.114~115

1 favor / No problem

2 Can you help me to wash the dishes

3 Why don't we have some ice cream?

　What about having some ice cream?

　Let's have some ice cream.

4 Why don't we go to the movies tomorrow

5 How about playing soccer after school

교과서 대화문 익히기

Check(√) True or False
p.116

1 F　2 T　3 T　4 T

교과서 확인학습
p.118~119

Listen & Talk 1 A

can, help me / What are, going / going to donate

Listen & Talk 1 B

with / broke it / a hurry, fell down / Is there, can do / can you help

Listen & Talk 1 C

can you help, wash them / but, to feed, don't you / ask you a favor / Can you help / have to

Listen & Talk 2 A

kinds of volunteer / don't we clean up

Listen & Talk 2 B

As, was, don't we raise, at, on, bring, donate, give a hand, need

cleaned up, we going to / don't we visit, it up / to do,
hold / What / serve / about playing / like

to do / don't, volunteer activities, make / is / who has
volunteered / has volunteered, help us find / search
for, don't we check

시험대비 기본평가 　　　　　　　　　　p.120

01 ②	02 ⑤	03 ③	04 ②

01 특정 행동을 같이 하자고 제안할 때는 'Why don't we ~?'로
　시작하는 표현을 쓴다. 'How about ~?'이나 'What about
　~?' 'Let's 동사원형 ~.' 등의 표현도 쓸 수 있는데 'Why don't
　you+동사 ~?'는 함께 하자는 것은 아니고 상대방에게만 권유
　하는 것이다.

02 ⑤는 '내가 도와줄까요?'의 의미이고, 나머지 보기들은 상대방
　에게 도움을 요청하는 말이다.

03 상대방에게 도움을 요청할 때는 'Can you help me ~?'로 시
　작하는 문장으로 표현할 수 있다. 이 때 can 대신 will을 쓸 수
　있으며 would나 could를 써서 'Could you help me ~?'나
　'Would you help me ~?'라고 말하면 공손하고 정중한 느낌
　을 준다.

04 what kinds of ~: 어떤 종류의 volunteer: 자원봉사의; 자원
　봉사자 / 어떤 종류의 봉사 활동을 할 수 있느냐는 질문을 했으
　므로, 구체적인 봉사 활동의 예시를 들며 같이 하자고 제안하는
　것이 어울린다.

시험대비 실력평가 　　　　　　　　　p.121~122

01 ①, ③	02 ③	03 ③	04 ④
05 ②	06 Can you help me buy a train ticket?		
07 ③	08 give	09 bring your items and	

donate them　10 ④　　　　　11 ④　　　　12 And
how about playing some music?　　　　13 ②

01 help는 5형식 동사로 '~이 …하는 것을 돕다'의 의미로 사용된
　다. 목적격 보어로 to부정사와 동사원형을 쓸 수 있다.

02 (B) be going to 동사원형: ~할 것이다 (C) these books를 받
　는 인칭대명사가 와야 하므로, 복수형 them이 어울린다.

03 fall down: 넘어지다 / 기차를 타려고 서두르다가 길에 넘어졌
　다는 말이 연결되어야 자연스럽다.

04 ① 어떻게 남자아이가 여자아이를 도울 것인가? ② 언제 여자
　아이가 다쳤는가? ③ 왜 여자 아이가 서둘렀는가? ④ 그들은 어
　디를 갈 것인가? ⑤ 여자아이는 무엇을 부러뜨렸는가?

---

05 ② 도와준다는 말에 내가 할 수 없다고 말하는 것은 어색하다.
　Can I give you a hand? → Can you give me a hand?

06 help 목적어 (to) 동사원형: ~가 …하는 것을 돕다

07 as: (접) ~과 같이, ~하는 대로 as you know: 아시다시피

08 give: 주다 give a hand: ~을 돕다

09 item: 항목, 물품 donate: 기부하다

10 ① 특별 행사의 목적 ② 특별 행사가 어디서 열리는지 ③ 특별
　행사가 언제 열리는지 ④ 어떤 품목을 기부할 수 없는지 ⑤ 특
　별 행사에서 모금한 돈이 어디로 주어지는지

11 양로원에서 청소를 하자고 제안하자 좀 더 재미있는 걸 하고 싶
　다고 이야기했으므로 ③은 답이 되지 않는다. 빈칸 (A) 다음 문
　장에서 여자아이가 'What can we do at the party?(우리가
　파티에서 뭘 할 수 있지?)'라고 말했으므로 파티를 열자고 제안
　한 것을 추리할 수 있다.

12 How about (동)명사: ~하는 게 어떨까?

13 ① 여자아이는 무슨 악기를 연주할 수 있는가? ② 어떤 음식을
　양로원에 있는 사람들에게 대접할 것인가? ③ 언제가 봉사 활동
　의 날인가? ④ 그들은 봉사활동을 위해 어디로 갈 것인가? ⑤ 양
　로원에서 그들은 무엇을 할 것인가?

서술형 시험대비 　　　　　　　　　　p.123

01 (D) → (B) → (A) → (C)
02 (A) → (C) → (B) → (D)
03 ④ which has volunteered a lot → who[that] has
　　volunteered a lot
04 can you help us find some good places?
05 do
06 of

01 다리에 무슨 문제가 있는지 묻는 질문에 (D) 지난주에 부러졌다
　고 대답한다. (B) 어떻게 된 일인지 질문하자 (A) 기차를 타려
　고 서두르다가 길에 넘어졌다고 답한다. (C) 이에, 정말 끔찍하
　다고 말한다.

02 봉사 활동의 날에 무엇을 할 건지 묻는 질문에 (A) 양로원에 가
　서 청소를 하자고 제안한다. (C) 이 제안에 나쁜 생각은 아니지
　만 좀 재미있는 걸 하고 싶다고 말하며 파티를 여는 것을 제안하
　고 (B) 좋은 생각이라고 답하며, 파티에서 무엇을 할 수 있는지
　질문하자 (D) 음식을 대접할 수 있다고 대답한다.

03 선행사인 수민이는 사람이므로 주격 관계대명사 who나 that이
　적절하다.

04 Can you help 목적어 (to) 동사원형 ~?: 목적어가 ~하는 것을
　도와주겠니?

05 do volunteer work: 자원 봉사를 하다

06 take care of: ~을 돌보다 short: 짧은 / tail: 꼬리

---

22 정답 및 해설

핵심 Check
p.124~125

1 (1) whom　(2) which

2 (1) sleeping　(2) exciting　(3) written　(4) excited

시험대비 기본평가
p.126

01 ①, ②, ③

02 ④

03 (1) who → which[that]

　　(2) which → who[whom/that]

　　(3) exciting → excited

04 The chicken salad which my mom made is very delicious.

01 선행사가 The only food로 사물이며 find의 목적어 역할을 할 수 있는 목적격 관계대명사 that이나 which가 적절하다.

02 감정을 나타내는 타동사의 과거분사는 '~한 감정을 느끼는'이라는 의미로, 주로 사람을 주어로 하며, 현재분사는 주로 사물을 주어로 하여 '~한 감정을 유발하는'의 의미를 나타낸다.

03 (1) 선행사가 동물이므로 who를 which나 that으로 고쳐야 한다. (2) 선행사가 사람이므로 which를 who나 whom 또는 that으로 고쳐야 한다. (3) 사람이 주어이며 '신나는 감정을 느끼는' 것이므로 과거분사가 적절하다.

04 '우리 엄마가 만든'을 관계대명사절로 하여 '치킨 샐러드'를 수식하는 구조로 쓴다. 선행사가 사물이므로 목적격 관계대명사로 which를 쓴다.

시험대비 실력평가
p.127~129

01 ②　　　　02 ③　　　　03 ③

04 There is a dress in the box (which[that]) Alex sent (to) me.

05 (1) that　(2) who　(3) whom　(4) interested

　　(5) interesting

06 ④　　　　07 ①　　　　08 ②

09 (1) scared　(2) embarrassing　(3) shocked　　10 ③, ⑤

11 (1) who　(2) that　(3) which is　　　　　　　12 ④

13 (1) Audrey Hepburn is a person who[whom/that] my partner respects a lot.

　　(2) This is the ID which[that] the spy used before.

　　(3) The letter which[that] you sent to me last week made me happy.

　　(4) Do you remember the girl who[whom/that] I met at the party?

　　(5) I like the music to which I often listen. 또는 I like the music which[that] I often listen to.

　　(6) Do you know the girl to whom Ann is talking? / Do you know the girl who[whom/that] Ann is talking to?

14 ③　　　　15 ④

16 (1) She was shocked because their lives were very difficult.

　　(2) I can't forget the tiger which I saw on safari.

　　(3) Are you satisfied with your job as a tour guide?

17 (1) amazed　(2) amazing

01 <보기>와 나머지는 목적격 관계대명사이지만 ②번은 주격 관계대명사이다.

02 모두 목적격으로 사용된 관계대명사 that이 들어갈 수 있지만 ③번은 소유격 관계대명사 whose가 들어가야 한다.

03 감정을 나타내는 타동사의 과거분사는 '~한 감정을 느끼는'이라는 의미로, 주로 사람을 주어로 한다.

04 'Alex가 나에게 보낸 박스'에서 목적격 관계대명사를 이용하여 '박스'를 'Alex가 나에게 보낸'이 수식하는 구조로 만들어 준다.

05 (1) 선행사가 사물이므로 that, (2) 선행사가 사람이므로 who, (3) 전치사 with가 있으므로 that은 쓸 수 없다. (4) 내가 흥미를 갖게 되는 '수동'의 의미이므로 과거분사 interested가 적절하다. (5) the game이 흥미롭게 만들어 주는 '능동'의 의미이므로 현재분사가 적절하다.

06 아이들이 놀라게 되는 것이므로 '능동'의 frightening이 아니라 '수동'의 의미를 나타내는 frightened가 되어야 한다.

07 ① 목적격 관계대명사는 생략될 수 있다. ②, ④ 관계대명사의 선행사가 사람이면 who, whom이나 that을 쓰고 사물이면 which나 that을 쓴다. ③ 관계대명사가 접속사와 대명사의 역할을 하므로 목적어로 쓴 it을 삭제해야 한다. ⑤ 전치사가 관계대명사 앞에 올 경우에는 관계대명사 that을 쓸 수 없으며, 관계대명사를 생략하지 않는다.

08 ②번은 접속사이지만 나머지는 모두 관계대명사이다.

09 감정을 나타내는 타동사의 과거분사는 '~한 감정을 느끼는'이라는 의미로, 주로 사람을 주어로 하며, 현재분사는 주로 사물을 주어로 하여 '~한 감정을 유발하는'의 의미를 나타낸다.

10 선행사가 사물이므로 which나 that을 이용하고 목적격이므로 목적어로 쓰인 it은 쓰지 말아야 한다. 또한 목적격 관계대명사는 생략될 수 있다.

11 목적격 관계대명사와 '주격 관계대명사+be동사'는 생략할 수 있다.

12 Everyone feels depressed at some time or another. 사람이 주어로 우울해지는 것이므로 과거분사가 적절하다. some time or another: 이런저런 때에, 언젠가

13 목적격 관계대명사는 선행사가 사람이면 who나 whom, that

을, 사람이나 동물이면 which나 that을 쓴다. 일반적으로 목적격 관계대명사는 생략될 수 있다. 목적격 관계대명사가 전치사의 목적어인 경우 전치사는 관계대명사절의 끝에 오거나 관계대명사 앞에 올 수 있다. 전치사가 관계대명사절의 끝에 올 경우에는 관계대명사를 생략할 수 있다. 전치사가 관계대명사 앞에 올 경우에는 관계대명사 that을 쓸 수 없으며, 관계대명사를 생략하지 않는다.

14 감정을 나타내는 타동사의 현재분사는 주로 사물을 주어로 하여 '~한 감정을 유발하는'의 의미를 나타낸다. 의미상 영어가 나를 '신나게 하는' 것이 아니라 '지루하게 만드는' 것이 자연스러우므로 boring이 적절하다.

15 관계대명사 that은 전치사 다음에는 쓸 수 없다. that → whom

16 (1) '충격을 받은'은 '수동'의 뜻이므로 과거분사를 쓴다. (2) '사파리에서 보았던 호랑이'를 '사파리에서 보았던'이 호랑이를 수식하는 관계대명사절로 수식하도록 한다. (3) be satisfied with: ~에 만족하다

17 감정을 나타내는 타동사가 '어떤 감정을 느끼게 하면' 주로 사물을 주어로 하여 현재분사를 쓰고, '어떤 감정을 느끼면' 주로 사람을 주어로 하여 과거분사를 쓴다.

서술형 시험대비
p.130~131

01 Playing, excited

02 (1) I didn't know you were interested in Latin dance.
(2) Emma was disappointed at her test score.
(3) I think these highway signs are very confusing.
(4) No one knows that I am worried about such a thing.
(5) For me he was not boring, so I was not bored.

03 that → which

04 (1) Jayu Park is a park which[that] my grandfather often visits.
(2) *Tom and Jerry* is a cartoon which[that] my little sister often watches.
(3) That is the girl who[whom/that] I saw this morning.
(4) The girl who[whom/that] I wanted to meet did not participate in the meeting.
(5) The woman who[whom/that] Mom is talking to is Ms. Larson. 또는 The woman to whom Mom is talking is Ms. Larson.
(6) Mariel took pictures of Ben and his car that were on the crime scene.

05 (1) King Sejong is a person who/whom/that my brother respects a lot.
(2) This is the bridge which/that they built about 20 years ago.
(3) The girl talked to a boy whom she met at the

party.
(4) I don't like the movie which I saw yesterday.
(5) There are many subjects about which people feel little interest. 또는 There are many subjects (that/which) people feel little interest about.

06 (1) I felt very tired all day because I didn't sleep well last night.
(2) I was scared to be left at home alone.
(3) Watching a baseball game makes me bored.

07 (1) *The Smurfs* is a cartoon.
(2) Let me introduce my friend.
(3) Laura was looking for the key all day long.
(4) I cannot speak about it for the reason.

08 (1) He put me in a very embarrassing situation.
(2) My mom was surprised at the news.
(3) It was shocking that he lied to me.
(4) We were all excited because my brother made a goal in the soccer game.

01 주어로 동명사 Playing을 쓰고 '내가 신이 나게 되는' 것이므로 과거분사 excited를 쓴다.

02 (1)~(4) 감정을 나타내는 타동사의 과거분사는 '~한 감정을 느끼는'이라는 의미로, 주로 사람을 주어로 하며, 현재분사는 주로 사물을 주어로 하여 '~한 감정을 유발하는'의 의미를 나타낸다. (5) 주어가 사람일 때도 현재분사를 쓸 수 있다. '나에게 그가 따분하게 만들지 않아서 내가 따분하지 않았다'는 의미이다.

03 관계대명사 that은 전치사와 함께 쓰이지 않는다.

04 (1), (2) 선행사가 사물이므로 관계대명사 which나 that, (3), (4) 선행사가 사람이므로 관계대명사 who, whom이나 that, (5) 목적격 관계대명사가 전치사의 목적어인 경우 전치사는 관계대명사절의 끝에 오거나 관계대명사 앞에 올 수 있으며 전치사가 관계대명사절의 끝에 올 경우에는 관계대명사를 생략할 수 있다. 전치사가 관계대명사 앞에 올 경우에는 관계대명사 that을 쓸 수 없다. (6) 선행사가 '사람+사물'이므로 관계대명사 that을 써야 한다. 목적격 관계대명사는 생략될 수 있다. crime scene: 범죄 현장

05 (1) 선행사가 사람이므로 who, whom이나 that, (2) 선행사가 사물이므로 which나 that, (3) 관계대명사가 접속사와 대명사의 역할을 하므로 him을 삭제해야 한다. (4) 관계대명사가 접속사와 대명사의 역할을 하므로 it을 삭제해야 한다. (5) 전치사가 관계대명사 앞에 올 경우에는 관계대명사 that을 쓸 수 없으며, 관계대명사를 생략하지 않는다.

06 감정을 나타내는 타동사의 과거분사는 '~한 감정을 느끼는'이라는 의미로, 주로 사람을 주어로 하며, 현재분사는 주로 사물을 주어로 하여 '~한 감정을 유발하는'의 의미를 나타낸다.

07 목적격 관계대명사는 접속사와 목적어 역할을 하며 선행사가

사람이면 who나 whom, that, 사물이나 동물이면 which나 that을 쓴다. 목적격 관계대명사절에는 동사 뒤에 목적어가 없다는 것에 주의한다.

08 (1), (3) '난처하게 만드는 상황', '충격을 주는'의 뜻이 자연스러우므로 현재분사, (2), (4) '놀라게 되는', '신나게 되는'이 자연스러우므로 과거분사가 적절하다.

교과서 Reading

확인문제
p.132

1 T　2 F　3 F　4 T

확인문제
p.133

1 F　2 T　3 F　4 T

확인문제
p.133

1 T　2 F　3 F　4 T　5 T　6 F

교과서 확인학습 A
p.134~135

01 Spirit
02 During, were
03 The only, that, was
04 felt scared
05 Luckily, thanks to
06 One of the groups that, was
07 a worldwide movie star
08 Her name
09 a symbol of beauty
10 because of, such as
11 which she wore
12 still love
13 a turning point
14 an international music festival
15 donated money
16 Thanks to, more, than
17 realized that, a UNICEF Goodwill Ambassador
18 went to
19 brought, to
20 shocked, lives
21 volunteered
22 to hand out, support
23 to, passed away, following
24 praised, real beauty
25 To honor
26 who, keep, alive
27 favorite saying
28 *As, get*
29 *One, yourself, the other, others*

교과서 확인학습 B
p.136~137

1 The Spirit of Audrey
2 During World War II, a little girl and her mother were hungry and sick.
3 The only food that they could find was grass.
4 The little girl felt scared all the time.
5 Luckily, the girl survived, thanks to the help of others.
6 One of the groups that helped her was UNICEF.
7 Later, the girl became a worldwide movie star.
8 Her name was Audrey Hepburn.
9 When she grew up, Hepburn became a symbol of beauty.
10 She was very popular because of her hit movies, such as *My Fair Lady and Roman Holiday.*
11 The little black dress which she wore in a movie is famous even today.
12 Many people still love her style.
13 The autumn of 1987 was a turning point in Hepburn's life.
14 She went to an international music festival in Macau.
15 Many people donated money at the festival, and the money went to UNICEF.
16 Thanks to her fame, UNICEF collected more money than ever before.
17 Hepburn realized that her fame could help others, so she became a UNICEF Goodwill Ambassador.
18 First, Hepburn went to Ethiopia in 1988.
19 There, she brought food to hungry children.
20 She was shocked because their lives were very difficult.
21 After that, she volunteered in other countries.
22 In 1990, she visited Vietnam to hand out medicine and support clean drinking water programs.
23 Her last trip was to Somalia in 1992, and she passed away the following year.
24 Many people praised her beauty and style, but Hepburn's real beauty was her heart.
25 To honor her, UNICEF made a statue, *The Spirit of Audrey.*
26 People who respect her keep her mission alive.
27 Her favorite saying shows her mission.
28 *As you get older, remember you have two hands.*
29 *One is for helping yourself, and the other is for helping others.*

01 (A) During (B) was (C) was
　　02 a little
　　girl and her mother　　03 ③　　04 Later
05 like　　06 fame　　07 ①, ⑤　　08 ③
09 ③　　10 ②　　11 ⑤　　12 ②
13 ①　　14 was → were
15 before → after　　16 ③　　17 ②, ④
18 ③　　19 ⑤　　20 ②, ④　　21 ②
22 ③　　23 ②　　24 ④, ⑤
25 It made a statue, *The Spirit of Audrey.*

01 (A) during+ 특정 기간을 나타내는 명사, while+주어+동사
(B) 주어 The only food를 서술하는 동사를 써야 하므로 was
가 적절하다. that they could find는 주어를 수식하는 관계대
명사절이다. (C) 문장의 주어는 groups가 아니라 One이므로
was가 적절하다.

02 '한 어린 소녀와 그녀의 어머니'를 가리킨다.

03 ⓑ: ~ 덕분에, ~ 때문에, ①, ②, ④, ⑤: ~ 때문에, ③ ~ 대신에

04 late: 늦은; 늦게 / later 나중에

05 such as = like: ~와 같은

06 famous의 명사 'fame'을 쓰는 것이 적절하다.

07 ⓒ와 ①, ⑤번은 접속사, 나머지는 다 관계대명사이다

08 ③ 1987년 가을은 헵번의 인생 '전환점'이었다.

09 주어진 문장의 that에 주목한다. ③번 앞 문장의 내용을 받고 있
으므로 ③번이 적절하다.

10 ⓐ와 ①, ②, ④: 동명사, ③, ⑤: 현재분사

11 위 글은 ⑤ '전기'이다. ① (신문·잡지의) 기사, ③ 독후감, ④
수필

12 ② 헵번은 에티오피아에서 '굶주린 아이들에게 음식을 가져다주
었다.'

13 ① how: 어떻게, 어떠하게, ⓐ 제2차 세계 대전 중에 당신의
삶은 '어땠나요?' ⓒ '어떻게' 유니세프를 위해 일하기 시작했나
요?

14 주어가 My family and I이기 때문에 were로 고치는 것이 적
절하다.

15 1987년 마카오의 한 음악 축제가 오드리의 인생을 바꾼 것이기
때문에, 1987년 '이후에' 아프리카와 아시아의 몇 나라들을 방
문해서 봉사했다고 고치는 것이 적절하다.

16 ⓐ bring A to B: B에게 A를 가져다주다, to Somalia: 소말
리아에[로], ⓒ for helping: 돕기 위한

17 ⓑ 부사적 용법(목적), ① 부사적 용법(결과), ③ 부사적 용법
(원인), ⑤ 부사적 용법(목적), ② 명사적 용법, ④ 형용사적 용
법

18 ③ 헵번이 배우로서의 성공 여부는 본문에 언급되어 있지 않다.

19 ⑤ 유니세프가 '오드리의 정신'이라는 동상을 어디에 만들었
는지는 대답할 수 없다. ① In 1988. ② She brought food

to them. ③ To hand out medicine and support clean
drinking water programs. ④ In 1992.

20 ② 실제로, ④ 적어도, ⓐ와 나머지: 마침내

21 ① 의지가 강한, ② 이기적인, ③ 다정한, ④ 자선을 베푸는, 궁
핍한 사람들을 돕는, ⑤ 관대한

22 ③ 글쓴이의 엄마가 언제 행복하게 느끼는지는 알 수 없다.
① The writer's mom. ② She smiles a lot and tries
to see the good in everything. ④ She had a serious
car accident. She was in the hospital for six months.
⑤ Because she always helps people in need and she
donates money and does volunteer work.

23 오드리 헵번이 방문한 국가와 그곳에서 한 활동을 소개함으로써
필자는 '헵번의 진정한 아름다움이 그녀의 마음이었음'을 설명하
고 있다.

24 ⓐ와 ④, ⑤번은 동명사이다. 명사를 수식하더라도 목적이나
용도를 나타낼 때는 동명사이다. drinking water: 식수, be
fond of: ~을 좋아하다, 나머지는 다 현재분사

25 그녀를 기리기 위해, 유니세프는 '오드리의 정신'이라는 동상을 만
들었다.

01 World War Two 또는 the second World War
02 that
03 (A) the help　　(B) movie star
04 (A) music festival　　(B) UNICEF Goodwill
　　Ambassador
05 donated　　06 (A) Thanks to (B) collected (C) than
07 As[Because]
08 (A) shocked　　(B) keep　　(C) *the other*
09 (A) volunteered　　(B) her heart
10 ⓐ died ⓑ *become* 또는 *grow*
11 your life during World War II
12 others
13 (A) help　　(B) help

01 로마 숫자를 포함하고 있는 단어를 영어로 읽을 때 '단어+
기수' 또는 'the+서수+단어'로 읽는다. 단, Elizabeth II는
Elizabeth the second로 읽는다.

02 선행사에 수식어 the only가 있을 때에는 보통 관계대명사 that
을 사용한다.

03 오드리 헵번은 다른 사람들의 '도움' 덕분에 제2차 세계 대전에
서 살아남았고 후에 세계적인 '영화배우'가 되었다.

04 매우 인기 있는 여배우였던 헵번은 1987년 가을에 마카오의 한
국제 '음악 축제'에 갔다. 그 때 그녀는 자신의 명성이 다른 사람
들을 도울 수 있다는 것을 깨닫고, '유니세프 친선 대사'가 되었
다.

05 donate: 기부하다, 자선단체에 주다 / 과거시제로 쓰는 것이 적절하다.

06 (A) 그녀의 명성 '덕분에'라고 해야 하므로 Thanks to가 적절하다. in spite of: ~에도 불구하고, (B) 더 많은 돈을 '모았다'고 해야 하므로 collected가 적절하다. correct: 바로잡다, 정정하다, (C) 어느 때'보다도' 더 많은 돈이라고 해야 하므로 than이 적절하다. then: 그때, 그 다음에

07 'so' 대신에, 이유를 나타내는 접속사 'As[Because, Since]'를 맨 앞에 쓰는 것이 적절하다.

08 (A) 그녀가 '충격을 받은' 것이기 때문에 shocked가 적절하다. (B) 주어가 복수(People)이므로 동사는 keep이 적절하다. (C) 두 개의 손 중에 다른 한 손을 가리키므로 the other가 적절하다. the other: 둘 중 나머지 하나, another 셋 이상 중에서 두 번째 것을 가리킨다.

09 헵번이 많은 나라들을 방문하고 그곳에서 '봉사한' 것으로 판단하건대, 헵번의 진정한 아름다움은 '그녀의 마음'이었다. judging from ~으로 판단하건대[미루어 보아]

10 ⓐ pass away 죽다, ⓑ get[become, grow]+형용사의 비교급: 점점 ~해지다

11 '제2차 세계 대전 동안 당신의 삶'을 가리킨다.

12 other people은 others로 바꿔 쓸 수 있다.

13 제2차 세계 대전 동안, Audrey의 가족과 Audrey는 굶주리고 아팠고 다른 사람들의 '도움' 덕분에 살아남았다. 1987년 마카오의 한 음악 축제 이후, Audrey는 자신의 명성이 다른 사람들을 '도울 수 있다'는 것을 알게 되었고, 유니세프를 위해 일하기 시작했다.

영역별 핵심문제 p.145~149

01 ③ 02 (1) (m)oment (2) (p)raised
   (3) (r)ealized (4) (c)ollecting   03 ④

04 (1) hold (2) fell (3) clean (4) raise

05 can you help me wash them?

06 (A) Why, (B) What   07 ③

08 Shall we raise money and help the people there?
   Let's raise money and help the people there.

09 ⑤

10 can you help me (to) move these books?

11 donate   12 ②

13 Doing[To do] yoga makes me relaxed.

14 ③   15 ④   16 ②, ③   17 ③, ⑤

18 (1) interesting, bored (2) tired

19 (1) The man (who/whom) I saw at the café was
       Park Jisung.
   (2) I love the dog (which) my grandmother adopted.
   (3) Jason didn't know about the party, so he was
       really surprised.

(4) We were so shocked when we heard about the
    accident.   20 which   21 ②

22 People who[that] respect her keep her mission
   alive.   23 ⑤

24 (1) 에티오피아(1988년), (2) 베트남(1990년), (3) 소말리아
   (1992년)   25 (A) terrible (B) changed (C) what

26 working   27 ④

28 helped young students with math homework

29 are → is

01 ① homeless: 집 없는, 노숙자의 ② elderly: 나이가 지긋한 ③ worldwide: 세계적인 ④ international: 국제적인 ⑤ following: (그) 다음의

02 (1) moment: 순간, 잠깐 (2) praise: 칭찬하다 (3) realize: 깨닫다, 알아차리다 (4) collect: 모으다, 수집하다

03 fame: 명성 / 유명한 상태

04 (1) hold a party: 파티를 열다 (2) fall down: 넘어지다 (3) clean up: ~을 치우다, ~을 청소하다 (4) raise money: 돈을 모금하다

05 Can you help 목적어 (to) 동사원형 ~?: 목적어가 ~하는 것을 도와주겠니?

06 Why don't you ~?: ~하지 그래? What: 무엇

07 남자아이 1이 'Can you help me wash these dogs?(이 개들 씻기는 거 도와줄 수 있니?)'라는 묻는 질문에 'Sure. But I have to walk these dogs first. After that, I will help you.(그럼. 근데 나 이 개들 산책 먼저 시켜야 해. 끝나고 나서 도와줄게.)'라고 대답했으므로, 개 산책을 시킬 것이다.

08 특정 행동을 제안할 때는 'Why don't we ~?'로 시작하는 표현을 쓴다. 'Shall we ~?', 'Let's ~' 등의 표현도 쓸 수 있다.

09 ① 어떻게 어려움에 처한 사람들을 위해 돈을 모금할 것인가? ② 어디서 특별 행사가 열리는가? ③ 언제 특별 행사가 열리는가? ④ 어디서 큰 불이 있었는가? ⑤ 언제 Mapletown에서 큰 불이 있었는가?

10 Can you help 목적어 (to) 동사원형 ~?: 목적어가 ~하는 것을 도와주겠니?

11 donate: 기부하다 / 사람들을 돕기 위해 무언가를 주다

12 오늘 오후에 무엇을 하기를 원하는지 묻는 질문에, 테니스를 같이 치자고 제안하는 것이 적절하다. Why don't we ~?: ~하는 게 어떨까?

13 내가 느긋해지는 것이므로 relaxed로 써야 한다.

14 감정을 나타내는 타동사의 과거분사는 '~한 감정을 느끼는'이라는 의미로 주로 사람을 주어로 하며, 현재분사는 주로 사물을 주어로 하여 '~한 감정을 유발하는'의 의미를 나타낸다.

15 ④ Susan is the woman (who/whom/that) I helped on the street.

16 ① The little girl felt scared all the time. ④ Riding

a roller coaster makes me excited. ⑤ It was very exciting, and I became interested in hockey!

17 ③, ⑤번은 주격 관계대명사이고, 나머지는 모두 목적격 관계대명사이다. run into: ~을 우연히 만나다

18 감정을 나타내는 타동사의 과거분사는 '~한 감정을 느끼는'이라는 의미로, 주로 사람을 주어로 하며, 현재분사는 주로 사물을 주어로 하여 '~한 감정을 유발하는'의 의미를 나타낸다.

19 (1), (2) 관계대명사의 선행사가 사람이면 who, whom이나 that을, 사물이면 which나 that을 사용한다. (3), (4) 감정을 나타내는 타동사의 과거분사는 '~한 감정을 느끼는'이라는 의미로, 주로 사람을 주어로 한다.

20 목적격 관계대명사 which를 생략할 수 있다.

21 ② 많은 사람이 '여전히 그녀의 스타일을 사랑한다.'

22 주격 관계대명사 'who'나 'that'을 보충하면 된다.

23 ⓑ와 ⑤번은 (비례) ~함에 따라, ~할수록, As you get older: 나이가 들어갈수록, ① 같은 정도로, 마찬가지로, ② ~처럼, ~하는 대로, ③ ~할 때, ④ ~이므로, ~이기 때문에

24 에티오피아(1988년) → 베트남(1990년) → 소말리아(1992년) 순서로 방문했다.

25 (A) 제2차 세계 대전 동안 나의 삶은 '끔찍했다'고 해야 하므로 terrible이 적절하다. terrific: 아주 좋은, 멋진, 훌륭한, (B) 마카오의 한 음악 축제가 인생을 '바꿨다'고 해야 하므로 changed가 적절하다. exchange: 교환하다, (C) 당신은 '무엇을' 했습니까?'라고 해야 하므로 what이 적절하다. how를 쓰면 do 다음에 목적어를 써야 한다.

26 begin은 목적어로 to부정사와 동명사를 둘 다 쓸 수 있다.

27 ④ 마카오의 음악 축제에 Audrey가 참가한 이유는 알 수 없다. ① It was terrible. ② Thanks to the help of others. ③ In 1987, a musical festival in Macau changed her life and she learned that her fame could help other people. ⑤ Some countries in Africa and Asia.

28 앞 문장의 내용을 가리킨다.

29 주어가 동명사 helping이므로 단수로 취급해야 하고, helping이하는 일반적인 사실을 나타내기 때문에 현재시제로 써야 하므로 is로 고치는 것이 적절하다.

단원별 예상문제　　　　　　　p.150~153

01 favor **02** ④ **03** What **04** ②, ⑤
05 ③ **06** ⑤ **07** ① **08** ⑤
09 nursing home **10** ② **11** ③
12 Why don't we check the volunteering website for teens?
13 (1) This is the cell phone (which/that) I broke yesterday.
　　(2) The speed at which everything moved felt strange.

---

　　(3) The girl who I met the other day was very pretty.
　　(4) I was very worried about his health.

14 (1) excited (2) interested
15 ②번, excited → scared 또는 frightened **16** ③, ⑤
17 (A) because of (B) is (C) turning **18** ④
19 she realized (that) her fame could help others
20 volunteered **21** helping others
22 *you → yourself*
23 We survived thanks to the help of others.
24 in some countries in Africa and Asia **25** ⑤

01 주어진 보기는 명사와 형용사의 관계이다. beauty: 아름다움, 미(美) beautiful: 아름다운 favor: 호의, 친절 favorable: 호의적인

02 friendly: 친절한 gentle: 온화한 curious: 호기심 많은 polite: 공손한 careful: 주의깊은 outgoing: 외향적인 patient: 끈기 있는

03 What kinds of ~: 어떤 종류의 What about 동명사 ~?: ~하는 게 어떨까?

04 thanks to: ~ 덕분에 because of: ~ 때문에 due to: ~ 때문에, ~ 덕분에

05 (B) 책을 옮기는 것을 도와줄 수 있느냐는 질문에 (C) 도와줄 수 있다고 대답하며 책으로 뭘 할지 질문하자 (A) 어린이 도서관에 기부할 거라고 대답한다.

06 (C) 어린이 병원에서 봉사 활동을 할 것을 제안하자 (B) 좋다고 대답하며, 거기서 뭘 할 수 있는지 질문한다. (A) 아픈 아이들을 위해 음악을 연주할 수 있다고 대답한다.

07 저번에 봉사 활동으로 공원을 청소했으므로 이번에는 무엇을 할지 묻는 질문이 연결되는 것이 자연스럽다. 또한 주어진 문장에 대해 양로원에 가서 청소하는 것을 제안하는 내용이 나오는 ①이 적절하다.

08 ⓐ visit ⓑ clean it up ⓒ to do ⓓ something fun ⓔ hold

09 nursing home: 양로원 / 너무 나이 들거나 병이 들어서 스스로를 돌볼 수 없는 사람들이 사는 장소

10 주어진 문장은 봉사활동에 대한 부가적 설명으로, 봉사활동을 제안하는 말에 이어 나오는 것이 적절하다.

11 do volunteer work: 자원 봉사를 하다

12 Why don't we ~?: ~하는 게 어떠니? check: 확인하다

13 (1) 선행사가 사물이므로 which나 that, (2) 전치사가 관계대명사 앞에 올 경우에는 관계대명사 that을 쓸 수 없으며, 관계대명사를 생략하지 않는다. (3) 관계대명사가 접속사와 대명사의 역할을 하므로 목적어 her를 삭제해야 한다. (4) 감정을 나타내는 타동사의 과거분사는 '~한 감정을 느끼는'이라는 의미로, 주로 사람을 주어로 한다.

14 (1) excite는 타동사로 '흥분시키다'라는 의미이다. 경기가 나를

22 outside, walk around

23 on, piece, scary

24 mean, painting   25 it, rooster

26 crow every   27 crowing, that, beginning

28 evil, away, crows

29 never heard, before

30 Actually, afraid, spirits   31 draw, for

32 draw, rooster   33 Put, above, protect

34 Yes, will   35 so, that, longer

36 all, traditional, in

37 understand, lot   38 want, visit, with

---

01 Traditional, Symbols

02 visiting, to meet, from

03 going to stay at, for

04 When, arrives, guest room   05 will stay here

06 is full of traditional   07 Look at

08 three things   09 bats

10 Bats on, pillow, scary

11 symbols of luck, long life

12 Western countries, remind, of darkness, scary

13 shows, grandfather's room

14 meet, greet each other

15 Have, seen, kind of look

16 haven't, so, that, can't

17 For a long time, have thought

18 don't close, when, sleep   19 interesting

20 watch over, why, looks like

21 Now understand

22 go outside, walk around

23 on the piece, looks scary

24 mean, rooster   25 is it

26 crow every morning

27 means, beginning

28 have believed, go away when, crows

29 never heard, before

30 Actually, afraid of, evil spirits

31 Could, draw, for   32 draw, for

33 Put, above, will protect   34 will

35 so, that, to stay longer

36 traditional Korean symbols   37 a lot of

38 want to visit, with

---

1 전통적인 한국의 상징물

2 피터는 자매 학교 친구인 미나를 만나기 위해 한국을 방문 중이다.

3 피터는 일주일간 미나네 할아버지 댁에 머무를 것이다.

4 그가 도착하자, 미나가 그에게 손님방을 보여준다.

5 피터, 넌 여기에 머무르게 될 거야.

6 이 손님방은 한국의 전통 물건들로 가득 차 있어.

7 이 베개를 봐.

8 이것들은 뭐야?

9 그건 박쥐들이야.

10 내 베개 위에 박쥐가? 그거 겁나는데!

11 그렇지 않아. 한국에서는 박쥐가 행운과 장수의 상징이거든.

12 그거 놀라운 일인데. 서구의 많은 나라들에서 박쥐는 사람들에게 어둠과 무서운 것들을 상기시키거든.

13 미나는 피터에게 할아버지의 방을 보여준다.

14 피터와 미나의 할아버지가 만나서 서로 인사한다.

15 안녕, 피터! 너는 이런 종류의 자물쇠를 전에 본 적 있니?

16 아니요, 본 적 없어요. 그 자물쇠는 너무 오래되어서 사실 알아볼 수가 없는데, 그건 물고기인가요?

17 맞아. 오랜 세월 동안, 한국인들은 물고기가 훌륭한 파수꾼이라고 생각해 왔단다.

18 물고기는 잘 때도 눈을 감지 않거든.

19 그거 재미있군요.

20 우리는 물고기가 귀중품을 지킬 수 있다고 생각해. 그것이 이 자물쇠가 물고기 모양으로 생긴 이유란다.

21 이제 이해가 되는군요.

22 그들은 밖에 나가서 정원을 걷는다.

23 저 종이에는 무엇이 그려져 있는 거죠? 무서워 보여요.

24 이 수탉 그림을 말하는 거니?

25 오, 그게 수탉이에요?

26 응, 그렇단다. 수탉은 매일 아침 울지.

27 수탉의 울음은 새로운 날이 시작하는 것을 의미해.

28 오랫동안 한국인들은 수탉이 울 때 악령이 물러간다고 믿어 왔단다.

29 우리의 점심은 항상 건강에 좋고, 맛 또한 좋습니다!

30 정말요? 전 그런 말을 들어본 적이 없어요.

31 미나야, 날 위해 수탉을 그려 줄 수 있니?

32 물론이지. 내가 널 위해 커다란 수탉을 그려줄게!

33 그 그림을 네 문 위에 걸어 놓으렴. 그러면 그게 널 지켜 줄 거야.

34 네, 그럴게요.

35 난 이번 여행이 매우 즐거워서 더 오래 머무르고 싶다.

36 난 이 집의 모든 전통적인 한국의 상징물들이 아주 마음에 든다.

37 나는 이제 그것들을 많이 알게 되었다.

38 난 우리 가족과 함께 한국을 다시 방문하고 싶다.

1 Traditional Korean Symbols

2 Peter is visiting Korea to meet a friend, Mina, from a sister school.

3 Peter is going to stay at her grandfather's house for a week.

4 When he arrives, Mina shows him the guest room.

5 Peter, you will stay here.

6 This guest room is full of traditional Korean things.

7 Look at this pillow.

8 What are these things?

9 They're bats.

10 Bats on my pillow? That's scary!

11 Not really. In Korea, bats are symbols of luck and a long life.

12 That's surprising. In many Western countries, bats remind people of darkness and scary things.

13 Mina shows Peter her grandfather's room.

14 Peter and Mina's grandfather meet and greet each other.

15 Hi, Peter! Have you ever seen this kind of lock before?

16 No, I haven't. It's so old that I can't really tell, but is it a fish?

17 Yes. For a long time, Koreans have thought that fish are good guards.

18 Fish don't close their eyes, even when they sleep.

19 That's interesting.

20 We think fish can watch over valuable things. That's why this lock looks like a fish.

21 Now I understand.

22 They go outside and walk around the garden.

23 What is on that piece of paper? It looks scary.

24 Do you mean this painting of a rooster?

25 Oh, is it a rooster?

26 Yes, it is. Roosters crow every morning.

27 Their crowing means that a new day is beginning.

28 For many years, Koreans have believed evil spirits go away when a rooster crows.

29 Really? I've never heard that before.

30 Actually, I'm afraid of darkness and evil spirits.

31 Could you draw a rooster for me, Mina?

32 Sure. I'll draw a big rooster for you!

33 Put the drawing above your door. Then it will protect you.

34 Yes, I will.

35 I'm enjoying this trip so much that I want to stay longer.

36 I love all the traditional Korean symbols in this house.

37 Now I understand a lot of them.

38 I want to visit Korea again with my family.

Think and Write

1. traditional Chinese dances
2. There are
3. For example, are, fan
4. One of, dances is
5. dress, act like
6. usually, on, such as
7. dance moves, great
8. to practice, someday

Presentation Time

1. have a good time
2. follow
3. take off, when, go into
4. bow, others
5. give something to older people
6. blow your nose, point at
7. Lastly, call, by, first names

Think and Write

1. Do you know about traditional Chinese dances?
2. There are many kinds.
3. For example, there are a lion dance, a fan dance, and an umbrella dance.
4. One of the most famous dances is the lion dance.
5. In this dance, two dancers dress and act like lions.
6. They usually dance on special days, such as New Year's Day.
7. I think their dance moves are great.
8. I hope to practice this dance someday.

Presentation Time

1. Do you want to have a good time in Korea?
2. Then follow these steps.
3. First, please take off your shoes when you go into people's homes.
4. Next, bow when you greet others.
5. Also, use two hands when you give something to older people.
6. And do not blow your nose at the table and do not point at people.
7. Lastly, do not call older people by their first names.

11 feed, 먹이를 주다　12 documentary, 다큐멘터리
13 grow, 재배하다　14 waste, 쓰레기, 폐기물
15 plate, 접시　16 experiment, 실험

단어 TEST Step 1　p.21

01 온난화
02 낭비하다; 쓰레기, 폐기물
03 끔찍한
04 두다, 놓다
05 지구의
06 해수면
07 사라지다
08 선풍기, 부채
09 초조한, 긴장된
10 환경
11 토양, 흙
12 충분한; 충분히
13 대신에
14 과정
15 흥미로운
16 오염
17 뚜껑
18 기르다, 키우다
19 섭취하다, 먹다, 소모하다
20 생산하다, 만들다
21 바닥, 맨 아래
22 고정하다
23 물을 주다
24 공간
25 정원 가꾸기, 원예
26 건강한, 건강에 좋은
27 연결하다
28 도움이 되는, 유용한
29 실험
30 해결책
31 (신문) 기사
32 생산적인
33 먹이를 주다, 먹이다
34 화학 물질
35 점점 ~해지다
36 제자리에
37 올라가다, 상승하다
38 (전기, 가스, 수도 등을) 끄다
39 (시간이) 다 되다
40 위험에 처한
41 A에게 B를 상기시키다
42 A를 B로 바꾸다
43 버리다

단어 TEST Step 2　p.22

01 plate
02 problem
03 bottom
04 documentary
05 warming
06 island
07 terrible
08 air conditioner
09 speech contest
10 solution
11 pollution
12 information
13 article
14 clay
15 amazing
16 sew
17 grow
18 feed
19 process
20 anywhere
21 pot
22 experiment
23 chemical
24 traditional
25 productive
26 hang
27 solve
28 environment
29 disappear
30 consume
31 helpful
32 gardening
33 global
34 connect
35 fill A with B
36 go up
37 in danger
38 turn A into B
39 cut A into B
40 remind A of B
41 throw away
42 turn on
43 be worried about

단어 TEST Step 3　p.23

1 produce, 생산하다　2 raise, 기르다, 키우다
3 consume, 먹다　4 repeat, 반복하다　5 hole, 구멍
6 fix, 고정시키다　7 connect, 연결하다　8 water, 물을 주다
9 chemical, 화학 물질　10 productive, 생산적인

대화문 TEST Step 1　p.24~25

Listen and Talk 1 A

leave, on their plates, worried about wasting food / should not put / right, shouldn't

Listen and Talk 1 B

watch, last night / didn't, What, about / global warming, is getting, going up, worried / heard about, disappearing, are losing / terrible / way to stop / turn off, instead of / try to

Listen and Talk 1 C

look nervous, wrong / worried about, are about / are, going to / soil pollution, enough information / What about, worried about, to do something / isn't there / in danger, enough water, in the near future / will talk about, solutions, for your advice

Listen and Talk 2 A

Look at, how to / for thirty minutes, turn on, anywhere / interesting

Listen and Talk 2 B

Where, get / made, myself / yourself, amazing / Why don't, not difficult / how to make / Cut, into, pieces / sounds easy, as, present

Listen and Talk 2 C

Have, heard of / haven't / global environmental, turn off, for an hour / Why, do / remind, of / such a / how to join / turn off, in March / will join

Do It Yourself

look upset, going on / worried about, about saving / how about using / how to use / Add, choose / sounds easy, try

대화문 TEST Step 2　p.26~27

Listen and Talk 1 A

B: In my school, students leave so much food on their plates. I'm worried about wasting food.
G: Right, that's a big problem. We should not put too much food on our plates.
B: You're right. We shouldn't.

Listen and Talk 1 B

G: Did you watch the documentary last night?

B: No, I didn't. What was it about?

G: It was about global warming. The Earth is getting hotter, and sea levels are going up. I'm worried about the Earth.

B: Oh, I've heard about that problem before. Some islands are disappearing, so people are losing their homes.

G: Yes. It is terrible.

B: Is there any way to stop it?

G: We can save energy. We should turn off the lights when we don't need them. We should also use fans instead of air conditioners.

B: Those are great ideas. I'll try to do those things.

Listen and Talk 1 C

B: You look nervous. What's wrong?

G: I'm worried about the speech contest next week. The speeches are about environmental problems and their solutions.

B: What are you going to talk about?

G: I want to talk about soil pollution, but I can't find enough information.

B: What about water problems instead? I read an article, and it said we don't have enough water. I'm really worried about it. I think we have to do something about that problem.

G: But isn't there enough water for everyone?

B: No. In some countries, people are in danger because they don't have enough water. Our country could have this problem in the near future.

G: Oh, I didn't know that. I will talk about that problem and its solutions. Thank you for your advice!

Listen and Talk 2 A

G: Look at this ball. Can you tell me how to use it?

M: Just play soccer for thirty minutes, and the light will turn on. You can use the light anywhere.

G: Wow, that's interesting.

Listen and Talk 2 B

B: I like your bag, Jenny. Where did you get it?

G: I made it myself.

B: You made it yourself? That's amazing.

G: Why don't you make one? It's not difficult.

B: Really? Can you tell me how to make it?

G: Sure. Find some old jeans. Cut them into small pieces. Then sew the pieces together.

B: That sounds easy. I'll make one as a birthday present for my sister.

Listen and Talk 2 C

G: Have you heard of Earth Hour before?

B: No, I haven't. What is it?

G: It's a global environmental event. People turn off their lights for an hour.

B: Why do they do that?

G: They do it to remind people of our environmental problems. They believe such a small action can change the world.

B: Oh, I see. Can you tell me how to join it?

G: Sure. Just turn off your lights from 8:30 p.m. to 9:30 p.m. on the last Saturday in March.

B: That's easy. I will join the next Earth Hour.

Do It Yourself

G: You look upset. What's going on?

B: I am worried about my science homework. I need to make a short video about saving the environment. But making a video is difficult.

G: Well, how about using this application? It's easy.

B: Can you tell me how to use it?

G: Sure! Open the application. Add your photos and choose some music. Then it will make a video with your photos.

B: Wow, that sounds easy. I'll try it now. Thanks.

본문 TEST Step 1   p.28~29

01 Science Project, Home
02 What, reading
03 reading, article about
04 growing, without soil
05 grow, raise, system
06 Is, possible
07 see, try, at
08 bacteria, main parts
09 After, feed, waste
10 turned into, by
11 clean, by consuming
12 process, repeated, again
13 Home, by
14 How, make, at
15 Why, good
16 From, to
17 tank, tube, cutter, clay
18 holes, bottom, pot
19 Then, put, in
20 lid, put, in
21 fixed, in, with
22 another, hole, through
23 put, in
24 used, connect, to
25 filled, with, put
26 turned on
27 grew, raised, with
28 fed, grown, in
29 stay healthy, all, time
30 things, learned, experiment
31 saved because, watering
32 for, because, used
33 Finally, anywhere, space
34 out, produce, raise
35 choose, far easier, gardening

36 much, productive, growing

37 much, soil, saves

38 produced, way, because, healthy

본문 TEST Step 2   p.30~31

01 Science Project   02 What, reading

03 reading, article about

04 growing, without soil

05 grow, raise, system   06 Is, possible

07 see, try, at   08 bacteria, main parts

09 After, feed, waste   10 turned into, by

11 clean, by consuming

12 process, repeated, again   13 Home, by

14 How, make, at   15 Why, good   16 From, to

17 tank, tube, cutter, clay

18 holes, bottom, pot   19 Then, put, in

20 lid, put, in   21 fixed, in, with

22 another hole, through   23 put, in

24 used, connect, to   25 filled, with, put

26 turned on   27 grew, raised, with

28 fed, grown, in   29 stay healthy, all time

30 things, learned, experiment

31 saved because, watering

32 for, because, used

33 Finally, anywhere, space

34 out, produce, raise

35 choose, far easier, gardening

36 much, productive, growing

37 much, soil, saves

38 produced, way, because, healthy

본문 TEST Step 3   p.32~33

1 나의 과학 프로젝트: 가정용 아쿠아포닉스

2 무엇을 읽고 있니?

3 아쿠아포닉스에 관한 기사를 읽고 있어.

4 흙 없이 식물을 재배할 수 있는 방법이야.

5 또 한 가지 장치만으로도 식물과 물고기를 동시에 키울 수 있어.

6 그게 가능하니?

7 곧 알게 될 거야. 내가 과학 프로젝트로 집에서 해 볼 예정이거든.

8 물고기, 박테리아, 식물이 아쿠아포닉스의 주요 부분이다.

9 물고기에게 먹이를 주면, 그것들은 배설물을 만들어 낸다.

10 이 배설물은 박테리아에 의해 식물의 먹이로 바뀐다.

11 식물은 그 먹이를 먹음으로써 물을 정화한다.

12 이러한 과정이 계속해서 반복된다!

13 가정용 아쿠아포닉스   에릭 잭슨

14 질문: 집에서 아쿠아포닉스 장치를 어떻게 만들 수 있을까?

15 아쿠아포닉스가 왜 좋은가?

16 기간: 5월 15일부터 8월 15일까지

17 재료: 화분과 작은 돌들, 어항, 플라스틱 관, 수중 펌프, 식물, 물고기, 커터칼, 찰흙

18 절차: 화분 바닥에 구멍들을 뚫었다.

19 그런 후에 화분에 작은 돌들을 넣고 식물을 심었다.

20 어항 덮개에 큰 구멍을 내고 구멍에 그 화분을 넣었다.

21 찰흙으로 화분을 제자리에 고정하였다.

22 덮개에 또 다른 구멍을 하나 만들고 그 안에 관을 넣었다.

23 어항에 수중 펌프를 넣었다.

24 관을 이용하여 펌프를 화분에 연결하였다.

25 어항에 물을 채우고 물고기 몇 마리를 거기에 넣었다.

26 그러고 나서 펌프를 작동하였다.

27 결과: 이 실험으로 나는 아쿠아포닉스로 식물과 물고기를 키웠다.

28 나는 그저 물고기에 밥만 주었는데도 식물은 석 달 동안 17cm나 자랐다.

29 물고기는 건강을 유지하며 물은 항상 깨끗하다.

30 결론: 아쿠아포닉스에 관한 몇 가지 중요한 사항이 이 실험에서 발견되었다.

31 첫째, 식물에 물을 줄 필요가 없으므로 물이 절약된다.

32 둘째, 화학 물질이 사용되지 않으므로 아쿠아포닉스는 환경에 이롭다.

33 끝으로, 넓은 공간이 필요하지 않으므로 당신은 어디에서나 아쿠아포닉스를 쉽게 할 수 있다.

34 나는 알게 되었다...몇몇 농부들은 채소를 생산하고 물고기를 키우는 데 아쿠아포닉스를 이용한다.

35 그들은 아쿠아포닉스가 전통 재배 방식보다 훨씬 더 쉽기 때문에 그것을 선택한다.

36 또한, 아쿠아포닉스는 식량을 재배하는 훨씬 더 생산적인 방법이다.

37 식물들이 흙에서 자라는 식물보다 훨씬 빠르게 자라고 공간도 절약한다.

38 그것은 우리와 환경에 훨씬 건강하기 때문에 나는 미래에 더 많은 식량이 이런 방식으로 생산되기를 희망한다.

본문 TEST Step 4-Step 5   p.34~37

1 My Science Project: Home Aquaponics

2 What are you reading?

3 I'm reading an article about aquaponics.

4 It's a way of growing plants without soil.

5 We can also grow plants and raise fish in just one system.

6 Is that possible?

7 We'll see. I'm going to try it at home for my science project.

8 Fish, bacteria, and plants are the main parts of aquaponics.

9 After you feed the fish, they produce waste.

10 The waste is turned into food for the plants by bacteria.

11 The plants clean the water by consuming the food.

12 This process is repeated again and again!

13 Home Aquaponics   by Eric Jackson

14 Questions: How can I make an aquaponics system at home?

15 Why is aquaponics good?

16 Period: From May 15 to August 15

17 Materials: a pot & small stones, a fish tank, a plastic tube, a water pump, plants, some fish, a box cutter, clay

18 Steps: I made holes in the bottom of a pot.

19 Then I put small stones and plants in it.

20 I made a big hole in the lid of the fish tank and put the pot in the hole.

21 I fixed the pot in place with clay.

22 I made another hole in the lid and put a tube through it.

23 I put a water pump in the fish tank.

24 I used the tube to connect the pump to the pot.

25 I filled the fish tank with water and put some fish in it.

26 Then I turned on the pump.

27 Results: From this experiment, I grew my plants and raised fish with aquaponics.

28 I just fed the fish, but the plants have grown 17 centimeters in three months.

29 The fish stay healthy and the water is clean all the time.

30 Conclusion: Some important things about aquaponics were learned from this experiment.

31 First, water is saved because the plants don't need watering.

32 Second, it is good for the environment because no chemicals are used.

33 Finally, you can do aquaponics anywhere because it doesn't need much space.

34 I found out... Some farmers use aquaponics to produce vegetables and raise fish.

35 They choose aquaponics because it is far easier than traditional gardening.

36 Also, it is a much more productive way of growing food.

37 The plants grow much faster than plants in soil, and it saves space.

38 I hope more food is produced in this way in the future because it is healthy for us and the environment.

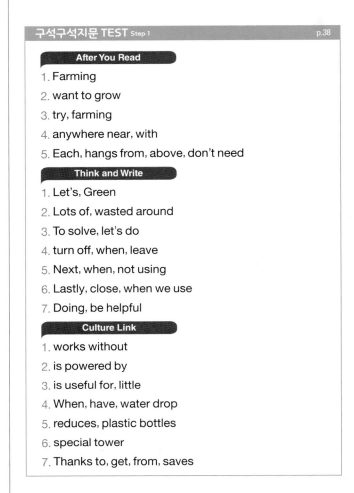

구석구석지문 TEST Step 1   p.38

After You Read

1. Farming
2. want to grow
3. try, farming
4. anywhere near, with
5. Each, hangs from, above, don't need

Think and Write

1. Let's, Green
2. Lots of, wasted around
3. To solve, let's do
4. turn off, when, leave
5. Next, when, not using
6. Lastly, close, when we use
7. Doing, be helpful

Culture Link

1. works without
2. is powered by
3. is useful for, little
4. When, have, water drop
5. reduces, plastic bottles
6. special tower
7. Thanks to, get, from, saves

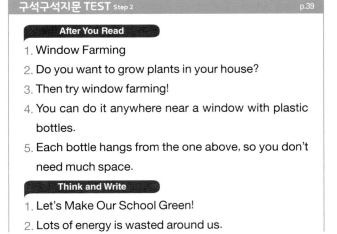

구석구석지문 TEST Step 2   p.39

After You Read

1. Window Farming
2. Do you want to grow plants in your house?
3. Then try window farming!
4. You can do it anywhere near a window with plastic bottles.
5. Each bottle hangs from the one above, so you don't need much space.

Think and Write

1. Let's Make Our School Green!
2. Lots of energy is wasted around us.

3. To solve this problem, let's do these things.

4. First, we should trun off the lights when we leave our classrooms.

5. Next, we should turn off the classroom computers when we are not using them.

6. Lastly, we should close the doors and windows when we use air conditioners.

7. Doing these things will be helpful to our school and the environment.

Culture Link

1. This refrigerator works without electricity.

2. It is powered by dirty water.

3. It is useful for countries that have little electricity.

4. When you need water, just have this water drop!

5. It reduces the use of plastic bottles.

6. This special tower is the Warka Water Tower.

7. Thanks to this tower, people can get water from the air. It saves water.

Lesson 5

10 turning point, 전환점   11 honor, 예우하다, 존중하다
12 mission, 임무, 사명   13 statue, 조각상
14 survive, 살아남다, 생존하다   15 volunteer, 자원 봉사자
16 nursing home, 양로원

단어 TEST Step 1 p.40

01 사고	02 명성	03 아름다움, 미(美)
04 순간, 잠깐	05 마음, 정신, 영혼	06 모으다, 수집하다
07 나이가 지긋한	08 살아남다, 생존하다	
09 존경하다	10 (그) 다음의	11 친선 대사
12 조각상	13 깨닫다, 알아차리다	
14 눈 먼, 장님의	15 국제적인	16 살아 있는, 존속하는
17 세계적인	18 먹이를 주다	19 항목, 물품
20 약	21 기부하다	
22 운이 좋게도, 다행스럽게도		23 (음식을) 제공하다
24 양로원	25 자원봉사의; 자원 봉사자	
26 집 없는, 노숙자의	27 칭찬하다	28 임무, 사명
29 들어 올리다. (자금을) 모으다		30 예우하다, 존중하다
31 전환점	32 속담, 격언	33 호의, 친절
34 지지하다, 원조하다		35 늘, 내내
36 넘어지다	37 나누어 주다	38 죽다, 사망하다
39 ~ 덕분에	40 ~을 치우다, 청소하다	
41 ~을 돕다	42 ~을 찾다	43 ~을 돌보다

단어 TEST Step 2 p.41

01 respect	02 blind	03 saying
04 serve	05 worldwide	06 beauty
07 mission	08 moment	
09 goodwill ambassador		10 favor
11 following	12 statue	13 hold
14 accident	15 raise	16 elderly
17 realize	18 collect	19 nursing home
20 spirit	21 fame	22 honor
23 alive	24 turning point	25 support
26 praise	27 luckily	28 grass
29 medicine	30 survive	31 donate
32 homeless	33 volunteer	34 feed
35 pass away	36 fall down	37 take care of
38 hand out	39 thanks to	40 give a hand
41 in need	42 clean up	43 all the time

단어 TEST Step 3 p.42

1 fame, 명성   2 blind, 눈 먼, 장님의   3 accident, 사고
4 collect, 모으다, 수집하다   5 praise, 칭찬하다
6 realize, 깨닫다, 알아차리다   7 support, 지지하다, 원조하다
8 respect, 존경하다   9 donate, 기부하다

대화문 TEST Step 1 p.43~44

Listen & Talk 1 A
can / help me move / What are, going to / going to donate

Listen & Talk 1 B
wrong with / broke it / happened / a hurry to catch, fell down / terrible, Is there, can do / can you help me carry

Listen & Talk 1 C
can you help, wash them / but, can't, to feed / Why don't you ask / ask you a favor / What / Can you help, wash / have to walk / Thank you

Listen & Talk 2 A
What kinds of volunteer / don't we clean up / right, Let's

Listen & Talk 2 B
As you know, was, Why don't we raise, at, on May, bring your items, donate, give all the money to, give a hand, in need

Listen & Talk 2 C
cleaned up, we going to / don't we visit, nursing home, clean it up / bad idea, to do something fun, Why don't we hold / What / can serve / how about playing / can play the cello / sounds like

Do It Yourself A
want to do on that day / Why don't, volunteer activities, help others, make, better / sounds great, is / who has volunteered a lot / has volunteered, help us find / usually search for, don't we check / good idea

대화문 TEST Step 2 p.45~46

Listen & Talk 1 A
B: Mia, can you help me move these books?
G: Sure. What are you going to do with them?
B: I'm going to donate them to a children's library.

Listen & Talk 1 B
B: Hey, Minji! What's wrong with your leg?
G: I broke it last week.
B: Really? What happened?

G: I was in a hurry to catch a train. But I fell down in the street.

B: Oh, that's terrible! Is there anything I can do for you?

G: Well, can you help me carry this bag?

B: Sure.

Listen & Talk 1 C

B1: Wow! These dogs are so dirty. Jay, can you help me wash them?

B2: Allen, I'm sorry, but I can't. I have to feed the cats now. Why don't you ask Nicky?

B1: Okay! Nicky, can I ask you a favor?

G: Sure, Allen. What is it?

B1: Can you help me wash these dogs?

G: Sure. But I have to walk these dogs first. After that, I will help you.

B1: All right! Thank you.

Listen & Talk 2 A

G: What kinds of volunteer activities can we do?

B: Why don't we clean up our town's streets?

G: All right! Let's do it.

Listen & Talk 2 B

G: Good morning, students! As you know, there was a big fire in Mapletown. Why don't we raise money and help the people there? Come to our special event at the school grounds on May 3! Please bring your items and donate them. We will sell your items. Then, we will give all the money to Mapletown. Please give a hand to people in need.

Listen & Talk 2 C

B1: Next Wednesday is Volunteer Day. We cleaned up the park last time. What are we going to do this time?

G: Why don't we visit a nursing home and clean it up?

B2: That's not a bad idea. But I want to do something fun. Why don't we hold a party for the people there?

G: That's a good idea. What can we do at the party?

B1: We can serve some food.

B2: And how about playing some music? I can play the piano.

G: And I can play the cello.

B1: It sounds like a good plan.

Do It Yourself A

G1: We have a class activity day next Friday. What do you want to do on that day?

B: Why don't we do some volunteer activities? We can

help others and make our community better.

G1: That sounds great, but choosing a good place is not easy.

B: We need someone who has volunteered a lot.

G1: I know Sumin has volunteered a lot. Sumin, can you help us find some good places?

G2: Sure. I usually search for information on the internet. Why don't we check the volunteering website for teens?

B: That's a good idea.

01 Spirit, Audrey 02 During, little, were

03 that, find was 04 felt scared, time

05 Luckily, thanks to

06 groups, helped, was

07 Later, became, worldwide

08 Her name

09 When, up, beauty

10 because of, such as

11 which, wore, even   12 still love, style

13 turning point, life

14 went, international, festival

15 donated money, went

16 Thanks to, more, than

17 realized, fame, others   18 went to, in

19 There, brought, to

20 shocked because, lives

21 After, volunteered, other

22 visited, hand out, support

23 to, passed away, following

24 praised, beauty, real, heart

25 To honor, statue

26 respect, keep, alive

27 favorite saying, mission

28 As, get, remember

29 *One, yourself, other, others*

01 Spirit of Audrey

02 During, little, were hungry, sick

03 The only, that, was

04 felt scared all the time

05 Luckily, thanks to, others

06 One of the groups that, was

41

07 a worldwide movie star

08 Her name was

09 grew up, a symbol of beauty

10 because of, such as

11 which she wore, is famous

12 still love her style   13 a turning point

14 an international music festival

15 donated money, to UNICEF

16 Thanks to, collected more, than

17 realized that, help others, a UNICEF Goodwill Ambassador

18 went to Ethiopia

19 brought, to hungry children

20 was shocked because, lives

21 volunteered in other countries

22 to hand out medicine, support

23 to, passed away, following year

24 praised, real beauty was her heart

25 To honor, made a statue

26 who respect, keep, alive

27 favorite saying, her mission

28 *As, get older*

29 *One, yourself, the other, others*

17 헵번은 자신의 명성이 다른 사람들을 도울 수 있다는 것을 깨닫고, 유니세프 친선 대사가 되었다.

18 먼저, 헵번은 1988년에 에티오피아로 갔다.

19 그곳에서, 그녀는 굶주린 아이들에게 음식을 가져다주었다.

20 그녀는 그들의 삶이 매우 어려웠기 때문에 충격을 받았다.

21 그 후, 그녀는 다른 나라들에서도 봉사하였다.

22 1990년, 그녀는 의약품을 나눠 주고 깨끗한 식수 프로그램을 지원하기 위하여 베트남을 방문하였다.

23 그녀의 마지막 여행은 1992년 소말리아에 간 것이었으며, 이듬해 그녀는 사망하였다.

24 많은 사람이 그녀의 아름다움과 스타일을 칭송했지만, 헵번의 진정한 아름다움은 그녀의 마음이었다.

25 그녀를 기리기 위해, 유니세프는 '오드리의 정신'이라는 동상을 만들었다.

26 그녀를 존경하는 사람들이 그녀의 사명을 이어 나가고 있다.

27 그녀가 가장 좋아했던 구절은 그녀의 사명을 보여 준다.

28 나이가 들어갈수록, 당신에게 손이 두 개가 있다는 것을 기억하라.

29 한 손은 자신을 돕기 위한 것이고, 다른 한 손은 타인을 돕기 위한 것이다.

1 오드리의 정신

2 제2차 세계 대전 동안, 한 어린 소녀와 그녀의 어머니는 굶주리고 아팠다.

3 그들이 찾을 수 있었던 유일한 음식은 풀뿐이었다.

4 어린 소녀는 내내 겁에 질려 있었다.

5 다행히도, 소녀는 다른 사람들의 도움 덕분에 살아남았다.

6 그녀를 도왔던 단체 중 하나는 유니세프(국제 연합 아동 기금)였다.

7 후에, 소녀는 세계적인 영화배우가 되었다.

8 그녀의 이름은 오드리 헵번이었다.

9 그녀가 자랐을 때, 헵번은 아름다움의 상징이 되었다.

10 그녀는 〈마이 페어 레이디〉와 〈로마의 휴일〉과 같은 흥행 영화들로 인해 매우 인기가 있었다.

11 그녀가 영화에서 입었던 아담한 검은 드레스는 심지어 오늘날까지도 유명하다.

12 많은 사람이 여전히 그녀의 스타일을 사랑한다.

13 1987년 가을은 헵번의 인생 전환점이었다.

14 그녀는 마카오의 한 국제 음악 축제에 갔다.

15 많은 사람이 축제에서 돈을 기부했고, 그 돈은 유니세프로 보내졌다.

16 그녀의 명성 덕분에, 유니세프는 어느 때보다도 더 많은 돈을 모았다.

1 The Spirit of Audrey

2 During World War II, a little girl and her mother were hungry and sick.

3 The only food that they could find was grass.

4 The little girl felt scared all the time.

5 Luckily, the girl survived, thanks to the help of others.

6 One of the groups that helped her was UNICEF.

7 Later, the girl became a worldwide movie star.

8 Her name was Audrey Hepburn.

9 When she grew up, Hepburn became a symbol of beauty.

10 She was very popular because of her hit movies, such as *My Fair Lady* and *Roman Holiday*.

11 The little black dress which she wore in a movie is famous even today.

12 Many people still love her style.

13 The autumn of 1987 was a turning point in Hepburn's life.

14 She went to an international music festival in Macau.

15 Many people donated money at the festival, and the money went to UNICEF.

16 Thanks to her fame, UNICEF collected more money than ever before.

17 Hepburn realized that her fame could help others, so she became a UNICEF Goodwill Ambassador.

18 First, Hepburn went to Ethiopia in 1988.

19 There, she brought food to hungry children.

20 She was shocked because their lives were very difficult.

21 After that, she volunteered in other countries.

22 In 1990, she visited Vietnam to hand out medicine and support clean drinking water programs.

23 Her last trip was to Somalia in 1992, and she passed away the following year.

24 Many people praised her beauty and style, but Hepburn's real beauty was her heart.

25 To honor her, UNICEF made a statue, *The Spirit of Audrey*.

26 People who respect her keep her mission alive.

27 Her favorite saying shows her mission.

28 *As you get older, remember you have two hands.*

29 *One is for helping yourself, and the other is for helping others.*

Presentation Time

1. a great person
2. priest, also
3. built, for
4. took care of, taught classes
5. From, that, should help, in need

After You Read B

1. How, during
2. tell me about
3. terrible, were hungry, sick
4. survived thanks to, others
5. begin to work
6. changed my life
7. that, could help other people
8. After that, did, do
9. visited some countries, volunteered there

Culture Link

1. Talking Books
2. program that makes, blind
3. was started
4. record your voice
5. are given, for free

Presentation Time

1. Lee Taeseok was a great person.
2. He was a priest and also a doctor.
3. He built hospitals and schools for the people of Tonj.
4. He took care of them and taught classes.
5. From this person, I learned that I should help people in need.

After You Read B

1. Reporter: How was your life during World War II?
2. Can you tell me about it?
3. Audrey: It was terrible. My family and I were hungry and sick.
4. We survived thanks to the help of others.
5. Reporter: How did you begin to work for UNICEF?
6. Audrey: In 1987, a musical festival in Macau changed my life.
7. I learned that my fame could help other people.
8. Reporter: After that, what did you do?
9. Audrey: I visited some countries in Africa and Asia and volunteered there.

Culture Link

1. Talking Books Program
2. This is a program that makes audiobooks for blind people.
3. It was started in 1931 in the United States.
4. You just read books and record your voice.
5. These audiobooks are given to blind people for free.

43

MEMO

적중100

영어 기출 문제집

정답 및 해설

능률 | 김성곤